CC 75
.H3

Hammond, Philip C
 Archaeological techniques for amateurs. Princeton, N. J.,
Van Nostrand [1963]

 329 p. illus. 21 cm.

1. Archaeology—Methodology. 2. U. S.—Antiq.—Bibl. 3. Canada—
Antiq.—Bibl. 4. Archaeology—Bibl. I. Title.

CC75.H3   913.018   63–4293

001065

DISCARD

ARCHAEOLOGICAL TECHNIQUES FOR AMATEURS

ARCHAEOLOGICAL TECHNIQUES FOR AMATEURS

➔ ➔ ➔ ➔ ➔

PHILIP C. HAMMOND

D. VAN NOSTRAND COMPANY, INC.
PRINCETON, NEW JERSEY

TORONTO　　　　　NEW YORK　　　　　LONDON

D. VAN NOSTRAND COMPANY, INC.
120 Alexander St., Princeton, New Jersey (*Principal office*)
24 West 40 Street, New York 18, New York

D. VAN NOSTRAND COMPANY, LTD.
358, Kensington High Street, London, W.14, England

D. VAN NOSTRAND COMPANY (Canada), LTD.
25 Hollinger Road, Toronto 16, Canada

Published simultaneously in Canada by
D. VAN NOSTRAND COMPANY (Canada), LTD.

PREFACE

This short manual is intended for practical field use, as a complement to theoretical, academic archaeology. For some time there has been a need for a guide to excavating *method* both for the amateur working under the direction of the professional archaeologist and for the anthropologically oriented professional whose training is largely in cultural evaluation—not in excavating. The manuals now on the market are largely out of date or often too complex for an introduction to technique.

As a result of this need, and more especially because of contact with enthusiastic amateurs whose desire for "collections" sometimes gets the better of them, this manual has been put together. It is hoped that it will point out that *real* archaeology is an exact science, for which training and scientific awareness are the prime requisites. Lest, however, the "professionals" decry the opening of the mystery of archaeology to "amateurs," it must be remembered that *all* science must be communicated to be of any value. It is our hope that the amateur will become aware of his need to be trained and directed by skilled professional leadership—and that his awareness will not lessen the enthusiasm which created the science itself and sustained it in its infancy.

Moreover, this manual has been written for another reason—the introduction of the Wheeler-Kenyon method of stratigraphic excavation to the American scene by an American. Both Sir Mortimer Wheeler and Dr. Kathleen Kenyon have written much concerning their technique, and the latter has trained many Americans in it, but it has remained largely a Near Eastern phenomenon. The merits of the technique, along with certain modifications which this author feels are indicated from his own experience in testing it, are hereby shared and recommended for other geographical areas. What Near Eastern archaeologists have learned by extensive excavations in the past and present can well be adapted for the American scene. Not all of the techniques are applicable, but enough of them are usable to justify their presentation here.

This manual does not presume to be the final word on technique, but it represents the experience of a number of workers in the field, passed down in the course of the last sixty years and developed particularly by W. F. Albright from the American side, and Kathleen Kenyon from the British, into a surprisingly exact field. From the pages that follow, the beginning professional can at least get started, and the amateur can learn to whom to turn for trained leadership.

A good part of this manual was written during the author's immediate contact with the North Central

Chapter of the Society for Pennsylvania Archaeology, and thanks must be expressed to that group of splendidly curious amateur diggers for their personal welcome to a Near Eastern archaeologist. A special bit of recognition is also due Lycoming College, Williamsport, Pa., for the use of its facilities and its support during the author's stay there. Appreciation is further to be accorded to those who kindly read the manuscript of this book and gave their suggestions for its improvement as a field reference and guide. To the various professional archaeologists throughout our own country and Canada, from whom information was received concerning individual state archaeological work, special thanks must be given. Then material in Section II of this manual needed to be gathered and it could only be secured from those actually engaged in state archaeological endeavors. Responsibility for the manner in which it is presented, the specific content, and related matters rests entirely on the author, however. It is hoped that the data so presented will help to meet the needs and fulfill the aspirations and plans expressed by those people and that they will find mutual encouragement and support from rereading these pages. Analysis, organization, and presentation of the material in Section II was the work of Margaret L. Hammond, with the assistance of the author.

PHILIP C. HAMMOND, JR.

Princeton, New Jersey

CONTENTS

ILLUSTRATIONS

SECTION I

HISTORY AND METHODS
OF ARCHAEOLOGY

1

AN INTRODUCTION TO
ARCHAEOLOGY

Archaeology is, by definition, the scientific study of antiquity, and, in particular, the study of the material remains of ancient human occupation. Whether it is indeed a branch of the newer science of anthropology remains to be debated. In any case, archaeology embraces the whole range of ancient culture—architecture, epigraphy, art, ceramics, institutions, cult, industry, and history—seen in the interrelationships of man.

Although archaeology now employs all the tools of modern science, and is itself based on purely scientific principles, it still involves subjective judgment in evaluation of data—or lack of it. Thus it must continue to refine its methodology, accumulate precise data, and develop more precision in its discrimination of results. The last word, or even the first one, has not yet been said in regard to all of these facets of the discipline.

Archaeology is also a science which has attracted the interest, attention, patronage, and participation of laymen (nonprofessionals) far beyond the limits observable in most other similar fields. This has had both positive and negative results, some of which will become clear in the material to follow.

In any case, archaeology, whether it be Near Eastern, European, Asian, African, American, or any other type is here to stay. We are looking back into the past to see where we came from—and how we have made our way from the Stone Age to the Space Age.

General History of Archaeology

A history of archaeology would involve tracing the development of the science not only from its "beginning", but also from its beginning in each area. Some of these area beginnings have been built upon long experience in other places; others have been matters of chance without any previous development or investigation.

C. W. Ceram, in his book, *The March of Archaeology,* has called Johann Winckelmann the "Father of Archaeology," insofar as he, as an art typologist, reawakened interest in antiquity in the mid-eighteenth century. But it was Thomas Jefferson who is accredited as the first scientific excavator to report his work (*Notes on Virginia*), as Sir Mortimer Wheeler points out in his *Archaeology From The Earth*. His excavations, toward the end of the eighteenth century, were concluded with the first record of "stratification" as an archaeological phenomenon, and represent the first realization of it. By the time Jefferson had started his work on burial mounds in Virginia, however, excavation had also begun in a vaster burial ground—the ancient city of Pompeii. Chance art finds awakened interest, as well as cupidity, in this ancient city, and Alcubierre began operations on a large scale in 1748. Pompeii's sister-city, Herculaneum, also buried by the eruption of Vesuvius in A.D. 79, followed in turn, and felt the excavator's shovel.

Perhaps the most ambitious archaeological project ever undertaken was that related to Napoleon's attempt to conquer Egypt, and an army of scholars accompanied the army of soldiers on that campaign. The volumes resulting from that twofold thrust have never been equalled in sheer bulk of material (*Description de l'Egypte,* 1809–1826). Time has shown the uncritical nature of the material collected, but it still remains a valuable reference library on Egyptian art and architecture.

The lure of Bible lands was felt in archaeological circles, especially, after the work of Botta, Layard, Rawlinson, and others produced not only museums full of art objects—some single items weighing tons—but also scientific materials: histories, records, new languages, data inscribed on stone and clay. A new world of scholarship was opened, and it is still being explored. Unfortunately much of the same collector's fever which had been, and was still characterizing work in Egypt, made itself felt in Mesopotamia, and excavators began to dig, mainly in order to find inscribed materials.

This same type of motivation is to be seen in the story of one of history's most colorful characters— Heinrich Schliemann, a businessman with an archaeological passion, superior intelligence, and unlimited wealth which enabled him to conduct singlehandedly a prescientific excavation. Although his results have needed extensive revision, the work at Troy remains a stepping stone in archaeological advance.

The Americas were largely in the hands of learned travelers who collected vast amounts of data, but hardly sifted truth from sheer phantasy. Yet even in their accounts, which finally reached Europe for popular reading, a great deal of important information was set down which might otherwise never have been known, particularly the works of Bernardino da Sahagún, Alexander von Humboldt, Lord Kingsborough, Guillaume Depaix, and J. W. Waldek. This development culminated in the more technical work of John Stephens, Frederick Catherwood, and Charles Brasseur in the second half of the nineteenth century, as Ceram notes.

Many of the scholars represented in the early history of archaeology were British, and Great Britain had not been neglected at home. The vast remains of Roman Britain were on every side, and walls, burial mounds, camp sites, and other remains were investigated. The greatest contribution arising out of these endeavors was that made by one Pitt Rivers

(General Lane Fox), however. As part of his interest in the barrows found on his estate, Rivers developed a system of recording still in use today.

By the end of the nineteenth century, the stage was set for the real development of scientific archaeology throughout the world. All that was required was another man of genius to tie together all that had been learned up to that point about actual excavation, and to provide the key to its interpretation.

Fortunately that man was at hand, and had been excavating in Egypt for quite some time. In the course of his work, Sir Flinders Petrie had developed and refined the technique of recording. As a consequence, Petrie gradually began to relate pottery types and levels of occupation. It was not until he arrived in Palestine in 1890, however, that the final association between the pottery, the strata, and chronology was made. Digging for only six weeks at a relatively obscure site called Tell el-Hesy, Petrie established the beginning of the "ceramic index" which revolutionized archaeological research by providing a new method of dating. A body of pottery was able to be dated by Petrie because of its relationship to other dated objects. This pottery then became the basis for further datings as other pieces were found in relationship to it. Finally, it was realized that dating could be done accurately by pottery fragments (sherds) alone. From Petrie's original work, the index in the Near East, and ultimately similar ones all through the world, became a standard of chronological determination.

Since 1900, and especially since the middle of this century, scientific archaeology has been developing new methods, new tools, and an ever-widening horizon. It is really to this segment of archaeology's history that the work in the United States, and in the Americas in general, really belongs.

Archaeology in the United States

It must be admitted, however, that much that is called archaeology in this country has been simply glorified relic collecting. In spite of increased general knowledge and highly specialized professional awareness, American archaeology has undergone a long period of site-stripping and relic-hunting which can be rated only as unscientific. Only within the last few decades have Americans interested in their own culture, on a popular level, taken a deeper interest in preserving it scientifically.

American archaeology has been, and now is, basically anthropological in its orientation. That is, the emphasis in professional work and professional training has been on cultures and cultural patterns, rather than on site stratigraphy, historical impact, and ceramic relationships. This is in contrast to both classical archaeology and Near Eastern archaeology, where the emphasis is placed upon the precise history of a site, the wide historical context, pottery, numismatics, epigraphy, and other factors, as well as upon the cultural patterns, shifts, and interrelationships.

An apparent cleavage between professionals and nonprofessionals is more acute at the academic level than any other. At the practical field level, professionally trained public personnel, academicians, and local societies of amateurs rub shoulders and talk the same language, with no friction.

In addition, almost all work being reported in the United States today by so-called amateur groups, is being done directly under the supervision of trained professionals. Thus much of the outcry against nonprofessional field work is basically uninformed.

The growing cooperation of professionally trained archaeologists and the far larger number of nonprofessionals is to be seen not only in the closer supervisory roles played by the former, but also in the educational area. State personnel travel widely on lecture tours or for special meetings with amateur groups; professional motion picture films, film strips, and taped lectures are available; state and local museums feature special exhibits; academic institutions offer special courses and summer-school field work. All these bring the nonprofessionnal into closer understanding of the viewpoint of the scientifically trained and oriented professional. At the professional level, too, interdisciplinary instruction, field seminars, conferences, and discussions have helped to broaden viewpoint and perspective. Governmental branches are also cooperating with both professional staff personnel and nonprofessional groups to preserve historic materials. State conservation departments, the National Park Service, and state archaeological societies have been most prominent in such relationships.

It has become more and more apparent to the nonprofessional, however, that there is an obvious need for extension of professional leadership so that the nonprofessional can contribute as much as possible to the field. Professional protests against destructive and unscientific work by the amateur were well founded in the past, but the practical fact remains that there are too few professionals to do all of the work that needs to be done. As a consequence, there is a need to continue the development of systems of excavation and reporting wherein the best use can be made of professional supervision and of nonprofessional interest, skills, and enthusiasm. The system offered in this volume—used and refined over a number of years in India, Britain, and the Near East, first by the British and now more and more by Americans also—is one workable solution to the problem. By using a professional director over the work of a selected group of nonprofessionals (students, trainees, and amateurs), by establishing standard routines of excavations, and by rigidly controlling recording, this method permits learning while working. Thus a great deal of scientifically accurate excavation can be carried out, the results are professionally reported, and training in field methods accomplished without loss of valuable data or materials.

Along with further cooperation and interrelationship between the professional and the amateur, there is also the need to remove secretiveness from the approach of both sides. At its worst, this has resulted in a desire on the part of some professionals not to reveal the "secrets" of the profession to the amateur —lest he be overwhelmed by a little knowledge of methods and excavate on his own! That this might be true in a few cases does not overbalance the good that awareness of scientific needs in the field might bring. The amateur, in turn, often distrusts the professional who speaks of museums as repositories for relics and not for private collections. Fortunately this situation is becoming less of a problem, and many fine museum collections are the results of amateur interest and insight. The matter of site discovery is another area where secretiveness becomes almost pathologic. In a sort of cloak-and-dagger way, sites are privately marked, secretly coded, or not even reported, by both professional and amateur. The fear of looting is expressed by both sides, and there is even some feeling that the danger of "poaching" will be lessened if sites are not recorded. Unfortunately, this practice often leads either to more private collecting or to total loss of a site through lack of official recognition of it. Site maps, duly protected by antiquities laws, are mandatory if the flow of cultures, the ceramic index, and general historical relationships are to be clarified. Neither the fear of vandalism nor the desire to hoard "points" is a valid reason to ignore scientific principles (see Chapter 2, "Site Surveys").

From the professional standpoint it is also necessary that American excavation techniques be overhauled. As was noted above, American archaeology is generally anthropological in its orientation, with a consequent high level of cultural evaluation evident in American results. However, it is now also necessary that increased attention be paid, in a more organized way, to modern stratigraphic techniques, to ceramic analysis and drawing, to classification and typology, and to the relationship of all facets to a more definite chronology. An analysis of the literature up to the present indicates a growing trend in these directions, and it is to be hoped that it will continue and accelerate.

The Amateur Digger

Who is the "amateur" or "nonprofessional" archaeologist in the United States? He or she may be a teen-ager or a venerable elder in the community. Generally, and preferably, he is a member of one of the local branches of a state archaeological or historical society, whose aim it is to assist in preserving antiquity sites through community effort. Over 70 per cent of our states have such groups, with membership ranging up to 1300 or more. Almost all of these groups are at the present time doing some work with professional guidance and supervision.

The local societies may be composed of members who themselves qualify as professionals in the fields of archaeology and anthropology. Often, too, societies may have members whose long acquaintance and deep interest in the local culture have made them recognized specialists and experts.

The amateur is usually eager for both information and help in learning more about the field. Not very often, today, is the acknowledged vandal or looter welcome, although some unwitting destruction is still occasionally the result of a well-meaning but misinformed desire to "fill out" a private collection. Rather, there is a widely voiced desire for more technical publications, more motion pictures on backgrounds and cultures, and more professional lectures on specific areas of interest. The demand is for more media which will make the relationship between professional and nonprofessional more meaningful and more effective.

The American amateur differs from his counterparts in the areas of classical or Near Eastern archaeology, in particular, in that the latter usually has some specific professional background which archaeology actually rounds out. Hence the amateur in those fields may not, in his daily or professional life, be so totally unrelated to the archaeological situation as are amateurs in the American field.

Today's amateur may still simply "collect," via surface finds, purchase, or trading. But the trend is toward scientific classification, planned discussions, and more formal workshops in which collection is scientific and a prelude to organized results and proper recording of sites. Likewise, the amateur used to excavate in plowed fields, or eroded river banks, or, unfortunately, actually undertake clandestine digging. Today he is usually part of a locally sponsored expedition working over a period of years on a local site with definite scientific archaeological ends in view, under trained professional leadership. As a consequence, the results of his work are not hidden away or displayed on his wall, but grace the pages of scientific reports, well written, well documented, and of significance for the cultural history of his area. By such means, the fullest use is made of the amateur's enthusiasm, and the greatest scientific benefits achieved.

Equipment, costly for the single amateur, can also be more efficiently secured, organized, and employed on a group basis. Upper-echelon procurement, storage, and allocation allows the use of more expensive and more efficient tools to achieve the best results. State and federal agencies can also be better enlisted, by a group, for special needs. Thus the loss of valuable data is precluded and their destruction through the use of improper equipment minimized.

As a result of these trends, amateur archaeology in the United States has been radically changed for the better, with startling contributions being made today by the nonprofessional. Some of these contributions may be seen in the increasing number of state laws designed to protect antiquities and historic sites. Most states now have some legislation, and newer laws are becoming increasingly severe, not because professionals are agitating for more controls but because amateur groups are demanding that our national heritage be preserved. More and more state legislatures are being made aware of their responsibility toward America's past by vocal, nonprofessional archaeological societies within their borders. This can indeed be a major contribution of the amateur society at any level, for affairs of a more contemporaneous nature often drive questions of antiquity from the minds of busy lawmakers until it is too late.

Another amateur contribution to archaeology in the United States has been in the realm of personnel. The awareness of the need for professional assistance has brought with it interest in securing professionally trained state and federal staff archaeologists and anthropologists to fill supervisory, regulatory, and resource positions on a full-time basis. Now, over fifty per cent of the states have such professional personnel, with specific functions. This improvement, again, has come about largely through nonprofessional pressure and interest.

Likewise, an increasing awareness of American culture, stimulated by the local amateur groups, has brought with it a recognition of the need for permanent, properly set-up repositories for archaeological materials. That need is being met in the creation of many local, state, and federal museums for the display, in the form of exhibits, of America's past. Many of these museums are under the care of nonprofessional groups, with the guidance of upper-level professionals. Many now offer traveling exhibits which may be used by local societies for educational purposes. This, of course, has had a spiraling effect: the greater the initial interest, the greater the resultant insight and action—and the conservation of America's past has become a public affair.

The nonprofessional can contribute to service, as well. He can be the eyes of archaeology in his local region: spotting, carefully recording, and reporting sites, remains, and even collections which come to his attention. This is being recognized more and more in the growing number of site maps, "news notes," and catalogues resulting from amateur action, individually and collectively. The nonprofessional can also contribute valuable service by volunteering his time and skills. Often museums can benefit by volunteer guides (or guards!), skilled nonprofessional technicians and work crews of all kinds. Many valuable collections have been organized, catalogued, and kept in shape by such means. Volunteers can also serve on local excavations, of course, but the *real* work begins after the digging is over. Here again, the interested amateur can furnish valuable scientific assistance in classifying, photographing, drawing, and otherwise preparing the data of an excavation for publication. Here the professional in other fields often is of great help—so that chemists, draftsmen, architects, engineers, and similar specialists may render signal service.

Another major area of contribution by the amateur is being made in terms of reporting. The bulletins, news-letters, and monographs produced by local, state, and associated archaeological societies are of such a high level that they often represent

"standard works" on specific areas of field archaeology, ceramic cultures, artifact typologies, and similar subjects.

It is for these reasons that the role of the nonprofessional in American archaeology, in particular,
must not be ignored. That the direction of archaeological work must be a professional concern is not
to be denied, but the amateur is an important link
in the chain which binds popular interest, public administration, and professional skill.

Archaeology As a Career

What about archaeology as a career? This is a
question often asked the professional, especially in
the academic situation. Here the plain fact of job
scarcity must be bluntly faced. The professional
archaeologist, particularly the field archaeologist, is
generally limited to teaching, program and institu-
tional administration, or public service positions. The
number of such opportunities is extremely limited,
though growing, and openings are relatively few.
Hence the usual approach to the problem of interest *versus* vocation is by indirection. That is, the
person interested in archaeology will usually special-
ize in a related field, in which job opportunities are
more abundant. Very often the specialty is aimed
at the teaching field, wherein a number of interests
can usually be related. Among a number of possibilities are Near Eastern languages, literature, and
history, the whole realm of classical studies, ancient
history, cultural anthropology, American, Asian, or

European area studies, museum administration, special technical fields, and many others.

It must be stressed, however, that regardless of the concentration, or the geographical focus, the archaeologist, professional or amateur, must first of all be thoroughly grounded in the history of his particular sphere of interest. Without a firm basis in the general historical development, the broad stages of historical and cultural interrelationships, and the specific details of the history of the local culture involved, excavation or evaluation cannot even be contemplated.

Unless this basic background is first assimilated, valuable remains may be ignored or overlooked, traces and clues may be lost, and thus the sequence connections of the stratigraphy of a given site totally misconstrued. Archaeology is essentially destructive, and once evidence is lost or mangled it cannot easily be restored.

Archaeology As an Avocation

As an avocation, archaeology can be part of the interest and energies of almost anyone. If the amateur status is kept in mind, and its relation to the professional field understood, the nonprofessional will find himself able to have a most rewarding avocation in archaeological work. Contributions can be made to the history of man at a most exciting level—that of actually seeing history unfold beneath the spade and trowel. This experience has often opened up to people working in the diplomatic and military fields, in geology, metallurgy, education, and other professional ranks. But it can also be part of the recreational life of the "man in the street" as well. The areas of service described above are not limited to people with profound educational backgrounds, or unlimited time. That archaeology should not be "fun," or should be completely devoid of aesthetic appreciation is a view both pedantic and unscientific. One cannot be accurate where interest is not sustained; one cannot interpret where the spirit of a culture is not understood and recognized. "Fun" and "aesthetics" interpreted as ends in themselves do not make "archaeology," but neither can archaeology divest itself of interest and understanding.

With all of this in mind, then, the following chapters of this manual are offered as a description of archaeological technique as it may be practiced in the field. Our intent is not to encourage promiscuous excavation by either the amateur or the professional. Rather, our purpose is to make it plain that we have passed from the prescientific days of both relic collection and nonstratigraphic digging to a new era of scientific outlook. In this new day, the amateur must understand technique and its requirements fully, if he is to be the necessary partner of his professionally trained colleagues—and if together we are to preserve and understand the cultural history of the discipline.

2

THE THEORY OF
EXCAVATION

Stratification

The modern archaeologist works according to a general theory concerning the manner in which the material remains of ancient civilizations were deposited in the course of successive occupations. This theory is known as "stratification" and, simply put, means that the remains of one occupation (or lack of it) pile up on that accumulated by the occupations which preceded it. In short, man dumps his garbage and trash, builds his buildings, and lives his life on a series of "levels" or "strata," which, in the course of time, raise the surface level of an area in a sort of "layer-cake" arrangement. Thus, if the archaeologist cuts into this accumulation, the oldest materials should be at the bottom, the latest at the top. This does not always work out so neatly, of course, since many things may disrupt the sequence of the strata. Holes may be dug into the accumulation so that the older materials are brought to the surface, there may be spotty dumping on the surface, there may be floods which wash away entire traces of life, there may be earthquakes and other natural phenomena which put the theoretical sequence in total disorder (see Chapter 4). Yet, in spite of all of these possibilities, the general theory holds, and the exceptional situations can be spotted and taken into account while excavating.

Basic to this theory is the idea that individual strata of occupational evidence can be identified and separated from those below and those above. This idea is based on the variations caused by the very situations and circumstances responsible for the accumulations in the first place: the variations of successive occupations.

It becomes the job of the archaeologist, therefore, to excavate these strata, one by one, carefully sorting out the sometimes subtle variations among them. When these are all defined, therefore, the chronology or "time-table" of the total accumulation will be made clear. This chronology is of two kinds—a relative one (*i.e.* the lower the level, the older the occupation which caused it to be laid down), and an absolute one (*i.e.* the actual "date" of the occupation, arrived at by dated or by dateable finds, comparisons, and other methods.)

For example, the remains found directly on bed-rock will normally be earlier than those found on the surface. This allows everything in between to be given a rough relative chronological relationship to all other things. This relative chronology does not give a date to the individual finds, however. That is done by the absolute relationship of all items to a dated or dateable artifact. For example, a coin found in a level will constitute an "absolute," in terms of dating—and also furnish a relative chronology for the levels below and above it.

Thus the place of accurate recording—of levels, of finds, of area, and of other details—becomes obvious. Once a given level is removed, it ceases to exist, except in the mind—and better, in the notebook and other records—of the excavator.

When the excavation is completed, either finally or seasonally, the accumulated data must be analyzed and interpreted. Here the records again count, for they accomplish the basic demands of scientific archaeology: the interpretation of the relationship of all parts of the excavation to each other, to the whole, and to all else that has been done of a similar nature. This is a large task, but it is the responsibility of the archaeologist, amateur or professional, to his fellow workers (see Chapter 5).

Not only must the actual artifacts, the stratigraphy, and all the physical data be considered, but the archaeologist must be prepared to bring local history —and sometimes even folklore, local customs, and other similar background—to bear on the subject. His own background, therefore, must be as extensive as possible; however, no one can reasonably know all the answers, hence consultation with a variety of experts has become a necessity today.

Clearing of Levels

Under this general theory of stratigraphic excavation, then, we may answer the question of how actually to go about digging. If occupations are superimposed, one above the other, to indicate a span of time, we need only dig down, from top to bottom, to expose them in sequence, one by one, in any given area. In order to pass from one level to another safely, however, we must carefully note the fine differences which characterize the various strata of accumulation, or we shall be digging more than one occupational level at a time. We must note differences in color, in texture, in soil composition, in hardness, and a host of other minute indications respective of each level. Here practical experience can be the guide, with certain built-in controls which will be suggested below. When one level is located and cleared, the excavator is ready to begin the next. All the materials from each separate level are, of course, kept isolated from one another, just as the levels from which they originally came were separate from one another in the soil.

The actual digging depends upon the situation. In the Near East, where archaeology has had its greatest heyday, large groups of laborers, directed by skilled supervisors, are employed to do the actual work. On the other hand, an American Indian site may be worked by an individual or by a small group, with or without paid labor crews. British excavations often hire local manual laborers in the neighborhood of an excavation. Whatever the work crew, however, the method, in its simplest form, is basically the same. A small amount of earth is loosened by pick, trowel, or other tool, and then cleared away by basket, wheelbarrow, or other means, until a given archaeological level has been removed and the surface of the next level revealed. It is essential that *all* of a given area (aside from control points and other exceptions noted below) be cleared from the surface of the next level *before* the latter is begun. If this is not done, the risk of mixing levels is great—with resultant confusion as to the precise level from which any given find comes. In this regard it must be noted that few levels are really *level*. Tracing any given stratum generally results in a surface far from flat, or even vaguely horizonal. A number of factors enter here, and cause this situation—as a look at the ground surface in any area will illustrate, even before any excavation. Here, too, it can be noted that it is better to penetrate a bit into a *lower* level in excavating than to allow even a slight amount of earth from a higher level to remain with the level below it. This is because earlier artifacts are better mixed with later ones, in dating, than to risk the reverse situation (see Chapter 3 "The Test Trench").

Sites

The question of "how" to dig also involves the general one of "where" to dig. This again depends upon the situation. There are many ways that an area for excavation (the "site") is located. In the

Near East tremendous mounds known as "tells," the results of perhaps thousands of years of occupational accumulation, mark the sites of ancient cities and other remains of man. At the same time, in the same areas, there are almost unnoticeable sites, unmarked by great heaps of earth, which are of comparable age! In South and Central America, jungle-shrouded monuments attest to former human habitation. In England, mounds, wall lines, and the outlines of military installations are clear evidence of potential archaeological reward. In North America, less obvious clues are apt to exist, although the cliff houses of desert Indians, the mounds of others, and the shell heaps of still others point to rich archaeological sites. In every area, too, chance finds, surface pottery, and other artifacts (the usual collectors' guide), local traditions, historical references, or even standing monuments, along with a general clue to ancient habitation always provided by a water supply, are all means by which a site can be discovered and chosen.

Having chosen a site, the archaeologist must secure permission to excavate. This is a professional nicety often overlooked by the amateur, but which may be forcibly brought to the attention of the digger by an irate owner, or by law enforcement agencies. Securing digging rights may be a simple word-of-mouth affair, or it may involve payments of hundreds of dollars and reams of legal documents. If a site is particularly important, specific aspects of excavation privilege should be worked out in the beginning to preclude later embarrassment or even legal complications (see below). Where, when, by whom, and other aspects must always be considered. Neighbors are often also to be considered, particularly in such matters as right-of-way to the site, boundaries, and so forth. Visitors are also a problem because, although shared enthusiasm should be fostered, damage claims, destruction of finds, casual excavation, and similar vexations are troublesome and may be costly. Some serious thought must be given to these matters in chosing a site, therefore.

Antiquities Laws

In addition to local or owner's permission to excavate, the matter of state or national law must also be investigated and obeyed prior to excavating a site. In most foreign countries, a well-developed system of national antiquities laws has been developed to control the excavation and export of antiquities. In the United States the necessity for this type of restriction is just becoming recognized. The amateur, and sometimes the professional as well, is often irritated by the red-tape surrounding such legal controls. However, each nation and each area have not only the right, but the responsibility, for preserving the traces of its national heritage. Too often in the past priceless antiquities were exported by the boat-load, or ruthlessly destroyed in the search for collector's items (see Chapter 1). In the United States, the search for relics has too often led to the confusion or total loss of

scientific data of considerable importance. In an effort to correct this situation, however, individual
states have been taking note of the problem and
drafting proper legislation. In the appendix to this
manual a summary of the current legislation, where
ascertainable, has been included. The observance of
those laws and pressure to exact even further controlling legislation, are a positive public responsibility of
every archeologist, amateur or professional. The state
archaeological societies can render the effect of their
collective voice in securing such necessary legal action from their state legislatures.

At this point the question "Why dig?" may well
be raised. To the professional this is an unnecessary
question—its answer lies in his chosen career. To the
amateur the question is also not really raised—
archaeology can be an outlet for talents and interest
which combine recreation with a contribution to
man's knowledge. To the onlooker, however, the
sight of people, armed with trowels and notebooks,
intently peering at trench walls, avidly sorting pieces
of broken crockery, spending time and investing vast
sums of money makes archaeology and archaeologists appear a bit odd! "What are you looking for?"
is the inevitable question of the visitor, and simply
cannot be answered outside of an appreciation for
the total sweep of man's history, past, present, and
future. Archaeology advances human knowledge by
looking back; hence, the need for scientific care must
be stressed.

Scientific Methods

Scientific methods were finally introduced into archaeology, especially as a result of the development of the stratigraphic theory, following the work of Sir Flinders Petrie in Palestine. But even at this stage a variety of methods present themselves today. Total denudation of a site has often been attempted, or discussed. By this method, an entire site is completely excavated. This means that the fullest view of any given level or phase of occupation can be seen all at one time. But this also means that the destruction of all of the evidence is also complete. Thus any mistakes made cannot be clarified by additional work, nor can more advanced methods be employed later on; hence, this method is not generally approved today.

Trenching

Another method of gaining a view of a large area is that known as "trenching." This method had its beginnings in the prescientific period when trenches were dug all over some sites in an effort to uncover the lines of walls or buildings. Today the method has been refined, and it is a valuable way of quickly determining the *extent* of an occupation in a given area. Essentially it is simply the removal of successive levels within a prescribed area, rectangular in shape. The length of the trench and its relative width are dependent upon the area to be excavated, the resources of the group, and the depth to which the

proposed excavation is to be carried. This latter factor is important, since extending a trench in width
is always a big operation, and work in the lower
levels must cease until all the trench is brought to a
single level to prevent mixing of materials. This
method is not solely a means of exploration as it has
been in the past, but is today a definite archaeological end in itself (called by Wheeler the "substantive
trench").

Grids

A variation of this same method is the one usually
called the "grid" system, but perhaps more properly
called the "square" system. This is excavation by
areas preset into squares. At first glance this method
seems to have certain inherent disadvantages—
mainly in the partial and restricted view it gives of a
given occupation area. This problem is met by the
extension of a given square to adjoining ones, wherever a fuller view is required. In some instances,
therefore, the addition of squares actually may result
in a rectangular extension, producing a trench. The
usual designation of this system by the word "grid"
refers to the practice of laying out at one time a
number of squares in lattice or grid-shape pattern.
Careful surveying and recording also extend results
of a single square through the rest of the grid, when,
even after the lapse of some time, additional squares
are excavated and notes compared. Extension, and
speed, may also be achieved by a "checkerboard" arrangement of excavated squares in any one area,

leaving unexcavated squares in between (see below under "controls").

Area

A still further adaptation of the trench grid system is that of area excavation, wherein the nature of the site precludes either a regularized grid or the straight extension of a trench. This type of excavation is irregular, and follows the contours or obstacles of the site. It makes for difficulty in both recording and digging and should be regarded as a strictly emergency method. The British fetish for neat, cleanly-cut squares and trenches, with straight, vertical walls is actually more than purely conservatism: it is the mark of conscientious attention, and repays the effort in meaningful records and results.

Soundings

A brief word should be said of the "sounding" (*sondage*) and "arbitrary level" methods in archaeology. The sounding is the random excavation of small pits to determine sequences beneath the surface of the ground. Such a method is useful if the proper stratigraphic techniques are followed, and, equally important, if a careful record is kept of the exact locations of such pits in order to prevent later confusion. The sounding is not, however, the same as the "control pit" or "test trench" which will be discussed below. The arbitrary level system is one widely used in some circles, today. It is a method of excavating by predetermined levels of a set depth. These are then

EXCAVATION PLOT PLAN AND TECHNIQUES

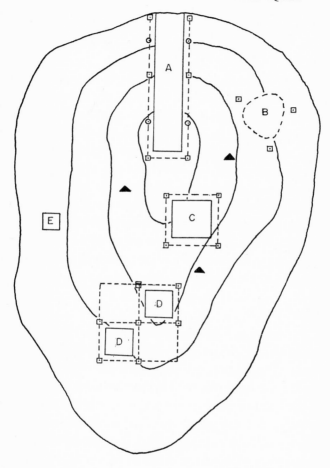

--- TRENCH LINE
—— EXCAVATION LINE
⊡ TRENCH OR OTHER RECORD STAKE
⊙ TEMPORARY PLOTTING STAKE
▲ SURVEYOR'S PERMANENT MARKER

A. TRENCH METHOD
B. AREA METHOD
C. SQUARE METHOD
D. CHECKERBOARD METHOD
E. SOUNDING

dated in terms of their own sequence ("seriation"). Except under most unusual circumstances, this method is to be avoided as being scientifically invalid, and almost totally meaningless.

Site Surveys

A final statement should also be made in regard to site surveys. Although these are not regularly excavations, soundings are occasionally made as part of the work. The site survey itself is merely the identification and recording of the presence of sites for the purpose of charting occupations and occupation zones, for noting particular cultures, for proposing the identification of historical sites, or for recording the location of possible areas for excavation. Field notes should be taken as accurately and as fully as possible on such surveys, preferably in some standard form.

The results of individual surveys are then plotted on an area "Site Distribution Map" (*i.e.* a map which shows where individual sites are to be found in a given area, with scale, local names and features of the landscape included for reference purposes), as a matter of record. Site survey work, on a national level, is being conducted by the National Park Service of the Department of Interior, with the assistance of other organizations. Sites of archaeological and historical importance should therefore be reported to the National Park Service if discovered.

Related to site survey of a purely record nature is also the survey work being done as part of the Inter-

Agency Archaeological Salvage Program, also administered by the National Park Service. Special attention is given by this project to those areas whose archaeological remains are threatened by water-control development. Detailed site recording has been done of over nine thousand sites in over forty states. Excavation has actually been conducted on almost seventy sites in thirty-one states.

Survey record sheets should be standard and complete. An excellent set has been assembled by the Carnegie Museum, Pittsburgh, Pa. This set records specific location, modern tenancy, physical features, artifact details (by class), burial notes, petroglyph data, and other information.

Succeeding chapters will deal with specific methods of excavating, recording, and other aspects of archaeology in the field.

SITE DISTRIBUTION MAP FROM THE FIELD

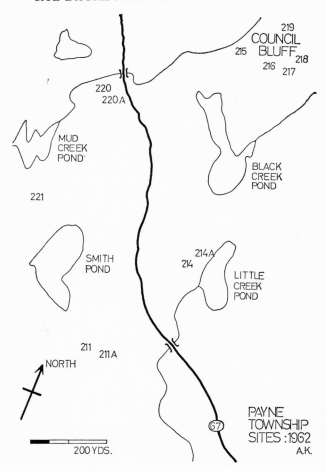

219
COUNCIL
215 BLUFF
216 218
217

220
220A

MUD
CREEK
POND

221

BLACK
CREEK
POND

SMITH
POND

214A
214

LITTLE
CREEK
POND

211 211A

NORTH

200 YDS.

PAYNE
TOWNSHIP
SITES : 1962
A.K.

67

3

THE METHODS OF
EXCAVATION

Once the site has been selected, in accordance with the possibilities mentioned above, preparations for excavation itself can begin. The precise method chosen will, of course, be determined by the specific particulars of site and its demands, but the general preparations for any site are roughly the same, and the stratigraphic method, regardless of how applied, requires the same preliminary steps.

Laying Out The Grid

The square (or its extended form, the trench) is the basic unit of excavation, and its size is determined by the terrain, the extent of excavation contemplated, and other general factors. The grid—that is, the pattern of a number of individual squares— must first be laid out on the ground, with the corners marked by securely implanted stakes or other markers. Occasionally large spikes are used for this purpose, along with angle-iron posts or even pipe, since metal markers can be driven into the soil easily and can, because of their durability, be reused.

After the first marker is established, a cloth or steel tape may be hooked to its top by a nail, and further linear measurements taken from there. Distances are laid off by suspending a plumb bob from the required point along the extended tape. Another marker is set beneath the point of the plumb bob, with a nail driven into its top to mark the exact distance required. In this fashion, the sides of the overall grid or trench are laid off.

The question of establishing right-angle corners always comes up, and the solution to the problem lies in elementary geometry: the "3-4-5 triangle." This is the triangle whose sides are in the ratio of 3:4:5, regardless of the unit of measurement. The peculiarity of this triangle, for archaeological purposes, is, of course, that the angle across from the longest side (the "5," or hypotenuse side) is always a right angle (90°). Thus, by measuring along one straight line already laid out, as indicated above, from one end (*i.e.* the turning point or "corner" point) three units (*e.g.* 3′) and establishing a temporary reference point (by setting in a surveyor's marker or arrow), one side of a 3-4-5 triangle can be set up. Tapes are then hooked on the temporary reference point and on the corner stake, and their free ends are brought together at the four-unit mark (*e.g.* 4′) on the tape from the corner stake and the five-unit mark (*e.g.* 5′) on the tape from the temporary reference point. The spot

A RIGHT-ANGLE CORNER IN AN EXCAVATION LAYOUT

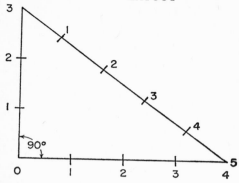

The "3-4-5 triangle" has its sides in a ratio of 3:4:5 units of measure, with a 90° facing the longest side.

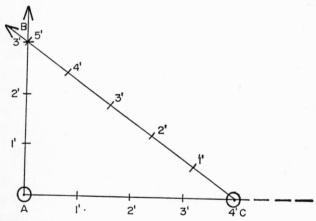

On the ground, 3 units (*e.g.* 3′) are laid out from a corner stake (A) along a previously laid out straight line to establish a temporary reference point (B).

Via tapes from (A) and (B) a point (C) is established by measuring four units (*e.g.* 4′) from (A) and five units (*e.g.* 5′) from (B), and intersecting the lines of measurement.

Since A-B = 3, A-C = 4 and B-C = 5, the angle facing B-C is 90° The line A-C may be extended as far as is needed to complete the new side.

over which this intersection takes place should be marked by the plumb bob and another temporary reference marker, and if that point is then joined with the corner stake by a string, a right-angle corner is established without difficulty. The new line is perpendicular to the original stake line, and may be extended indefinitely. This same procedure is followed for the other corners of the area being laid out.

To outline the entire excavation area, strings are secured to the nails on top of each stake or other support, and stretched from stake to stake, or from whatever marking device is used. These strings establish the edge of the excavating line (a sore point with archaeologists whose visitors step too close and break in the soil along that straight line). The easiest knot for this and all other archaeological work is the "clove-hitch." It is made by making two loops in a cord, in opposite directions, placing one above the other, and then placing both loops over the object to be secured. This knot holds well, but may be easily untied.

Accurate measurement is important in laying out the grid or the trench, since it speeds up the job of placing the excavation area on a plan or map later on. The sides need not be laid out with a transit, but a surveyor's compass or a similar instrument will help to ensure that a straight line is kept in every direction laid out on the ground. Orientation of the area often depends upon the terrain, or upon the site, but if at all possible, North-South, East-West lines are to be desired, and are usually used in American

THE CLOVE HITCH

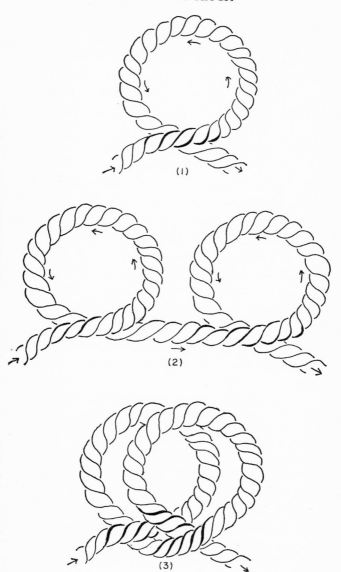

(1)

(2)

(3)

archaeology. Here again, later mapping can be simplified by a little forethought.

Record Stakes

The "Wheeler Method," used in Britain and in other areas, insists upon control areas of unexcavated soil ("baulks") being included within each given square. For example, "10′ squares" are really only dug to 8′on a side, with the remaining area of each one left unexcavated for control and reference. This also allows record stakes to be placed within the square, in the unexcavated portion. When adjoining squares are opened, therefore, a control area still remains unexcavated in each one, reducing the possibility of later error. It is suggested that the record stakes, from which measurements are taken for recording features within the individual square, be 2″ x 2″ stakes, placed diagonally, in order that the grid and square numbers, painted on the two sides of the stakes which face toward the square, can be seen from within the square itself.

In the case of trenches, the sides are marked off precisely in the same manner as the grid, but the record stakes are placed in a straight line at some convenient distance along one edge and set back from it. This facilitates measurements, since any two stakes can be used along the entire line. Definite numbers should be assigned to each stake from one end to another to facilitate reference in recording.

It is frequently worthwhile to build stone circles or huts around record stakes to prevent their being accidentally dislodged or removed. Temporary stakes for plotting purposes may sometimes be necessary, and these should also be protected.

Americans commonly use the trench position for all record stakes, regardless of whether the grid or trench method is being used. This has proved to be easier and just as accurate in practice. It is sometimes necessary, however, to place record stakes on more than one side of a single square, merely for convenience in measurement. On the prehistoric site of Abi Pataud, in southern France, a grid of jointed pipes was actually constructed above the excavation area, with plumb bobs suspended from corners. This might be worthwhile in some cases, but is a bit cumbersome and expensive to set up.

It is very important that the individual record stakes be carefully noted and as soon as possible in the site supervisor's "site notebook" (and in that of the surveyor, also). Thus a dislodged stake can be replaced, if necessary, by simply remeasuring.

Size of Square

The size of each square in a grid system depends upon questions of terrain and soil composition, among other things. In England and the Western Hemisphere, in general, the matter of soil consistency is not too much of a factor, but in areas where the soil is sandy, the size of the trench or square (see Chapter 2) must consider contemplated depth of excavation, in order to prevent cave-in as the work progresses. In cases where the excavation of a site may go down 60′ or more, insufficient width becomes dangerous, and walls may even have to be "stepped" to insure safety. Generally speaking, in American work 5′ squares will probably be adequate, since additional ones can be opened as the work progresses, and have become more or less customary.

Tools

Having laid out the area, the next step is the actual digging. Here, once more, much depends upon the site. The typical implements of the excavator are the pick, both large and small, the shovel or hoe-shovel, and a wide variety of small miscellaneous tools, such as broad-bladed knives, crowbars, sledge hammers for rocks, spades and shovels. The G.I. spade-mattock has also been found to be a useful tool, since it can be used for loosening as well as removing soil, and is an inexpensive item to secure. Added to these tools may often be wheelbarrows, portable cranes, hand-cars, or some other means of disposing of the excavated earth and debris of excavation. The hand-carried basket of the Near East is familiar there, but other means are generally employed in the West, where labor is not so cheap.

The Dump

The matter of earth disposal is an acute one, for a dump must be found which will not interfere with future work. Usually the excavator does not know where that "future work" may take him, and thus must gamble on his choice of a dump area. If the excavation has to be filled in again, a dump in the immediate vicinity of the work is preferable. Sometimes this problem is simplified by using the first excavated square as a dump for the next adjoining one opened, filling in the first hole when the entire work is completed (see also Chapter 2, "Grids"). If an excavation is on a large scale, the dump is generally at some convenient distance from the work, to preclude the need of removing it should the work be expanded. For dumping over a small hillside, the wheelbarrow or the small hand-car on tracks comes in handy. Where the excavation is on a small scale, dumping may be along the actual work edge, but far enough away from it so that excavated dirt (and missed artifacts) do not come tumbling back into the hole, or cave in after a rainstorm, or cascade down under the feet of the unwary visitor. If record stakes are in, dumping should be on the opposite sides of the excavation. If the soil is sandy, a leeward side will prevent dust settling back after each load is dumped.

The Test Trench

The area to be excavated is now cleared of surface debris and stones and the actual excavation begins. At once the problem of stratigraphy has to be considered. How can one dig if he does not know where the levels, that have to be so carefully kept separate, are? How deep does one go to begin? What should one expect in the course of going down? Here the "test-trench" or "control-pit" comes to the rescue (also see below). This is the method by which the archaeologist "sees" beneath the surface before he actually clears away a level. Before the larger area of the entire square is cleared, the archaeologist excavates a small area in which, if errors are made, they can be kept restricted. Sometimes preliminary soundings will have given some information as to the sequence of the individual levels, but each square has its own individuality, and the test-trench is necessary to examine the exact constitution of each. The test-trench may be simply a strip along one side of a square, or even a more limited segment, but regardless of its size, it furnishes the key to each level to be expected beneath the surface.

The procedure is simple: the test-trench is excavated until the first clearly defined level in the trench is uncovered, then this level is completely removed from the rest of the square as a whole, leaving the second level visible and ready to be excavated, and so on, until bedrock is finally reached. This "peeling" process is actually the entire job once digging has begun, for relationships within the levels are thus made clear, and the relationships between levels (*e.g.* of walls sticking up, or pits cutting down, "tip lines," or other features) are interpreted as the successive levels are removed. It must be emphasized, however, that each separate level must be completely cleared of the level above it before it is, itself, excavated. Often a new level surface will be swept, in order to be sure that no remains of a higher one remain upon it.

The Levels

The best method of removing the soil of a given level will depend on the soil itself, the depth of the level, the area involved, and similar factors. In the Near East, for example, a heavy pick is used to loosen the soil so that it may be removed, whereas on American sites a flat-edged shovel may be used for the same operation. In many cases the level may have to be removed with a small hand shovel, a trowel, or even a knife blade and paint brush. The tools to be used are generally determined by the precise situation. Too heavy equipment may completely destroy a valuable clue or fragile artifacts. Care must always be taken that succeeding levels are not destroyed, or even actually lost in the removal of those above them. In some situations massive earth-moving or clearing is necessary, but generally the strata of a site, no matter where it may be, requires more of a peeling operation than bull-dozing.

The top-most level of a site is its "surface" and although it must be carefully removed, it generally represents an entirely mixed mass of materials. It must be clearly marked and noted in the records, however. Usually the surface (and any levels below it which remained the "surface" for a long period) contains grass, roots, and other signs of vegetation. Sometimes this "surface" will go down a considerable depth, either as a result of a long period of undisturbed occupation, or lack of it, or as a result of deep plowing (c. 10″–14″) in a farmed area. Below this level will be the first undisturbed occupational remains which have been sealed off by the "surface level" in relatively recent times.

Numbering Levels

The succeeding levels should be numbered consecutively from top to bottom, in the order in which they are excavated (also see Chapter 5, "Site Notebook" and "Notation of Levels"). Relationships between levels and between squares are interpreted later, when the excavation has been completed. Obvious points of relationship and contact should be noted, but separate numbers retained in all cases. The site supervisor, or excavator, must therefore keep a notebook which describes each operation as it is carried out, with a complete description of each level as dug, along with important facts relating to it.

To assist in keeping things properly noted and to avoid general confusion, Near Eastern archaeologists place tags or labels in the wall of the actual excavation to mark each level (see Chapter 5, "Level Tags"). On the tag are noted the same basic data about the individual level as are noted in the notebook. Thus one can go back and trace a single level all around an excavated area. This is very important in terms of understanding relationships and generally checking results. Although most American digs are not so complex, this method still pays great dividends in efficiency in exchange for a bag of staples and a pile of tags.

Here also the matter of straight lines in archaeological excavation should be stressed. A square with neat edges, straight sides, and well-marked levels is apt to be more accurate in its presentation of evidence than one excavated without any concern for careful digging. Straight edges are secured by the simple device of marking those edges on the ground, using the stretched string on the boundary stakes as a guide. Keeping sides of an excavation vertical is simply a matter of being careful. To assist the excavator here, a plumb bob (or even a rock) can be suspended from a nail in the side of the area, and the sides of the excavation lined up with it.

The Excavation

In its basic form, therefore, this is the method of field archaeology. In theory, it is the removal, level by level, of a given area (the trench or square of a grid), until bedrock is reached. In reality, of course, many problems and obstacles may be encountered before the anticipated "bottom" of a hole is simply a bare stretch of bedrock. Some of these specific problems will be discussed in the next chapter.

Once any given square is cleared, or some level is reached that indicates it, the area may be expanded to surrounding squares. These are then cleared in the same manner as was the first one, in accordance with the stratigraphic method outlined above.

When more than one square is dug at a time by different excavators, the relationships between levels must be worked out if the squares are later connected.

Here the value of labels in the walls of the excavation is again evident.

If a trench is being dug by more than one excavator at the same time, the area must be subdivided into sections (practically the same as digging separate squares with a common line), with separate numbers assigned, and then the interrelationship of levels worked out as the excavation progresses.

Controls

The matter of check strips, or controls on the stratigraphy (called in Britain "baulks") depends upon the situation. In any case, wherever the relationship of levels to each other might be interrupted (*e.g.* a wall emerging close to the edge of a square, or cutting across it, etc.), an unexcavated area must be left so that the connections between levels are clear over the entire excavated area. It is generally considered wise to leave a baulk at corners, or along one side, or (less often) diagonally across, or jutting into, the area being excavated (see above, "Record Stakes"). When the situation becomes clear, the baulk can be cut out, if necessary. This kind of caution is essential, however, if the finished excavation is to make sense, since once a given section is excavated, it cannot be put back in again to rectify mistakes or to recheck connections.

Another very common control on the stratigraphy is the "checkerboard" type. This is more common in American work than the British baulk, but serves the same purpose—it gives a visual check on levels. The

technique is simply a matter of leaving an unexcavated square between excavated squares. The resulting pattern looks exactly like a checkerboard, with
excavated squares alternating with unexcavated ones.
Not only does this method permit rechecking of particular strata, but it also preserves an adequate sample
of each stratum for future excavation.

Protection of Sites

If the work being done on a given site cannot be
completed within the limits of one season, the question of protecting the excavated area against the elements becomes a problem. On the large site very
little can be done except to erect temporary structures
to cover important features. On the small site, a number of possibilities exist. The use of tarpaulin, pegged
down or weighted with stones, often serves to keep
out rain, snow, or sand. A larger area may be covered
with sheet plastic of heavy industrial gauge, available
now in rolls. This material may also be held down
with stones or planks. For a site of extreme importance, a temporary shelter may even be constructed—
either a shed, a tent, or a plastic "house." Such devices
often repay the effort expended in building them, in
terms of the protection offered and ease in beginning
the next season.

An expanded version of such seasonal protection of
sites has been made by at least one Danish archaeologist, who was bothered by the elements during his
excavation. This enterprising archaeologist simply
constructs a plastic-walled Quonset hut over the spe-

cific site he is working on. The hut is dismountable and is transported from site to site. While this is feasible for a small site, obviously it would prove too expensive for large-scale use.

4

SPECIFIC PROBLEMS
OF EXCAVATION

In this chapter consideration will be given to the problems and obstacles which arise in excavation. In addition, something will be said about methods to be used for more unusual excavating situations, such as earthwork mounds, burials, building sites, and other areas.

First of all, the problems of archaeology are not really "problems," if one understands the reasons for the levels being laid down in the first place (see Chapter 2, "Stratification"). But since certain situations do occur which are not covered by the simple formula of peeling off levels, they must be given specific consideration.

Fully realizing the danger of over-simplification, but in order not to complicate the matter unduly, we can say that the basic problem situations of stratigraphic excavation can be reduced to three general group headings: (1) distortions, (2) interruptions, and (3) disturbances. Roughly speaking, these are the over-all types of situations into which individual problems of excavating can be placed, and an understanding of the strategy for solving the general problem will allow the excavator to plot his attack on the specific problem encountered. These three general headings are presented in order of the difficulty of resolving them, although each one may present a more or less complicated problem when considered in terms of a specific situation. The apparent complexity of each, however, disappears with the understanding of what brought about the precise situation in the first place. The archaeologist is thus placed in the position of having to be a spectator to the original event in order to understand and thus interpret the results as he uncovers them.

Distortions

Distortions, in stratigraphy, refer to the fact that every excavator soon learns that "levels" are not level! Dumpings, tip-lines, subsurface slopes, fills, inversions, cave-ins, and a host of other phenomena resulting from every-day occupation cause given levels sometimes to become elusive, and often to disappear altogether. But, since we have said that a level must always be followed and thoroughly cleared, these distortions are handled by care in observing the rule of clearing each higher level completely from the one below it (see Chapter 3, "The Test Trench"). Often a given level will not run over the whole area of a trench or square. This is especially true when one is digging in a dump area where, in an earlier period, individual loads of dirt were flung on a pile. Each load thus constitutes a level or stratum in the records until the whole "dump phase" is understood. The relation of each level to succeeding levels must be carefully checked and noted.

Uneven filling, or "tip-lines," natural or accidental, can also produce horizontal distortions in the stratigraphy. This is often the case when an uneven area was leveled in ancient times, and the "pockets" of fill must be traced all over the trench or square being excavated. These pockets, if they are not completely cleaned out of lower levels into which they have been thrown, can cause error or embarrassment in the later identification and dating of artifacts and other finds. This is similar to the problem of pits, which will be discussed below. Often such fills were thrown against ancient slopes, which thus seem to protrude upward through succeeding (later) levels. Such a practice was designed to even off the surface of the ground, and, once seen in that light, becomes completely comprehensible. Here the chance for extremes of error in attribution of finds is possible, however, and great care must be paid to the untanglement of the separate layers of the filling processes.

Interruptions

Archaeological interruptions are simply those situations in which something artificial interrupts the horizontal progress of a given level. The most com-

THE EXCAVATION OF DISTORTED LEVELS

A. TIPPED LEVELS:

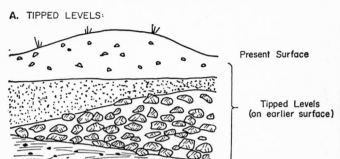

Present Surface

Tipped Levels
(on earlier surface)

Earlier Surface

B. DUMPS:

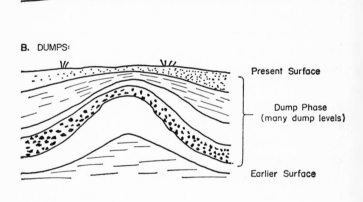

Present Surface

Dump Phase
(many dump levels)

Earlier Surface

C. FILLS:

Fills

Original
Surface

Original
Surface
(sloped)

mon of these is, of course, the presence of a wall or walls, but even natural obstacles like large stones or fallen timbers can as easily interrupt a level. The interrupted level (or levels, if the obstruction is large enough) appears to be cut vertically, and thus the relationship to other horizontal levels at the same depth becomes a problem. Is a level of red soil, on one side of a wall, for example, the same as a level of red soil on the other side, if the cross-over of the individual levels is not absolutely clear? This question, of course, must be answered by the careful recording of the entire situation.

As a general rule, where something vertical interrupts a level horizontally, the level or levels so interrupted are given separate numbers in the notebook, until another level is reached which again crosses the barrier (*i.e.* goes beneath it, linking the two parts of a level) and is horizontally unbroken. Even levels that look alike may later prove to be quite different, and if pottery and other artifacts are thrown together from such levels a confused mixture will result. The date of things *inside* a building may not be the same as the date of things in the immediate occupation levels *outside* that building (*e.g.* a museum is a fine example of radical differences in the dates of artifacts inside and outside, separated only by a wall).

In the case of walls especially, the vertical barrier interrupting horizontal levels may continue all the way to bedrock, necessitating separate numbering of many levels (see Chapter 5, "Notation of Levels").

THE EXCAVATION OF INTERRUPTED LEVELS

A. WALLS:

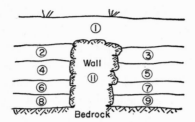

Levels numbered independently on each side of the interruption.

B. PARTIAL BARRIERS:

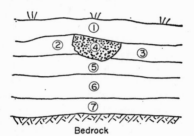

Levels numbered independently on each side of barrier until resumption of horizontal connection of levels.

C. FOUNDATION TRENCH AND POST-HOLE INTERRUPTIONS:

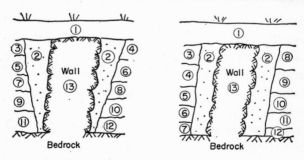

Levels numbered independently on each side
Level ② = foundation trench.

When the barrier is only partial, on the other hand, the continuation of separate numbering is greatly reduced, since ultimately a level will pass under or around the obstacle and the continuity of level numbers will be resumed over the entire area being excavated.

One very important point must be noted here in regard to interruption by man-made barriers, such as walls, timber fortifications, or similar works introduced into the surface level at some time in the past. This is the matter of the "foundation trench" which, one way or another, usually accompanies the building of a vertical barrier founded in the earth. Normally a wall is not simply built upon the existing ground surface, because of the instability of such a building procedure. Rather, a foundation trench (of a variety of individual types) must be dug in order to give the wall a firm base, and to prevent upper courses of it from falling down when lower courses settle under their weight. Witness of this fact is the depth to which foundations for modern buildings are sunk—depending upon the height, weight, and materials of the edifice being contemplated. In ancient times, too, the builders also had to take into consideration the fact that an enemy might dig under a wall, either to undermine it ("sapping"), or simply to get inside by tunneling underneath its foundation. This defense need often resulted in foundation courses being laid directly upon bedrock.

To accomplish this, a trench had to be dug into the existing surface, the foundation stones laid down,

and then the excavated space filled in again with soil
to securely strengthen the foundations. Likewise,
post-holes are often dug into the surface for the
erection of a building or a stockade. But, because one
cannot dig a hole exactly the size of a post, the extra
space is filled in with dirt or stone (or today, with
concrete) to make the post firm. These excavations
next to a barrier of this sort must also be watched for,
since they form, in effect, separate levels cutting into
the levels into which the barrier itself was originally
set. This, of course, interrupts the horizontal sequences of the regular levels. They have to be
watched for, and are then treated like the "pits" and
burials noted below. The varieties of these foundation trenches are many, and depend largely upon
local custom, soil conditions, and the originality and
energy of the builders.

Disturbances

The third major group of problems are the ones
that can be placed under the general heading of disturbances, although most of the problem situations
might well be so classified. In any case, these disturbances are vertical in their effect, as are the more
apparent group we have just discussed and of which
they really form a part, even though they also involve some natural interruptions as well. The difference lies in the more obviously solid nature of the
above interruptions, as against an often casual disturbance in a level being traced. These disturbances
include pits (storage, water catchments, and burials),

foundation and post-hole trenches as noted above, wash-outs and stream cuts, robbings, falls, and a variety of other possibilities. In any case, they are always the result of cutting into a given level or levels from the surface, thus allowing comparatively later material to get beneath the surface and thus inverting the stratigraphy in terms of artifacts. If the disturbance area is great enough, it can be recognized readily as the surface of a given level is cleared.

But, on the other hand, if the disturbance is limited, or the soil changes are more subtle, considerable stratigraphic damage may be done. Often these disturbances appear in the section, and can thus be seen, or show soil color changes (such as a hearth), or soil consistency changes (such as water-carried pebbles), or even are evident from a difference in soil hardness (*e.g.* soil tamped down after a hole has been dug in the surface and refilled). In any case, when early artifacts suddenly seem to be mixed with later ones, and *vice versa,* the excavator becomes acutely aware of a disturbance in his area.

These areas must be treated carefully, since caution will render them harmless, and sloppy treatment may well undo a vast amount of work. Here, again, the policy of "too much care" is preferable to "too little." The disturbed area must be isolated by leaving a "skin" around it—which is excavated separately from the surrounding (and earlier) levels. The untouched section must be adequate enough to provide for the entire area of disturbance, and presents no dating difficulty, since any nondisturbed soil excavated with that from a disturbance can only contain materials earlier than those in the disturbance itself. As noted above, an artifact is always dated in terms of the latest materials found with it, not by the earliest. Any disturbance level is given a new number and its relation to surrounding and succeeding levels noted.

Usually the nature of a disturbed area will indicate the cause of the original disturbance of the surface. Thus a shaped depression will indicate a pit, a burial will explain an entrance, remains of walls will clarify a robbing, fallen rock will suggest a building, and so on. Very often identification of the reason for a disturbance assists in excavating the area, since its limits can be predicted (*e.g.* walls and their foundation trenches, burials and their fillings, pit shapes, etc.).

These, then, constitute the major groups of problems encountered in actual digging. But even in "regular" excavation, following usual patterns and the usual stratigraphic theory, special situations will arise that require a particular technique and special precautions.

Buildings

Buildings, for example, be they the huts of American Indians or the monuments of kings, present the need for careful consideration and application of standard stratigraphic method. In the case of stone or brick walls, one cannot overlook their presence, although the accidental destruction of mud-brick is always a Near Eastern possibility, if not a common one elsewhere. How to go about dealing with these solid interruptions of stratigraphy is another question. In the case of camp and hut sites the delicate nature of the evidence is such that it may be missed completely. Thus normal excavation always includes the special situations, as well as the problems.

Camp and Hut Sites

To discuss the approach to the more primitive remains of ancient habitation first: the very nature of casual camp and impermanent hut sites precludes much in the way of spectacular results, or even of discernible plans. Since generally, in America, camp and hut sites were the temporary resting places of wandering, or at most semi-nomadic groups, the shelters erected on them were either portable (and hence not apt to leave tangible remains), or were of such a nature as to disintegrate easily when abandoned. Here must be excluded, of course, sod huts and other permanently walled enclosures (including village palisade walls) which fall into the brick-stone category below. A camp site poses the problem of extent of excavation, but this can be solved by gradual increase of the lateral expansion of squares as the evidence is uncovered and the over-all plan of the camp begins to emerge and to be clarified.

Of major interest, aside from the nature of the dwellings used, are the defense works, if any, including the access ways or gates, along with special use areas, such as religious shrines, factories, etc. As the plan of the camp site becomes clear, knowledge of local customs assists in determining the order of priority of excavation. At least one complete dwelling unit should be cleared, in order to restore (on paper) the type used on the site. Here, the presence of hearths, stone-edgings and curbings, post-hole molds, floors, dumps and fortifications, along with available pottery and other artifacts, all indicate the presence and nature of a given occupation. Here the stratigraphic method of peeling levels assists in assigning a particular period to a camp site as excavated over a large expanse. Thus care in determining and recording of levels is necessary.

In the case of huts and semi-permanent installations, such as corrals and pens, the situation is clarified a bit by the presence of solid structures. These are investigated in the same manner as are regularly built structures of any material, following the general rules of stratigraphic excavation. They can, therefore, be considered along with stone and brick constructions, even though some American Indian installations were partially dug into the ground, as well as built upon the surface.

All solid structures pose the problem of division or interruption of the horizontal levels, and at the same time also consist of a series of superimposed levels themselves. By that we mean that a wall, or an entire building, interrupts stratification by sticking up through a series of levels over a given segment of the excavation. The horizontal sequence of levels includes certain levels into which the original builders cut to set their foundations, as well as levels that, in the course of time, were accumulated all around— and eventually above—the finished structure. At the same time, the building has a complete stratigraphic history all its own—*i.e.* the floors which belong to it, the levels into which its parts were set, and the various phases and stages of repair, rebuilding, and restoration reflected in it.

Walls

Whether the wall or walls of a structure or of an entire village complex be sod, mud-brick, logs, stone, or cement, certain approaches must be made to determine meaning, relationships, and, if possible, use. The major difference between structures of different materials is simply a matter of relative durability, construction, and individual stresses to which the various parts of the structure in question has been put. These factors have some effect upon the archaeological evaluation of the residual materials. One of the most obvious problems to be met is the difficulty of distinguishing certain relatively perishable materials—such as sod, or mud-brick, or logs—from the soil surrounding them, since they may have been manufactured from that very soil in the first place, or may have since decayed into it. The distinction can be made, however, if care is paid to the whole matter of stratigraphic method. In the case of stone and other more durable materials, robbings, fall, or

reuse may cause some little confusion, but these too
are clearly indicated by careful excavation (*e.g.* by
density, outlines, soil color, etc.).

As excavation proceeds, if digging is done carefully, the difference between intrusive materials and
the complexion of a given level will be apparent, just
as any difference is picked up within a level, and
structures, regardless of material, will make themselves known by obvious formation. Here again, construction methods, determined by materials, often assist in declaring the presence of definite structures.
For example, masonry construction requires some
foundation or footing, in contract to mud-brick or
sod which may require little or none; hence, the
former generally is accompanied by foundation
trenches, etc., which assist in clarifying presence and
plan. The matter of decayed logs or post-walls is
closely related to that of post-molds, which will be
discussed below.

The usual method of excavating structures, regardless of material, is roughly the same. When a structure, or a part of it, has been uncovered, the interior
and the exterior sides must be considered as separate
areas. The levels must be given correspondingly different numbers, once the level which crosses (or,
strictly speaking, "seals off") the top of the structure
has been cleared away. Ultimately the next level
which crosses below the structure, unless the latter
goes clear to bedrock, will again relate all parts of a
given excavation area. Sometimes, however, a structure will extend down to bedrock, or to some other

solid impediment, and no real connection between interior and exterior is possible stratigraphically, unless it become clear through breaks in wall lines (*e.g.* doorways, windows, destructions, etc.).

Building Limits

When a structure has been found, certain other measures must be taken to prevent its "loss" archaeologically. Some clear idea must be gotten of the extent of a building, if possible; hence a wall may be traced laterally by the extension of excavation into adjoining squares or by the extension of a given area. This is not done *along* the line of a wall, however, since such an approach would destroy the connections of that wall with the levels on both sides of it. Rather, extent can be checked by cross-trenching, or opening of cross squares. When the limits of a structure are determined, the internal stratigraphy can be ascertained by the usual methods.

Here, however, the use of check areas (baulks) (see Chapter 3, "Controls") of unexcavated soil are very important—otherwise the excavator suddenly finds himself in an empty room, with four walls unrelated to anything he can check or even draw. By leaving an unexcavated area, either across a side, or in opposite corners, or in any area which develops unusual or complicated features, relationships can be checked and data clarified later. When all the information has been recorded and the situations are clear, the control keys can be cut out, if desired, but not until all the evidence has been evaluated. Excavation of buildings should, therefore, be at right angles to any given wall, to ascertain its relationship to levels coming up to the wall face itself.

Floor and Foundation Levels

The chronology of a structure is dependent upon its relationship to the levels with which it was connected as an occupation site, from its building to its destruction. Thus it is important to discover when a structure was originally erected, and how long it continued in use. These facts can be found from the foundation trench, or from the level on which the foundations actually rest, and from the floor levels within a structure. The first level which crosses over (or seals) a foundation trench marks the initial phase of occupation or use of a given structure. The floors—paved, hard-packed, or otherwise prepared for use—will mark the series of subsequent occupations to which the building was put. Here, the first floor which seals the foundation trench is, generally speaking, also chronologically the same as the exterior level which seals the foundation trench on the exterior side of the building wall. Other indications which assist in dating are artifacts, pottery, coins, etc. Successive floors, including intervening periods of disuse, however, do not necessarily correlate with the exterior levels of an area, since some floors tend to wear out rapidly and are replaced more or less continuously, while exterior levels accumulate more slowly.

Structural Features

When an entire structure is cleared, if that is to be done, other features must be noted in terms of dating and use. Changes in construction, rebuilds, and other clues are usually obvious from changes in original plan, reuse or change of materials, joints and bonds of corners and ends, additions, and a host of other structural indications. Here, again, knowledge of local building customs greatly assists the excavator, since these may also indicate datings, suggest reasons for changes, or even help to clarify an understanding of the general plan. Knowledge of general building techniques in all major materials, as well as of the special local variants, is essential to the over-all training of the archaeologist.

Finally, unless a structure is to be left permanently, the excavator must dismantle it in order to reach the lower levels. This process also serves as an additional dating check, since all materials, artifacts, etc., found inside a wall must predate its erection, or, at the latest, be contemporary with it. These, like the "foundation deposits" of the Near East, and the "corner-stone" deposits of modern times, are sort of built-in records of construction. In this regard, mud-brick walls are extremely profitable sources of data, since pieces of broken pottery (sherds) were often used in ancient times to help bind the brick material together, along with straw, grits, and other materials.

Hearths and Pits

In both camp sites and the more permanent structures of antiquity, hearths and pits are often encountered. Both of these are valuable indicators, but, at the same time, can cause great errors because they represent intrusions from higher (hence later) levels into lower (hence earlier) levels from a given surface. To excavate these intrusives features, care must be taken to clear them completely, in order to avoid mixing the contents of the level or levels into which they are cut. Hearths are generally shallow, and present little difficulty, particularly because of the accompanying discoloration of the soil which they produce.

Pits, on the other hand, may extend a number of feet into the surface, cutting into or through a number of levels, and often almost indistinguishable from the soil into which they were cut, since they may be filled again with that same soil (even though in an inverted order). Archaeologists differ as to the specific methods, but the safest approach is to let the situation dictate the precise method to be used in any given example. If a pit can be cleared out first, and then the succeeding levels excavated, this method is preferable since it gets rid of contaminating materials at once. If, however, the nature of the pit is obscure, or it is difficult to be sure of its extent, the safest method is that used in foundation trenches: isolation behind a thin skin of unexcavated soil, excavation of succeeding horizontal levels until the bottom of the pit area is reached, and then excavation of it.

Here, again, leaving earlier materials in company with later materials is permissible, but the reverse situation must be avoided and guarded against. When a hearth or pit can be excavated first, the preferable method is to excavate half of it, vertically, at a time, so that a clear picture of the internal stratification of the area can be preserved and connections with the other horizontal levels observed. This is particularly necessary when a storage pit has been in use over a long period of time. Once the first half of the pit has been excavated and properly noted, the other half can then be dug.

Post-molds

Post-molds (the residual impression left in the soil after the decay or destruction of dwelling posts) must be removed in the same manner as pits, since they also represent an intrusion into lower levels. Less care need be lavished in their removal, however, since they represent the mold of a solid stake or pole and thus have no chronological contribution to make. A great deal of care, however, must be given to an accurate description of the molds and their patterns, since they are, of course, the "image" in the surface of an occupational level of the buildings erected upon it.

In this case, careful measurement on a horizontal plane is the critical factor, along with careful measurement of mold size (to determine the size of the posts, and hence the weight-bearing capacity of the walls), and an attempt at determining the angle at which they were set (which clarifies the type of structure involved, in terms of roofing, general shape, etc.). Analysis of the wood samples, if any are preserved, may also be instructive, since this has something to do with the effectiveness of tools and craftsmanship of the builders. Related to such molds or impressions are decayed remnants of logs or post-walls. These must also be carefully measured and recorded, if the contours and structural features of the installation, or even village area, are to be determined.

Burrows and Roots

Some degree of confusion may sometimes be introduced into the stratigraphic picture when burrows or roots are encountered. These often resemble post-molds and may even be dug as such. Generally, however, it will soon become clear as to which phenomenon is being encountered. Both burrows and roots, or their molds, will finally identify themselves by branching off, curving, opening into a nest, or some similar variation, whereas the post-mold will generally be more or less smooth, straight-sided, and tapering at the end. It is better to err on the side of caution, however, than to ignore what might well turn out to be the only evidence for the plan of a dwelling. It is better to add a note in the notebook to the effect that what seemed to be a post-mold was really the remains of a root, rather than *vice versa!*

Burials

Burials are another of the special problems of archaeology which require special treatment and methods. A number of different practices were common in ancient times for disposal of the dead, and although they may have differed in terms of locality, chronology, and fashion, the sum total number of possibilities is so limited that most burials can be described in terms of a relatively few types. Dismemberment of the body, supine or prone burial, flexed or constricted burial, individual or group burial, tomb burials, jar burials, along with cremation by fire or chemicals—all seem to have had a rather general vogue throughout human history. Each of the categories involves special techniques, but the general approach is similar in every case.

Here, again, much time and effort can be saved (along with the preservation of the specimens, themselves) if one knows, in a general way, what to expect in any given locality or chronological period. Thus, in the Near East, the presence of large jars may indicate an enclosed skeleton, while, in America, a "bundle" at the bottom of a storage pit may indicate an Indian burial. Knowledge of the practice of "floor burials" will tend to make the excavator cautious within a structure. "Gables" of stone, or a "roof" suddenly appearing in the soil will be a signal in another context that a burial is near. Heaps of earth ("barrows" or mounds) are more conspicuous signs; while rings of stones likewise may signify funerary remains of a particular type.

Burial Registration

In any case, certain data must be secured in every burial find, regardless of the specific handling of the mortuary situation at the time (see Chapter 5, "Burial Reports"). What a burial may contribute, in terms of artifacts, will be of value only if the position of that burial, in a chronological sense, can be ascertained. Thus when any burial situation comes to light, how it got there becomes the main question. Few burials, including cremations, were made simply on the surface of the ground, and generally some attempt was made to conceal or protect the body, usually by excavation (*i.e.* a dug grave) or in a previously constructed resting place (*i.e.* a tomb, either excavated, or erected). Hence the entry pit for interment of body, bones, or ashes must be discovered, if possible, and its relation to the levels through which it cuts, along with the level which seals it, must be noted.

Clearing of Burials

When a burial is cleared, it should be photographed and planed before anything is removed. Often the relative position of grave furniture (*i.e.* the objects buried with the body) assists in reconstructing them. The skeleton must be cleaned thoroughly (with dull, flat-bladed knives, brushes, blowers, trowels, and other fine hand tools). If the bones are so weak that they tend to crumble, some means of strengthening them may be tried (see below), so that the skeleton may be "lifted" as a whole. If this is not possible, the skull, the long bones of arms and legs, and the pelvis should be saved and carefully preserved for future study by an expert. A variety of devices are suggested, here and there, for the lifting of burials, and which method is used must depend upon the situation and the materials available. Undercutting the burial and placing wood or metal supports beneath it is probably the simplest method, but the result is apt to be a burden far heavier than might be anticipated. Sometimes the bones are strong enough, or can be strengthened enough, to remove them separately and then reassemble the skeleton from photographs and drawings. If the burial is an important one, trained specialists are needed for the job. In that case, the skeleton should be covered with a waterproof cover weighted down with stones along the edges to keep animals and visitors away.

Cremations

Cremations are of such a nature as to preclude the salvaging of much of the bones, but the specific details of find-spot, arrangement, etc. have to be carefully recorded. Catastrophic cremations (*e.g.* volcano action, etc.) often allow of fuller detail when uncovered, and may even allow of reconstruction of skeletal outline, but these are the exceptions, not the general rule.

Tomb Burials

Once the entrance pit has been cleared, the excavation of tomb burials very often is less a matter of digging than one of care in recording, photography, and planing. The same attention to position and arrangement of furniture and body or bodies must be given as in cases of regular interment. Generally speaking, the entrance to a tomb or the pit of a deep grave will have been filled at one time, and nothing within the fill will postdate the burial. The danger of reused graves and tombs, in reference to the chronology of the fill, exists, however. In certain areas, such reuse by family or clan or simply through chance can continue over many generations. Again, caution must be used in regard to the off-hand dating of a complete grave area ("necropolis") on the basis of a single example, since all may not be of the same period. Some clue as to date is, however, of course afforded by the contents of the pit or grave fill, if carefully evaluated.

String Grids for Burial Registration

The planning and photographing of a burial, or a similar complex can be greatly assisted by the construction of a string grid over the area. String is stretched across the burial area in straight lines, equally spaced according to the size of the area involved. A second series of string lines is then stretched at right angles to the first, and spaced accordingly. This will result in a grid, on the basis of which greater scale in photographs may be attained. Using graph paper with printed squares, one can, with little effort, determine a scale and draw in details of a burial area. Where a number of burials are encountered, a simple wooden frame, with string girds already tacked in place, makes a handy portable drawing device. These frames can be quite cumbersome to handle, but can be made to be collapsible.

Burial Mounds and Defensive Earthworks

Still another type of special problem related to burials and pits is to be found in the burial mound (barrow), and its similar artificial formation, the defensive earthwork. These two, but especially the latter are encountered in almost every part of the world, since a simple earthwork probably is one of the earliest methods of defense used by man. Differing only in motive for use, the mound type of construction, whether for burial or defense, is of interest both for its contents and its architecture. Although a mound seems to be quite prosaic—merely a heap of earth and debris—it can exhibit a number of surprises and may even be extremely complex in its conception and execution. Further, although the mound or barrow seems to be stratigraphy in reverse (*i.e.* piled up *above* the surface), it still follows the regular rules of excavation and is to be seen as another example of levels accumulated stratigraphically. The only difference is that the mound or barrow is a smaller site spot built up artificially by man, and, usually, over a shorter period of time.

Section and Quadrant Excavation

The mound is attacked, archaeologically, from top to bottom, with the individual levels peeled off in regular sequence. In order to preserve the order of that sequence visually, the same control system is used as in ordinary excavation. Two possible variations of method are in use in excavating earthwork mounds, and the specific one to be employed is determined by the situation in each case. The first method is excavation by sections, slicing at right angles to the face of the mound and completely through it. This is preferable in dealing with a mound of some length, or with a defensive earthen wall. The second possibility is to remove segments (like the slices of a cake or pie), leaving baulks in between for control. This technique is called the "quadrant" method, and is preferable for grave mounds, especially, since it preserves a visual picture of the make-up of the mound in both directions.

In any case, once the mound or earthwork has been entered, the basic difference between burials and defenses becomes clear. The burial mound is simply a monumental covering for the grave (either a pyre, a hut, a grave-pit, or some other arrangement, with accompanying area), generally with some delineation of the sector (i.e. by a trench, a circle of stones, or some other sign). This grave may be of one individual (such as a chief, hero, or beloved citizen), or of a multitude (*e.g.* warriors fallen in battle). On the other hand, the defensive work has been erected for the sole purpose of preventing access, hence, it is generally reinforced internally (by timbers, debris, old walls, or even with new reinforcing walls) to preclude shifting or easy sapping. The reasons for excavating the two earthwork types, burial and defensive, are thus also different. In defensive work, the method of construction is the major interest; in the burial mound, construction is important, but content is more crucial. Although offerings or protective deposits may be distributed through the make-up of a burial mound, the major concentration of contents is usually on the surface level (*i.e.* the level upon which the mound itself was originally erected). This surface level, because of successive events, may even be considerably below the modern surface level, as is to be expected from the usual phenonenon of stratigraphic accumulation. Further, because of the nature of the burial mound (*i.e.* as a covering for something) the actual burial generally occupies the geographical center of the mound on the ancient surface level. About this center the ancient builders heaped their covering mound.

Architectural details of defensive works (such as ditches, revetment walls, particular measures taken for strengthening, sally points, entrance arrangements, etc.) should not be overlooked. These usually appear in the cross-section wall of an excavated earth-

THE EXCAVATION OF MOUNDS AND OTHER EARTHWORKS

A. SEGMENT METHOD:

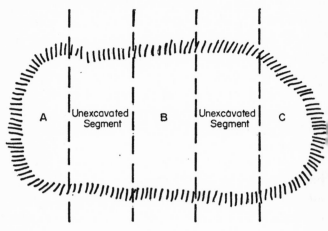

Segments (A, B, C) excavated through earthwork.
Unexcavated segments serve as controls.

B. QUADRANT METHOD:

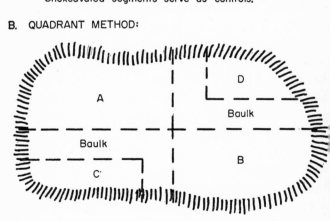

Quadrants (A, B, C, D) excavated, with control
baulks unexcavated.

work, but care should be taken not to miss signs of re-building and the relationships of all phases of the earthwork to each other and to the final product. Various periods of use will be plainly indicated in section also by the presence of signs of successive surface levels upon which vegetation grew annually ("turf lines"), or which were packed down by wear and then rebuilt. These, of course, have definite chronological implications for the interpretation of the total work.

Rock Shelters and Cave Sites

Rock shelters and cave sites often represent the very earliest homes of man, either as semi-permanent or as transit residences. Surfaces indications (location or surface flints) usually testify to the archaeological possibilities of such sites. In any case, if these sites are to be meaningful at all in terms of contents, they must be excavated stratigraphically—by either a trench or sector approach. Peeling off predetermined amounts of soil, over the entire site, is both arbitrary and unrewarding. Any site occupied by man will show strata and these must determine the levels, not an artificial number of inches or centimeters of soil.

Open Air Sites

Here is included a variety of "sites" rather difficult to pin down, except from careful observation of the surface area. Tent circles, boulder circles, quarry sites, betyles (standing stones), pictographs and sim-ilar remains are often right before one's eyes and remain unseen. Here background knowledge of an area and its cultural history comes into focus again. Knowing what to look for assists in finding it, and in recognizing its nature when once found. The corollary to identification is, of course, recording. Often valuable remains are "lost," or destroyed because they are not recorded and reported. This is another example of the great importance of site survey and site map records.

Archaeology, however, is more than simply excavating. To be sure, this is how the materials are actually uncovered, but "discovery" is worthless unless it is properly recorded so that relationships and meanings can be determined and understood. Without records, even the most careful digging is senseless. Often the poorest excavation techniques have been partially offset by a record of what was actually done. The best archaeologist, therefore, must always combine the best possible techniques of excavating with the best possible methods of recording. The next chapter will deal briefly with this subject in terms of the content and methods of recording necessary to achieve intelligible results.

5

THE RECORDING OF EXCAVATION

The key to accurate recording is clarity. What the excavator wants to record is the nature of his finds and their relationships to each other and to the entire excavation. All other information is superfluous and can be dispensed with.

Recording is done descriptively. That is, for each notation there must be a description of the facts, so written that they make clear to the reader what has been done. To assist in this aim, measurements and other indications of location, size, etc. are also included as part of the notation, along with soil descriptions, descriptions of structures, notations on frequency of pottery occurrence, etc. Thus find spots, levels, and areas can all be reproduced or checked on maps and plans, or on the ground by future excavators.

Site Notebook

In order to keep the approach to recording as simple as possible, we shall begin with the excavator at the actual site (the "site supervisor"), and then proceed to more detailed matters later. The site supervisor is actually the person who controls all the other records of excavation, since his notes and directions to others form the basis for permanent recording and interpretation of results. Normally the site supervisor keeps a "site notebook," which is merely an individual notebook in which he records the history of the excavation of his own trench, square, or other area unit. A bound, hard-covered notebook is probably the best to use, preferably with one side of each sheet plain or printed with graph lines for sketches. Looseleaf notebooks, no matter how reinforced, tend to lose their pages, since note-taking on an excavation may be in the middle of a storm, a high wind, or a labor argument! Once lost, a sheet of recorded notes means a gap in the entire picture of the excavation. The gain in neatness (via recopying of pages) in a loose-leaf notebook system is thus secondary to completeness and security. Notes should be taken in ink, preferably a waterproof variety. The ball-point pen has thus become the archaeologist's constant companion, providing both a nonleaking supply of ink and an unbreakable point.

Notation of Levels

The British have developed a rather intricate page-notation system, which is generally too cumbersome and, in actuality, requires undue attention. What is basic in page notation, is of course simple sequence, from page to page, of level notations as they occur. Where some interruption of the page sequence occurs, an index notation to the next page in sequence in a given section must be made. Basic to the entire system of notebook recording is the proper notation of the levels themselves by the simple method of giving each a separate number. No matter what number is assigned to a level in the course of excavating, the notation must be made of its place in the over-all sequence of the excavation. Next to each level number, a brief description should be written in the notebook of whatever has actually been given that number (*i.e.* regular levels of soil, walls as discovered, pits, hearths, etc.). These descriptions should cover general appearance, so that they may be identified and recognized "on the ground."

Following the description, the excavator notes anything unusual about the actual level itself (*i.e.* rocky, rich in artifacts, sterile soil, fire-burned, etc.). A brief form for the site notebook format is reproduced here, and each site will call for its own particular modification (see Chapter 2, "Sites"). The drawings and sketches of the site supervisor need not be measured ones (although measurements should be noted). The more refined measured drawings are the task of the surveyor and the draftsmen.

Level Tags

At the same time as the level is noted in the site notebook, tags or labels should be put into the wall of the excavation marking the actual presence of the level noted in the records. This system facilitates rapid identification and eventual section drawing, along with identification of pottery and other materials uncovered. The level tag is just that—a simplified version of the notebook description and identification of the individual level. The general site name (or code designation), the specific trench or square number, the notebook level number (often circled to identify it beyond any doubt), and a brief description of the individual level should be on each tag. These are then placed at intervals along the walls of the excavation, the number depending upon the situation. The large staples used by builders can serve to hold the tags in the wall, via a hole punched in the top.

"Find" Tags

The same kind of record must be made to identify finds. Record tags are again necessary, being a bit more elaborate and made out in duplicate in this case (so that one can always be attached outside, the other inside, containers in which the artifacts are stored). Here again appear the general site name, the year, the specific site locus, notebook level number, and a brief level description along with the date (in case of accidental mixing of levels or of storage containers as well as to identify specific batches of finds), and the site supervisor's name or initials. These are placed in the bottom of whatever receptacle is being used to collect finds (*something* should always be used—the casual heaping up of finds along the edge of a trench is an abominable habit, as well as being an invitation to the mixing of level materials). In the Near East, baskets serve for pottery fragments and kraft paper bags serve for other small finds, with boxes for the larger artifacts. This seems preferable to single containers with multiple compartments, wherein items are kept together and sorted later. It is important to check whether tags have been made out for each receptacle, to preclude losing the identity of materials once they have been removed from a given site. Sample level and find tags are reproduced here as guides. These, too, may require some modification for specific sites, or to fit a given situation, even though the total information required is the same. On a large dig, printed or stamped tags are used, with spaces for the individual data required.

SUMMARY: ADMINISTRATIVE RECORD FORMS

Sample Record Forms

SITE NOTEBOOK

Preferably 8½" x 11", hard-cover, bound book; ruled lines with scaled grid on reverse of each sheet for scaled drawings; includes

Level Number—consecutively numbered as excavated in each area, not necessarily successive in terms of position relationship; order and location of each specific level relation necessary.

Description—details of color, composition, make-up, and content of each level noted.

Remarks—all pertinent data relating to what was found, relation to whole work, unusual features, pottery frequency, possible importance, and similar data should be recorded.

Scaled Drawings—on scaled overleaf, or on added sheets. These are measured, but not to the degree of accuracy of the plans drawn by the surveyor.

Space must be left after *each* level notation for additional information, as larger areas are opened up; notation of the level should *never* be on a daily basis—but each day's work on a given level should *always* be noted under the primary notation, regardless of date.

Notations should be made in permanent ink; errors are simply crossed out.

References to other level numbers should be encircled.

SAMPLE NOTEBOOK ENTRIES

Level No.	Description & Remarks
3	Light-brown sandy soil, with small stones, under level ②; floor level of Wall #1(?); occupational level— N. B. burning marks on surface.
4	Hearth; charcoal & burned debris; gravel held in stone-built circle; cut into level ②—see sketch for size and location.
5	Hard red-black soil; under level ③; earlier floor level of Wall #1; high pottery frequency.
6	Wall #2; mud-brick (20 cm X 10 cm); mud mortar; staggered coursing; extending E-W; emerged in level ③; see sketch.

SUMMARY: ADMINISTRATIVE RECORDS

Sample Record Forms
Site Records

LEVEL LABELS

Executed by site supervisors; placed in trench wall as needed (suggested: every 50 cm.–1 m.); identify the levels as dug, and provide ready data for notebook recording and pottery tags: contain basic data only.

Site Name	PETRA
Expedition/Year	AEP 1962
Trench	Trench I.8
Level	Level 1
Description	Description: lt brn, sandy

POTTERY TAGS*

Executed by site supervisor; placed in each basket or other container used for finds; written in ink; always in *duplicate* (for added protection of locus identification and for future use on wrapped bags of samples—*i.e.* one inside package, another tied to exterior).

Site Name	PETRA	PETRA
Expedition/Year	AEP 1962	AEP 1962
Trench	Trench I.8	Trench I.8
Level	Level 1	Level 1
Description	Description: lt brn, sndy	Description: lt brn, sndy
Date	Date: 10/7/62	Date: 10/7/62
Site Supervisor	XYZ	XYZ

* The same form of tag is used for other artifacts uncovered, with a notation made as to type entered on the tag (*e.g.* stone, metal, etc.).

Burial Reports

In the case of burials, additional data is necessary. For this reason, the Burial Report (*i.e.* the description of any burials found) may take the form of a separate report sheet. Here must be included the findspot, the position (extended, flexed, etc.), the orientation (of particular importance in the Near East), the state of preservation, and a general description of the type of interment, ornamentation, furniture, and stratigraphic relationships (see Chapter 3, Burials). Measurement of the skeleton and a thorough plotting and photographing of the site must also be done. A sample Burial Report is given for guidance.

Section Drawing

The final job of the site supervisor in recording is that of drawing a "section" of his completed work, at crucial locations in his area. This simply means a scaled drawing of the vertical face of an excavated area (usually at a scale of 1:20 in the metric system, or 1:24 in the duodecimal system), which serves to tie the site notebook, the actual excavation, and the meaning of the excavator's notes together. It records the superimposition of levels so that, in later study and reference, they may be seen in their actual sequences. Thus the accent is on accuracy, but in a schematic fashion. Too much shown in a section drawing is just as bad as too little. Here the drawing

BURIAL REPORT (Site Supervisor)

_____
(Excavation Name)

B U R I A L   R E P O R T

SITE _____

LEVEL NO. _____

DATE _____

POSITION OF BURIAL (Extended, flexed, etc.)____

_____

ORIENTATION _____

STATE OF PRESERVATION _____

TYPE OF BURIAL _____

ORNAMENTATION, FURNITURE, ETC._____

_____

_____

STRATIGRAPHIC RELATIONSHIPS _____

PHOTOGRAPH NO._____

PLANNED BY _____

REMARKS _____

_____

_____

DISPOSITION _____

_____

_____
(Site Supervisor)

differs from a photograph, and serves quite a different purpose.

"Accuracy" in section drawing is in terms of presenting an understandable view, and is determined by the needs of the situation, the tools used, and the degree of complexity necessary to make the section clear. To some extent, therefore, the section drawing is conventional, and although important details will be recognizable when compared to the actual site, they are not drawn absolutely, either to scale or to texture, even though their identification is unmistakable. Conventional symbols for stone, soil, brick, masonry, etc. are all adapted to fit the needs of the particular drawing in question.

The method of section drawing is fairly simple:

1. A string is stretched across the face of the vertical area to be drawn, secured by nails or other means a few inches from the face itself. This string is then made level via a hand level in order to provide an arbitrary reference point for measurement and drawing. This is the "datum line" and is drawn to scale on scaled graph paper as a straight line. Along the actual string line is hung a measuring tape, preferably on another set of nails, in order to facilitate linear measurement along the datum line.

2. A series of vertical measurements are then made, at convenient horizontal distances along the datum line upward and downward to each of the levels and to outstanding features which stand out in the face of the section, or to which some reference has been made in the site notebook. The measure-

ments so secured are then noted on the graph paper
at the proper points along the datum line already
drawn in. All the separate points are then joined to
outline the levels, walls, pavements, or particular features visible in the face of the actual excavated section. Conventional renderings of each type of material are made to assist later visual identification;
level numbers and brief verbal descriptions are also
included, to coincide with the notebook descriptions.

3. The completed drawing is labeled as to site,
area, compass direction, site supervisor's name, and
any other information necessary for future reference.
The section drawings are usually done in pencil at
the site and then inked in with India ink for permanent reference.

A SECTION DRAWING FROM THE FIELD

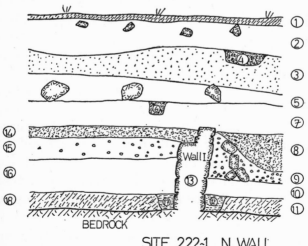

SITE 222-1   N. WALL
SECTION   1:20   A.K. '62

Tools for Section Drawing

This kind of drawing requires the use of a pocket-size steel tape for the vertical measurements from the datum line, a plumb bob to insure accuracy and to assist in getting over difficult places (such as walls), and a drawing board to hold the actual drawing itself. A triangular engineer's scale, of the appropriate scale, is also very handy, since it simplifies the conversion of measurements from the actual size to the scale of the drawn lines. A supply of nails, toothpicks, or wooden match sticks is also handy for temporarily keeping track of the levels as they are traced along from the datum line. This work can be done singlehanded, but a helper, either taking the actual measurements or recording the measured points on the drawing sheet, is of great assistance, and speeds up what can become, at times, a rather tiresome task. An extra set of hands to help with tapes and plumb bob, when both have to be used at one time, is also welcome!

Permanent Records

In theory, at least, the site supervisor does not have to concern himself with the permanent records of the excavation beyond those noted above. However, depending upon the personnel of a dig (which, in some cases, may be limited to the excavator alone), a general idea of the nature of other permanent records is necessary. To be concise, the following records constitute the minimum permanent history of any excavation, regardless of its size. The actual size of the records themselves will depend on the extent of the work, the number of levels and artifacts uncovered, and similar features. Sample formats of each of these records are included to serve as a guide, the precise type being determined by the situation (see also Chapter 5).

JOURNAL ("DAY NOTES")

_____
Expedition Name)

_____
(Date)

_____
(Site)

Director _____

Subdivision Number _____ Level: _____

General Progress _____

_____

New features, materials, etc. _____

_____

Special Features _____

_____

Photographs, Drawings, etc. Required _____

_____

_____

1. Journal ("Day Notes"): a general summary of the progress of an entire excavation, kept on a daily basis. This is usually the job of the director.

2. Register: the record of all individual finds which are retained by the expedition, with necessary information concerning them. These records are usually kept by the recorder, in duplicate, one copy for the expedition and another copy for local governmental or other authorities.

3. Small Finds Index: this is the record of all small artifacts, with the general exception of pottery vessels, maintained on three sets of index cards (by serial numbers, by site, and by the kind of object). This is again usually the job of the recorder.

Photographic Records

These records are supplemented by photographs and drawings of the pottery and other objects actually uncovered. Here again, the individual excavator is not supposed to have to assume the role of photographer or draftsman, but may well find himself doing it. The photographic side of archaeology is becoming a highly specialized branch and cannot be discussed here. The cardinal photographic principle to keep in mind is that any photograph taken must clearly indicate *what* is intended to be illustrated. To put it differently, an archeological photograph should declare at once to the viewer *why* it was taken at all. To achieve this effect, the photographer must examine the situation carefully, both archeologically and photographically. He must supply some means

REGISTER (recorder)

REGISTER

Page _____ Vol. _____ Year _____ _____ (Site)

Serial No.	Date	Square	Level No.	Description	Material	Measurements	Drawing/Photo

SMALL FINDS INDEX (Recorder): Three Cards

Object Card

Type of Object: _____ Drawing:

Site _____

Level _____

Serial No. _____

Date _____

Description _____

_____

Material _____

Measurements _____

Site Card

Site _____ Drawing

Level _____

Type of Object _____

Serial No. _____

Date _____

Description _____

_____

Material _____

Measurements _____

```
┌─────────────────────────────────────────────┐
│                  Serial Card                  │
│   Serial No.  _____  │
│   Type of Object _____   │
│   Site _____  │
│   Level _____   │
│                    etc.                        │
└─────────────────────────────────────────────┘
```

of suggesting scale to the viewer (via a scale stick, or ruler, preferably), and must be sure that the object of his photograph is both visible and obvious. Here the site supervisor can contribute by cleaning the area (with brushes and brooms), and by removing extraneous debris from the area to be photographed.

Scale sticks or rods are a must in archaeological photography, and the photographer must have enough variety in size to handle all situations. These can be made quite easily by taking 1″ x 1″ sticks, painting them white and then masking off every other unit of measurement with masking tape and spraying or brushing on black paint, making a scale stick easy to read and easy to photograph. "Sign boards" indicating the site, date, trench, level, and other information also help clarify a photograph. These may be made by using movable letters on grooved board, or by using gummed letters on cardboard, or some similar method.

Pottery Drawing

Pottery and artifact drawing are also quite specialized affairs, but even the amateur can eventually learn to do a creditable job. Again certain conventions have been established in the field which assist in making a drawing clear and meaningful. The proper drawing of a piece of pottery, particularly, cannot be replaced by a photograph and where one or the other is to be chosen, the drawing is preferable.

POTTERY DRAWING

Complete and Reconstructed Forms (1·2):

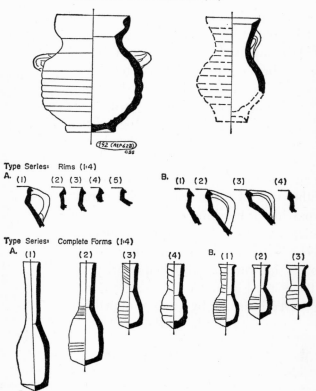

Type Series: Rims (1·4)
A. (1) (2) (3) (4) (5)   B. (1) (2) (3) (4)

Type Series: Complete Forms (1·4)
A. (1) (2) (3) (4)   B. (1) (2) (3)

In drawing pottery, a given piece is outlined, and then a vertical line through the center of the drawing separates the two sides, each of which is handled differently in the finished product. The right side of the drawing is shown as a cross-section through the edge of the particular piece. The left side of the drawing is rendered to show the external appearance of the vessel, including decoration or other surface treatment. The outline of the vessel itself may be actual or may be restored (via calculations). The cross-section is drawn from measurements, using calipers and other tools for assistance. This cross-section is of great importance, since it indicates specific rim formation, construction devices, joints, and other details. External decorations are carefully drawn so that comparisons may be made. Scaled drawings (*i.e.* drawings made less than full size) were common in the past, but most work done today is full scale (*i.e.* 1:1) and is reduced photographically for publication. When a drawing is done to less than full scale the irregularities, which may be invaluable for classification purposes, are too often either disregarded or lost entirely when the drawing is published. As a result, great care is taken in drawing to full scale to emphasize the important features for classification so that they are clearly evident when the drawing is reduced in size for publication. Actual tracing of contours is done wherever possible and accurate measurements are taken by calipers, or other means, when tracing cannot be fully carried out (*e.g.* interiors of small mouthed pieces, bases, handles, and other inaccessible areas). Often pottery drawings are done in the field as the excavation progresses, but unless staff size permits this, it usually becomes too cumbersome a task and is completed at a later time. Ultimately the Register should show drawings of all completed pieces, all reconstructed pieces (see Chapter 7, Pottery Restoration and Reconstruction), and unusual sherds, along with photographs. Each drawing should also show the registration number of the individual piece it represents, with the number encircled.

Drawing Aids

A variety of drawing aids, either for tracing or for more free-hand drawing of outlines, are available on

POTTERY DRAWING AIDS

Determination of Rim Size (Diameter): Scale Method

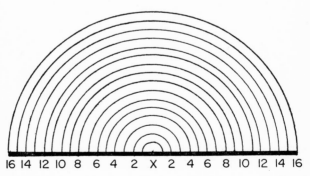

A measuring "scale" is made by drawing a series of half-circles from a single point (x) at increasing diameters.
Rim fragments to be measured are compared with scale until appropriate curve coincides, and "size" can be read.

Determination of Rim Size: Mathematical Method

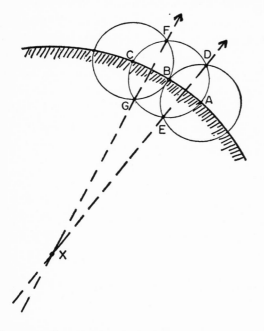

The outer edge of the rim fragment is traced on drawing paper. From any point along the curve (A) a circle is drawn with a compass.

From the point (B) where the first circle cuts the traced curve, another circle of the same size is drawn. Where the second circle again cuts the curve (C), a third circle of the same size is drawn.

Lines are drawn through the intersections of the three circles (D-E and F-G). Where those lines intersect (D-E-X and F-G-X) the center of a circle corresponding to the original size of the rim will be found (X).

the market and assist greatly in the task of drawing the pottery and other finds from an expedition's work. Scaled drawing papers (like graph paper), or open frames with a network of strings at set intervals, are sometimes used as guides. Common among older devices was the vertical stand with small horizontal rods protruding through holes at set intervals. The rods could be moved against the contours of a vessel to provide reference points for drawing. Another of the older devices still to be seen is the *camera lucida,* which is simply a box with sighting and viewing holes inside of which is a mirror or prism. This device causes the illusion that the reflected image of an object is actually projected, in reduced size, on the drawing paper, itself, where its outlines can be traced. Actual tracing of the contours of a vessel or other artifact is, however, always preferable. Devices for tracing rounded shapes are available and generally consist of a flat base which glides over the drawing sheet, with a vertical arm perpendicular to the base. The arm actually traces the outlines of the vessel and, at the point where the arm and base join, a pencil or pen transfers the contours to the drawing sheet. The rim size of a vessel should be determined whenever drawings are being made of sherds alone. The rim diameter of a piece of pottery can be most easily ascertained by the use of a very simple drawing aid. This device is constructed by scribing a series of half-circles on a sheet of drawing paper from a common center. The rim fragment to be checked is then placed against succeeding arcs until it fits, and thus indicates the rough size of the original rim diameter of the vessel. The same information can be determined by drawing a line around the outer edge of a rim sherd and then calculating the center of that arc by mathematical principles (see illustration). In any case, when drawing rim sherds their relation to the horizontal must be indicated, in order to show the angle at which they were originally joined to the complete vessel. Again, a very simple drawing aid comes to the rescue. The top edge of the rim fragment is held against a straight edge (a ruler, a flat piece of cardboard, or similar rigid object) and tilted back and forth until no light shows between the two. At this point the rim surface is horizontal, in terms of its original position, and the angle at which it joined the rest of the vessel may be seen, as well. The same trick will assist in determining the correct horizontal position of a base fragment. Once the original edge is determined, drawing is simple.

Flints and Other Lithics

Because of the great importance of flint projectile points, banner stones, rubbers, and other stone tools and weapons in American archaeology, a great deal of attention has been devoted to their classification and presentation. As a result of this widespread concern for such artifacts, it was felt unnecessary to dwell on them at length in this volume. It should be noted, however, that these artifacts, because of their chronological and cultural value, must be carefully noted in the course of excavation. Each item must be registered after it has been cleaned (see Chapter 7, "Lithics") and the registry number put on the artifact in waterproof ink, covered by collodion, as is done with ceramic pieces (see Chapter 7, "Pottery Marking"). Drawing of these pieces is usually less cumbersome a process than is the case with pottery, because of their smaller size, but it is also more difficult in terms of accuracy, because of the complexities introduced by marks of chipping, drilling, and other surface treatments. However, outlines must be carefully traced, if possible, and chipped faces carefully noted in the case of projectile points. This should be done in the most simple manner possible, with clarity the keynote of the drawings. Photographs should accompany the drawn forms wherever possible in publication. Classification of these artifacts is covered in the various excavation reports of local areas, to which reference must be made in order to understand both typology and chronology in that area.

Surveying: Triangulation

Full-scale surveying is again not the task of the site supervisor, and may well be beyond the limits of interest or technical ability of most amateurs. But certain aspects of survey techniques must be used as everyday recording practices in the field, aside from the major job of the official surveyor (see also Chapter 3). Most common of these techniques is the plotting of features or find-spots for recording in the site notebook. Although even here major features (such as walls, pavements, etc.) will be recorded in the permanent record plans by a visit from the surveyor, a reasonably accurate record of them should also be placed in the site notebook for handy field reference.

The simplest way to record a given feature is by means of a survey method known as triangulation. This means that from any two known points the third point of a triangle may be plotted. Here the "record stakes" along the sides of a trench or square come into use. Since the distance between any two stakes is known, they may be plotted on a scale drawing, and connected by a straight line drawn to scale. They become, therefore, two "known" points, and from them any third point may be located by taking measurements to it from both stakes with tape and plumb bob. These measurements are then transferred to the drawing by scale and compass and the point at which they meet is the "third" or "unknown" point on the ground.

Thus, by this method, any number of points may be located by multiplying the number of triangles on the ground. Surveyor's "arrows" (metal rods with finger loops) are used to great advantage here, since they may be moved from point to point easily, and serve as portable "points" for further measurements too far from stakes, or in places difficult of access from the stakes.

Site Surveying: Triangulation Grid

It is by a larger scale application of this same method that a given site is actually plotted on the plan of an expedition and related to known maps of the entire area or district. The surveyor establishes a "base-line," fixing two points at each end of a measured distance. From these two points further measurements are then taken to unknown points, which can then be plotted in the same manner as the site supervisor plotted the features of his smaller area. This continues, on the site itself, until a "triangulation grid" of the site is made. This is merely a series of interrelated triangles, indicated on the ground by semi-permanent markers (or "station points"), which covers the area to be excavated, and may also include some feature (*e.g.* a "bench-mark" or permanent mapping marker) already on a map of the area. Thus the site may have points relating its various parts and tying them into other recorded features.

If a transit is used, the surveyor need not even measure the distances from his base-points to the station points, since he can measure angles, and these furnish the same information mathematically since the base-line has actually been measured. All this data is then transferred to a drawn plan, generally at a scale of about 1:100.

Coordinate Grid

From the "triangulation grid" a further grid may be prepared which sometimes forms the basis for

STEPS IN TRIANGULATION

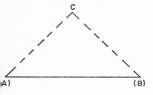

Points A and B known, distance A–B known, Point C to be located:

Distances A–C and B–C measured and plotted; intersection of lines A–C and B–C locates point C.

PREPARING TRIANGULATION GRID

The T.G. is made in order that the various sections of an area may be related to each other.

The T.G. is established by setting up semi-permanent markers on the ground ("station points"), which serve as the apexes of a series of interrelated triangles actually determined on the ground and transferred to a drawn plan.

The station points are tied in with bench-marks, or other similar permanent reference points in the area.

Smaller subdivisions of the triagulations may be made, as determined by the needs of the excavations.

"Station-points" established on the ground.

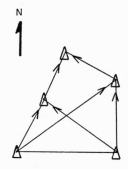

Triangulations to "Station-points—transferred to Plan.

recording the areas of the excavation as it progresses. This is the "coordinate grid," which is the super-imposition upon the triangulation grid of a series of parallel lines, laid out on the plan in North-South, East-West directions.

This is accomplished by taking any point on the triangulation grid and drawing a line through it either N-S or E-W (by compass bearing). From those lines, equally spaced parallel lines are then lined off on each side of the first drawn lines and perpendicular to them. This new grid now covers all the area which was only partially located via the triangulation grid and its fixed station points. Hence, any place in the area can now be referred to in terms of coordinate grid references. These references are usually designated by letters for the N-S lines and numbers for the E-W lines. Thus any given square can be fitted into its proper coordinate grid location and referred to in terms of it.

If this gridding is done at the very beginning of an excavation, the plan of the "excavating grid" can be made to fit that of the coordinate grid, and refer-ences generally simplified. It was for this reason that the suggestion was made above that the lines of excavation should be as close to N-S, E-W as possible.

Topographical Surveying

A further step in the survey of a site is the topo-graphical or contour map. This is a full-dress affair, however, and is generally to be left in the hands of a trained surveyor. Assistance is possible in most cases

PREPARING COORDINATE GRID

The C.G. furnishes a ready reference system for any given section or locus on the site as a whole.

The C.G. is superimposed on the T.G. by chosing any point on the T.G. and drawing N-S, E-W lines through the point chosen. "Grid" lines are then drawn parallel to the original N-S, E-W lines at set intervals. These are lettered in one direction and numbered in the other direction, or numbered in both directions. Apexes of the T.G. may be noted for reference purposes.

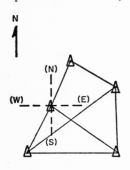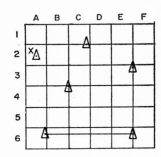

The location of the triangulation point marked "x" would therefore be noted, in terms of the coordinate grid references, as "A-2" or "1-2," reading first the N-S square reference number and then the E-W square reference number.

from national or other map-making agencies. Geodetic surveys, aerial maps (especially stereoptic ones), and other types of ground survey sheets are usually available. With these helps, a particular site can be tied down to official bench-marks or other permanent ground markers. The basic tools for this type of plotting are the *plane table,* the *dumpy level,* and the *transit.* These all come in a variety of types and the specific operation of each must be individually learned. The fine points of these operations are beyond the scope of this manual, but can be found in any surveying text.

Scales

The scales used in plotting vary with the particular job and its needs. A large area will allow a larger scale; a smaller area, or the details of a specific feature will require a smaller scale. In the metric system, the scales 1:100, 1:50, 1:25, and 1:20 are probably the most common archaeologically. Adaptations of these in feet and inches are made to suit the situation, with 1:100, 1:50, along with 1:12 common in the small scale range, with 1:1000 and downward used in large scale work.

Conventional Signs

In topographical surveying conventional signs are also a common factor. These are generally accepted symbols, looking vaguely like the features for which they stand, which are used to indicate natural and artificial aspects of terrain, features, and materials. Since these are also used by the site supervisor in making his sketches, and specifically in drawing his section, some acquaintance with these symbols is most desirable. Lists of them, with their meanings, can be found in books on camping and scouting, and are even part of the familiar highway touring maps of today.

Elevations

Elevations are drawings which show the elevated parts of a building, such as its walls, in distinction to

CONVENTIONAL SIGNS IN ARCHAEOLOGICAL DRAWING

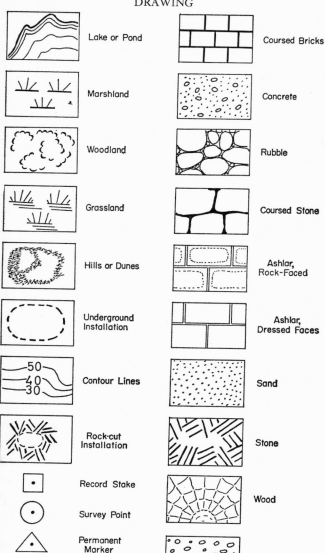

Lake or Pond

Marshland

Woodland

Grassland

Hills or Dunes

Underground Installation

Contour Lines

Rock-cut Installation

Record Stake

Survey Point

Permanent Marker

Trench Line

Coursed Bricks

Concrete

Rubble

Coursed Stone

Ashlar, Rock-Faced

Ashlar, Dressed Faces

Sand

Stone

Wood

Gravel

a mere plan, which shows only the foundation outlines. Drawing elevations to show how they appeared
in ancient times ("restorations") requires some artistic, architectural, and technical skill, as well as the
ability to handle drawing instruments. These drawings are therefore usually left to the trained surveyor
or draftsman, but even the amateur can learn to do a
creditable job by using some of the drawing aids
available. One of these is isometric paper, which
looks like the usual scaled paper used for graphs, but
its sets of parallel lines are printed at angles of 90°,
60°, and 30°, in terms of one side of the paper. The
actual measurements of a plan (length and width),
along with measurements indicating height, are
transferred to the lines of this paper to produce an
elevation. This type of elevation looks like a true
perspective drawing, but none of its lines diminish
in length, as they would in a true perspective drawing. In addition to simplicity, this type of drawing
also permits measurements to be taken directly from
it, since all of its lines are actual length. To use isometric paper to produce an elevation, any side of a
given plan is plotted to scale along one of the 60°
or 30° lines on the paper and then all other lines
are plotted along the appropriate parallel printed
lines, in relation to the first one. The vertical lines
which represent the height of the structure are plotted along the 90° lines on the paper. This same
method can be followed on plain drawing paper,
without the printed lines on it, by following the in-
structions given below.

PREPARING ISOMETRIC DRAWINGS

Isometric Drawings

Isometric drawings may be done simply from a given floor plan by the following method:

Choose any corner of the plan and draw a vertical line to represent the vertical corner from that point.

Draw two lines at the base of the vertical line in each direction at 60° from the vertical (30° from the horizontal). These now constitute the "isometric lines" from which to draw all other lines necessary for the finished "elevations."

Measurements along all sides and in all directions may now be made along the isometric lines, with additional lines (corners, etc.) *always drawn parallel* to the three original ones, as indicated by the shape of the plan being drawn.

Therefore to draw an isometric elevation of the following floor plan, the above steps would look like this:

Storage of Records

During excavation, all records should be kept in a safe place available at all times for use and consultation. On a "resident" dig, this is no great problem but in a situation where work is sporadic (e.g. the "weekend" dig) a safe storage place should be established on or near the actual site. A small safe or other chest, with a lock is to be recommended.

PREPARING ISOMETRIC DRAWINGS

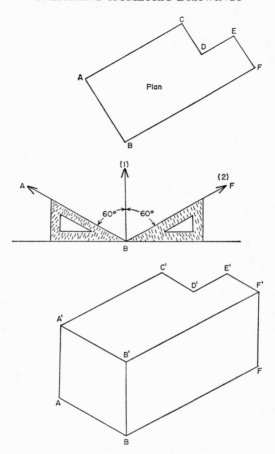

Draw corner edge for corner edge B.

Draw "isometric lines" from B to represent sides A-B, B-F at 60° from the vertical lines.

Measure along "isometric lines" the length of A-B, B-F, depending on the scale used.

Construct all other lines of the plan by direct measurement in the required scale, keeping all horizontal lines parallel to the "isometric lines" A-B, B-F. All vertical lines are kept parallel to the original vertical edge, and their length is determined by the "height" of the "elevation" being drawn.

Lengths of lines shown above are taken from the plan and indicated in terms of it in the "elevation" by A', B', C', etc.

6

THE ADMINISTRATION
OF EXCAVATION

Regardless of size, location, or type of archaeological work being conducted, some organization is necessary if things are to proceed smoothly and if the results are to be of any real value. Without some guiding framework, the expedition will be chaos.

The following "table of organization" is designed to handle all the needs of an archaeological expedition, and may be modified to fit the individual situation. The only thing which cannot be changed is the job itself, for someone, even on the smallest site, has to do the work. Therefore, if there are more parts of the job than there are individual members of the expedition's crew, someone has to do more than one part of the total task.

In some cases, outside help—especially that of technical experts—has to be sought, but even there, the need exists and cannot be ignored. It is usually surprising how much trained assistance will be given if it is only requested. Numerous national, international, and regional groups are glad to add to the resources of state and other local bodies where necessary (see Section II). Not every excavation will require the complexity of a big organization, but will be able to tailor its staff to its own needs.

The site will also dictate reductions in the extent of a given job in terms of accessibility, actual equipment needs, richness of finds, and other factors which have to be handled. Excavations in a local area will obviously be of a different type from those in some far-distant place. The excavation of an entire ancient city in the midst of a desert will be quite a different problem than a "backyard" dig of American Indian remains. Each situation calls for its own design.

Table of Organization

Basically, the organizational structure of any excavation project must provide for the duties, if not for the personnel, of the following staff members:

1. Director
2. Assistant Director
3. Technicians (Surveyor, Draftsman, Photographer, and Laboratory Staff)
4. Recorder
5. Pottery Assistant
6. Site Supervisors
7. Working Crew
8. Specialists

The director is entrusted with the over-all supervision and control of the excavation. Therefore he must be thoroughly trained in archaeological method in order to decide issues of technique and to report in final form, in consultation with his staff, the results of the entire excavation.

The assistant director is especially entrusted with the details of administration. That means that he is charged with the problems of logistics, equipment, finances, supplies, repairs, medical facilities, and general housekeeping. These areas may be decentralized, if the staff is large enough, but they are all individually vital to the success of the whole undertaking. Particularly on a large expedition to some secluded place, the task of the assistant director becomes difficult, since he must know local sources and their possibilities, and be able to out-guess factors of weather, unexpected needs, possible finds, and unlooked-for local variations.

The technicians on an expedition are not necessarily archaeologists, in the strictest sense, but they must be able to relate their own special technical ability to archaeological problems. Thus surveyors, draftsmen, photographers, and laboratory staff must all possess some knowledge of the particular applications of their field to the work at hand. They must also be aware of the problems of equipment, accomodations, and general conditions which field archaeology often poses.

The surveyor is charged with preparing grids, the general field plans, topographical and other specific maps, sections, and detailed plans of each excavated area. Generally speaking, there is no real need of level-by-level planning, unless the features are distinct in terms of permanent installations or structures which must be destroyed. These are usually put on the general plan as overlays or inserts. Nothing of importance should ever be destroyed until it has been plotted, but nothing should be plotted until its plan and its dimensions are clearly defined. Recognition of the latter responsibility falls upon the shoulders of the site supervisor. Speed, along with necessary accuracy, is one of the basic requirements for an archaeological surveyor.

The draftsman of an expedition is a supplement to the surveyor, and generally concerns himself primarily with the drawing of records—*i.e.* pottery drawing, small finds, tomb-planning, and similar work. He may also assist the surveyor in detail work, but not as a general rule. Artistic skill is here the major requirement, along with a general knowledge of the art forms of a particular area.

The work of the photographer is fairly obvious, and his specific tasks will be assigned by the director (see Chapter 5, "Photographic Records"). The archaeological photographer must be able to handle his equipment well, to improvise readily, and have the technical knowledge necessary for all darkroom procedures. Negatives are usually read wet, on a resident dig, to be sure that a given feature has been properly recorded before it is destroyed. Here again the site supervisor works closely with this staff member, as do also the surveyor and the recorder. Complete photographic records should be kept by an expedition, with full details as to film, exposure, orientation, area, site, level, and all other identifying data. General photographic coverage of an excavation, including its lighter and artistic sides is worthwhile also in terms of public relations. For archaeological work, plate cameras are an asset, because of their larger image size. However, the use of the 35 mm. camera is on the increase for the general record shots of an expedition. This camera size often makes up in versatility and ease of operation for other minor disadvantages. Single-lens reflex models with fast lenses and adequate lighting equipment are unmatched for archaeological photographic usefulness.

Laboratory staff is composed of all those who are responsible for the field preservation, treatment, and processing of finds (see Chapter 8). They must know both the specific remedies for all the maladies of time—rust, corrosion, decay, decomposition, and the rest—and how to apply those remedies to a variety of materials. Here again, archaeological training is not the major area of emphasis, but archaeological chemistry or museum training is a necessity, along with practical laboratory experience. The laboratory must be set up and stocked as soon as work begins upon an excavation. Here the laboratory staff, like the other technical people, must work closely with the assistant director to ensure that all the proper equipment is procured.

The laboratory staff also keeps detailed records of the specific treatment given any one item. This becomes part of that item's "personal history," and is entered into the permanent records, until the item reaches its final destination and permanent treatment can be given. It must be stressed that, owing to factors of time, expense, equipment, etc., the field laboratory does not give permanent treatment to artifacts or other finds. The work of this staff is to preserve and to forestall further deterioration of finds until they can be permanently cared for. This is in the nature of field emergency first-aid—not hospitalization!

The recorder is the "memory" of an expedition. It is the job of this staff member to maintain all of the records of the work done. Often parts of this task are parceled out to other staff members (site supervisors, the surveyor, the photographer, *et al.*), but the over-all responsibility falls upon the recorder to make sure that the director will ultimately have a complete record from which to derive his conclusions and make his final report. The register, journal, and card index noted above must be carefully maintained (see Chapter 5, Permanent Records). In most foreign areas, national antiquities laws require this record-keeping, and increasing pressure is being brought by American groups to enact the same type of legislation to preserve historic materials. (See Chapter 2, Antiquities Laws.)

Working closely with the pottery assistant, the recorder also is responsible for the marking and final packing of pottery and other major finds. These are generally marked with India (or if they are themselves dark, with white) ink, and then the marking is shellacked to prevent accidental smudging or removal. A code system is used for each excavation, usually a letter to designate the site, a year number or yearly numeral, followed by notebook location and level designations. This coded number is entered into the register. Only registered pieces are so recorded. The pottery assistant also handles pottery washing and lay-out (a daily affair on a large resident excavation), along with the collection, marking, and bagging of any sherds designated by the Director to be saved as samples from a specific level or area. Complete pottery pieces and small finds are usually cleaned individually, and are then marked and recorded as a matter of routine practice. Directions for field reconstruction, drawing, photographing, and other special treatment are also the joint tasks of recorder and pottery assistant.

The site supervisor is the actual excavator—the individual who is responsible to the director for the real job of digging. He has the direct supervision over his assigned site, and the task of overseeing its destiny. He controls his work by means of the test trench, records his actions in the site notebook, labels levels and tags pottery and other finds, confers with fellow staff members, and keeps the director aware of progress and of developments, both routine and unusual (see Chapter 5).

Generally the site supervisor has had at least some grounding in technique and is usually individually trained by actually working under the guidance of an experienced supervisor, or the director. The latter makes periodic checks on the progress of each supervisor, assists in clarifying problems and advises in matters of technique. Where language factors also enter in, the site supervisor may have the assistance of a native foreman, or of a more experienced senior supervisor. In American work, the site supervisor may often be his own crew—and must often fulfill other roles, as well. As the recorder is the "memory" of a dig, so the site supervisor, regardless of his other duties, functions as the "hands" which actually uncover the data later to be worked into final form by the Director.

The working crews differ in direct relation to the kind of excavation. In the Near East a standard work crew consists of one pickman, two hoemen, and five basket carriers. This unit crew is multiplied until the total number of workers have been secured. On a large dig the total may run around one or two hundred workmen. On a shoestring excavation, there may be only one or two crews at work. In England some work used to be done by hired diggers, unskilled laborers called "navvies," but the cost of such labor is getting prohibitive. In South American work, native work crews are used, just as in the Near and Far East.

In North America the general practice is against hired laborers, because of labor costs, although the staff may be a paid one. Much of the work done here is done by amateurs working under the guidance of an advanced member of the group, or under state or federal specialists. The danger in this system is not only the disillusionment caused by the actual effort expended in digging, which somewhat reduces volunteer enthusiasm, but in the possibility of "collector's fever" which besets the expedition very soon. This disease results in large, but totally unscientific, private collections!

Specialists include all those trained experts who must augment the archaeologist's store of knowledge by specialized information and techniques. This opens the door to practically every scientific and artistic discipline in the catalogue. Epigraphists, numismatists, anthropologists, zoologists, botanists, skin-divers, artists, linguists, architects, geologists, engineers, and many others are at the beck and call of contemporary archaeology. Often local industries or local educational institutions are a prime source for such specialized assistance. Sometimes specialists accompany an expedition in order to study some particular aspects of a culture or of an area. At other times specialized help must be secured on a fee basis. In any case, the modern archaeologist can, and usually does, enlist the training and background of specialized experts in many fields. In the course of time an amateur may even himself develop sufficient training in some specific area to qualify as a "specialist" and consultant in that field.

SUMMARY: STAFF AND DUTIES

DIRECTOR: Over-all supervision and control of expedition

ASSISTANT DIRECTOR:
general administration
logistics

finance and supplies
equipment care
medical facilities

TECHNICIANS
photographer: photography and darkroom
surveyor: grids, site surveys, final plans, sections, etc.
draftsman: pottery plates, special finds, tomb planning, etc.
laboratory: staff field laboratory, field treatments, record of treatments, suggestions for preservation, special lifting

RECORDER and POTTERY ASSISTANT
register and journal
card files (pottery notes and small-find index)
marking registered items
packing and storage
pottery cleaning and daily lay-out
sample collection
reconstruction and field treatment

SPECIALISTS
epigraphists, numismatists, anthropologists, zoologists, botanists, cartographers, area specialists

SITE SUPERVISORS
direct supervision of given site
supervision of "control pits" and "trial trenches"
maintenance of site notebook and other site records
marking of pottery, small finds, etc., as found
drawing of sections, sketch plans
consultation with director on site needs

7

THE PRODUCTS
OF EXCAVATION

This chapter will consider the actual finds uncovered in excavation, in terms of care, handling, and preservation. Obviously not every type, nor all aspects of any given type, of discovery can be discussed, but a general summary of materials and methods will be given for general guidance. These are the material remains which form part of the total picture of an archaeological excavation, and are often the only visible and tangible results, or products, in the eyes of laymen. They must therefore be carefully evaluated and their position, original use, condition, and state of preservation be related to the data of stratigraphy which together with them constitutes the impression of any ancient culture and becomes the "final report" of the excavation.

Finds

Broadly speaking, objects and materials uncovered in the course of archaeological excavations are listed simply as "finds" and "small finds." The latter grouping is a result of size more than any other criterion, and is used to ensure special care in handling. In the first category goes anything from a two-ton carving to a cooking pot. In the latter listing are placed special small vessels, unusual sherds, small articles of jewelry, figurines, coins, small cult objects, and other artifacts that are apt to be lost easily. Special records are kept of the small finds, and each is individually registered and numbered (see Chapter 5, "Permanent Records"). Under this arrangement, further breakdown may be made by material or use: *i.e.* bone, stone, glass, metal, as well as classifications such as beads, whorls, coins, fishhooks, etc., on down the line of possible human artifacts.

Archaeological finds of all sorts, regardless of use, must be considered in terms of materials when matters of cleaning, recording, and marking are discussed. For this reason, a brief summary is given here of material types, and the general approach to their handling in the field. In unusual cases, individual attention must be paid, but the basic approach will be similar, from the standpoint of material alone.

Lithics

Lithics are all artifacts made of stone. This includes, therefore, a wide range of both remains and material. Most common, of course, are the smaller objects made in primitive times, such as spear and arrow heads, knife and other blades, missile stones,

weights, and cultic objects, along with more specifically household utensils such as bowls, plates, store
jars, and mortars. Likewise, there is involved a wide
range of stone, from flints down to sandstones. Each
type requires its own particular treatment, depending
upon its strength, condition, and surface. In most
cases, however, cleaning with a soft brush and water
will cleanse the surface as fully as is needed in the
field, revealing details and any decorations which
may exist. Any further cleaning of stone should be
done in the laboratory, not in the field. Exceptions to
this rule are many, of course, particularly in the case
of harder stones, such as flint and basalt.

In every case, the objects should then be marked
in terms of the record system being used. India (or its
equivalent for dark objects, white) ink can usually
be used. It is generally wise to shellac the markings to
insure permanence. A separate section of the register,
devoted to "stone objects," may be used for these
materials, saving some time later on in classification
(see Chapter 5, Permanent Records). Very small
finds will, of course, be placed in the "small-finds
index." Restoration of stone work, beyond necessary
cementing of pieces to preclude loss or further damage (done with a cellulose cement) should be
avoided in the field. In the hurry of the usual expedition's work, too casual restoration may actually
confuse, rather than clarify, and, in some cases, may
even be permanently injurious to the object in question. Stone materials should never be coated with
plastic or shellacs, in any case.

Ceramics

Pottery finds mark the beginning of civilized living, and are usually the most common remains, either whole or in pieces ("sherds") on any site. In the Near East these finds are measured by the baskets-full. In American work there is less quantitative abundance, yet much has been recovered from Indian sites all over the Americas. In every case, however, pottery has a story to tell and is of major importance to the archaeologist. One aspect of this importance is the fact that pottery, made from a plastic substance and fired to a stone-like state, thus permanently reflects the changes in fashion of each age or group, as well as its artistic achievement up to that period. Pottery is, therefore, a chronological criterion, the "index" to which must be built up by careful observation of the stratigraphic results of a number of excavations (see Chapter 1, The History of Archaeology). Once the index has been established, and the various members of it have been fitted into their proper chronological sequence, a single sherd may contribute greatly to the understanding of a problem, although the usual solution will be the cumulative evidence of many sherds, as well as other factors.

Pottery Making

The excavator, to understand pottery properly, must also have a general knowledge of how pottery is made, in order to deal with it. Usually the ancient potter found a raw clay source suitable for his "factory" and then, depending upon experience, pottery types, or other factors, refined the raw material as needed. This was generally done by a process of settling out of impurities. The clay was then given added body by the inclusion of a binder (straw, famous from the Biblical story of Hebrew brick-making in Egypt, or some other substance, such as stone particles, pebbles, or even broken shells). The correct amount of the plastic material was then cut out, kneaded to remove air, and formed into a shape.

The simplest methods of building a vessel are the coil or rope techniques, in which the plastic clay is rolled into a thin, rope-like strand which was then coiled around one end to form a closed circle upon which the rest of the strand was coiled. This could be built up as high as needed. Generally the lines of the coil would be smoothed off, both inside and out. More sophisticated is the wheel-made pottery. Here a lump of plastic clay is placed in the center of a flat wheel, the wheel turned (by hand, feet, or machine), and the vessel shaped by hand and by tool as it rotates. This resulted in more delicacy of form and more symmetrical shapes. Other methods were also used in ancient times, including molding and pressing. Each area will exhibit its own typical varieties.

In every case, however, something had to be done to the raw clay vessel to make it stronger and capable of holding liquids or solids. Whether by accident or by experiment, the ancient potter discovered that his product could be hardened by fire. Over a long period of time, in every area in the world, therefore, potters fired their products to a rock-like state, their experience and facilities gradually producing better results. This is the same process in use today, and modern pottery ranges from flower pots to fine china. Technical terminology exists to define the precise nature and firing process of each type today, as well as to classify the product itself.

With technical skill in the production of forms and "ware" (the material from which the vessels were made), came artistic skill as well. This has made the archaeologist's task easier by the addition of distinctive decoration, body, rim and handle shapes, color variations, and even, in some cases, the signatures of the artists involved. These added features assist in the classification of individual pieces into general type headings and systems.

Pottery Cleaning

Since pottery is usually heat-treated, it can be handled almost like stone. Therefore, in field cleaning, pottery vessels and sherds are usually washed, and often scrubbed with a brush to remove surface dirt. However, it must be cautioned that not all pottery can stand rough treatment. Poorly fired pottery will crumble if left too long in water, and will lose its surface if brushed too vigorously. Likewise, painted pottery will often lose its decoration if washed too long, or at all! In any case, pottery finds are collected at a central location on an excavation and are usually washed to reveal their actual surface.

It is for this reason that labels are included with the baskets or bags from each site as noted above. If marked with a waterproof ink, the labels do not suffer when a given lot of pottery is dumped into the washing bath (see Chapter 5, "Find Tags"). Once washed, the sherds are laid out for drying and sorting (in the Near East grass mats serve for this purpose; elsewhere canvas or other matting is used). A rough sorting should be done, with rims, bases, and handles put to one side in each pile. From the total mass of sherds, samples are taken for further study and as illustrations of the types found in each level excavated. All complete pieces are, of course, kept, and are washed and handled separately. Miscellaneous body sherds, duplicate sherds, and indistinguishable fragments need not be saved, once samples have been taken. The residue can be dumped. The pieces saved from each lot are then packed, together with their individual labels.

One very workable system is to use kraft paper bags for each lot of samples saved, placing one identification label inside and tying one to the outside of the package. In this manner it is possible to place one's hands upon a particular lot of samples without much trouble later on. In the case of unusual sherds, they may become "small finds," and be entered into the register, just as complete vessels are entered. Usually the run-of-the-mill pottery is simply noted in a pottery record notebook kept by the director, with an ultimate classification by levels or phases into "type series," which are then drawn and described in the final report. Complete vessels are all entered into the register and are marked with a registry number by the recorder's staff as noted above.

Pottery Restoration & Reconstruction

In certain cases, and especially in the case of damaged vessels which are complete or near-complete, some restoration and reconstruction may be indicated. In the case of a rich level of pottery, this additional work may contribute additional complete pieces, as well. Reconstruction may take two forms, actual and theoretical. Both methods are important to the over-all results of an expedition. Actual reconstruction involves sorting out of broken pieces which resemble each other, or collecting the sherds of a single vessel which have been found together, and attempting to reassemble them. If a piece is merely damaged, or if there is evidence that most of the pieces of a vessel can be found, this is no great problem. Where one is faced with a vast number of vaguely similar sherds, however, the situation becomes like the beginning of a vast jig-saw puzzle.

In any event, broken pieces are matched together and their edges joined with a collodion cement (either commercial or homemade). Usually a box filled with sand is used to assist in steadying joined fragments and holding them firm until they are completely dry. To preclude difficulty in making the final "joins," care must be taken to observe general directions of curvature. This factor also arises in regard to the amount of cement to use, for if too much is used, the lines of a vessel will be distorted by a slight amount each time fragments are put together, until the shape of the vessel is, itself, distorted and, finally, pieces cannot be fitted together. When the available sherds in any reconstruction are exhausted, often a vessel can be "finished" with plaster-of-paris, but this is not a field exercise, and should wait for the home or museum work-shop.

Theoretical restoration of a vessel requires enough of the orginal so that height, curvature, rim diameter, and other factors can be shown in drawings, if at all possible (see "Pottery Drawing" and "Pottery Drawing Aids" on page 98).

SUMMARY: POTTERY RECONSTRUCTION

1. PHYSICAL RECONSTRUCTION (*i.e.* actual rebuilding)

   Fragments are collected and washed.

   Fragments are sorted and matching pieces joined with collodion cement, applied to both broken edges and allowed to become tacky; joined pieces are then placed in sandbox to support the union until cement dries.

   Gaps in repaired pieces are filled with Plaster of Paris molded to match curvature (by beeswax form), decoration, etc. of original piece. Patches may be painted or tinted.

2. MATHEMATICAL RECONSTRUCTION (*i.e.* calculation of form and drawing)

   Rim Features: determined by
   a) angle: hold stright-edge along rim edge and rotate rim to exclude light; or
   b) diameter: compare with scaled sizes on chart; or calculate geometrically.

Body Features: thickness of wall measured with calipers, outlines traced or drawn (see *Pottery Drawing*)

N. B. often decoration, etc. will indicate vertical orientation of body fragments; if not, body pieces generally tend to be reduced in thickness from base to rim.

With reconstruction of rim-angle, etc., vessels can often be wholly reconstructed on paper. Comparison with parallel pieces further guides reconstruction.

Base Features: base diameters can generally be determined by the same comparison techniques used for rims. In the case of rounded or other base treatments, approximations to the turn of the vessel can usually be made and verified by comparisons.

SUMMARY: POTTERY DRAWING
AND DESCRIPTION

DRAWING METHODS
a) Mechanical (with frames, grids, etc.)
b) Direct tracing of outline (1:1)

SCALES
Generally 1:1 with subsequent reduction to 1:4/1:2. Special decorations, etc. usually shown in larger scale details.

CONVENTIONS
Left side of drawing—exterior
Right side of drawing—interior and cross-section
Rims—right side section and inclination indicated
Handles—side and cross-section if significant
Bases—right side cross-section with horizontal indication

IDENTIFICATION OF DRAWINGS
Drawing sheets numbered consecutively
Individual items with registry numbers shown and encircled for reference

DESCRIPTION
All drawings must be supplemented by written descriptions indicating features of vessel in terms of:

Form (i.e. shape)
Ware (i.e. fabric of vessel)
Decoration (i.e. color, surface treatment, decorations, etc.)

Glossary of Common Terms

base	bottom or support upon which vessel rests
body	main part of vessel
bowl	shallow, open vessel
burnished	surface treatment done by polishing surface with hard object before firing
coil	a method of building a vessel by piling up rope-like pieces of wet clay in coils to shape desired
combed	a decoration made by a comb-like tool
core	center of the cross-section of a sherd
disc	base formed by a solid ring of clay
everted	an out-turned rim
ewer	pitcher type vessel
finger indented	decoration made by pressing finger into vessel surface or applied rope of clay to form a pattern
firing	the heating of clay vessel to harden it
flask	small-mouthed vessel for holding liquids
glaze	a clear, fired finish
incised	decoration in form of incisions in surface
inverted	an in-turned rim
jar	deep, broad-mouthed vessel
jug	deep pitcher-type vessel, small mouth, handles
loop	handle in form of loop
lug	handle in form of projection, no finger hole
neck	part of vessel between rim and shoulder
ribbon	handle formed from superimposed strips, or applied decoration in wavy form
ring	base formed from open ring of clay, by a coil or by cutting away a disc
rim	mouth of vessel, or border around mouth
rope	see coil
sherd	a fragment of a pottery vessel

shoulder	point of joining of rim/neck and body
slip	a clay wash, applied before firing
paint	a colored surface treatment
plastic	designation of clay solution applied to vessels as a separate part
plate	flat or semi-flat vessel, open
wash	an aqueous clay solution applied to a vessel after firing for decoration
wet smoothed	smoothing of vessel surface while still moist, before firing
wheel made	pottery made by turning on a flat wheel, in distinction to hand made by coil or rope method or by molding

Metal

Metal objects vary as to size, condition, and type of metal, along with the more obvious differences of purpose. Variations are extremely great here, and particular cleaning and care are dictated by the individual situation. Field cleaning is usually limited to brushing, or to only the most superficial cleaning necessary to clarify the metal and, if possible, the nature of the object. In the case of coins and other specific small objects, however, preliminary cleaning may involve laboratory methods as well. Copper- and iron-base items may be cleaned by boiling them in a solution of caustic soda (5%–10%) and granulated zinc, brushing with a soft brass brush and then thoroughly rinsing in distilled water. Silver-base materials may be cleaned by boiling in an ammonia solution (10%). Gold, since it does not corrode or tarnish, usually takes care of itself, but an ammonia treatment, such as suggested for silver, will remove surface discolorations.

Too much cleaning, however, of any metal object may permanently ruin a small find of great value which could have been saved by more controlled care. It should also be noted that some of the materials used for cleaning metals are extremely dangerous, and should only be used by those completely aware of the dangers involved. Occasionally some field preservation of metal objects is indicated, especially of those in immediate danger of further deterioration. In such cases, paraffine, plastic spray, lacquer, or even shellac may be used, since all can be removed later on when proper equipment is available for complete and permanent preservation methods.

Fragile Materials

In addition to these more solid materials, artifacts and remains will also be found in more delicate materials. Some of these, like bone, glass, mosaic or plaster, have to have their surface preserved in order to prevent further deterioration or damage. This also can be done by the use of paraffine, plastics, or shellac surface coverings. In other cases, further reinforcement must be made. For unusual problems, skilled assistance should be sought.

When wood, vegetable or animal textiles, or bone is uncovered, the problem of immediate solidification and strengthening may enter into the picture because of the danger of decomposition of such materials upon exposure to air after a long period of burial. Here, again, the surface treatments are safest. Hot paraffine is particularly valuable in these cases because of the ease with which it soaks into the open pores of such materials. Once hardened, the paraffine acts as a solid binder to strengthen and to reinforce, especially if it also is reinforced by cloth or other backing materials. By sealing the surfaces of organic materials from contact with air, paraffine fulfills another necessary function. The paraffine can later be removed by the application of heat, and more permanent preservatives used. The plastic known as polyvinyl is widely used, especially by British archaeologists, for both wood and bone, and especially for the latter in the case of burials.

Architectural Remains

Architectural and sculptured remains occur in all of the possible materials noted above, but special mention must be made of the importance of careful handling of this type of ancient artifact. Usually fragments are treated as "small finds," depending upon the material involved. Often, however, sheer size demands special treatment, and specialized help may well be needed, as, for example, in the removal of painted walls.

Recording of Treatment

Field treatment of all materials must be recorded carefully on the packing label of the particular item, and in the register, in order to ensure that proper note is taken of it later on and permanent treatment may be carried out. Care should also be taken in the field with the use of all chemicals since some, if casually handled can cause serious harm (*e.g.* caustic soda, the fumes from ammonia solutions, hot paraffine, etc.) (see Chapter 6, Specialists). First-aid kits are an integral part of the archaeologist's equipment, but "preventive" measures, such as proper storage, proper labels, and proper handling, are preferable to the need of repairing damage to necessary workers!

8

NEW TECHNIQUES
IN ARCHAEOLOGY

New techniques and trends are being developed or employed in current archeological work. Many of them are beyond the technical facilities of the average expedition, but a knowledge of their existence is desirable for reference purposes.

For purposes of discussion, we can divide the material into three main categories, dealing with *Site Discovery, Dating,* and *Analysis of Materials.*

Site Discovery

The usual methods of site discovery—*i.e.* by surface remains, pottery, known historical location, place means, and other similar indications—have now been supplemented by aerial reconnaissance. In this regard, the most fruitful technique is aerial photography. By this means an area may be surveyed for indications of ancient habitation rapidly and with a precision sometimes impossible from the close-up view of ground investigations. A larger area may be accurately plotted, in order to see interrelations of village sites, or even of parts of a single mound. In addition, a series of aerial views of the same area may, by virtue of shifting light and various viewpoints, disclose quite unexpected indications of occupation. This technique has been used to great advantage in the Near East, *e.g.* the mounds of Jericho, Hazor, Ezion Geber, and other individual sites, as well as the broader "survey" of Transjordanic, Iranian, Syrian, and other areas too vast to cover efficiently by land operations.

Of special value in the line of aerial photos are stereoscopic photographs *i.e.* two photographs of the same area, taken at a specified distance apart. These photographs, when viewed together through a binocular type instrument (like the stereoscopes used a couple of generations ago) are combined by the eyes into one view which reproduces the contours of the ground itself. There are now on the market modern cameras which provide the twin pictures, as well as projectors which focus them into a single view. The same result can be obtained by training the eyes to converge the twin images of two photos placed side by side. Such photographs call attention especially to barrows, earthworks, wall lines, and similar depressed or elevated features which might be investigated on the ground.

A similar effect can sometimes be achieved from photographs of an area taken merely from some high point in the vicinity. The angular line of vision necessitated by this method often precludes much in the way of results, however.

Related to aerial and stereoscopic photography are photogrammetric devices now used in map-making. These machines use stereoscopic views from which actual contours are traced. A separate unit then can actually reproduce the original contours in reduced form. The map-making feature is here the major one for site discovery and survey, but the modeling technique is of great importance for exhibitions and museum displays.

Another method of site "discovery" has recently been introduced from the electronic field. This method "plots," in a broad sense, subsurface remains through difference in electrical impedance measured from rods set into the ground at given intervals over a probable site. Differences in conductivity between rods is an indication of some variation in soil consistency between them. Hence a stone wall, or some large artifact, can be detected. This equipment is similar to the soil impedance gear used by soil engineers. The uneven performance of this technique does not yet seem to warrant very general use, however.

Still another new subsurface "seeing" technique is used in Italy, among other places, in the investigation of Etruscan tombs. When a tomb has been located from surface indications, a long drill is used to open a small hole from the surface down into the tomb chamber. A revolving camera, located in the lower end of the drill is then operated from the surface and photographs the entire chamber area. If the developed films indicate that the tomb has not been robbed in antiquity, or that it has desirable features worthy of investigation, the tomb is excavated. If the chamber is empty and without distinctive features, the labor of fruitless excavation is saved and the team can go on to the next tomb.

Miniature cameras and high speed "strobe lights" have made this and similar devices possible. Hence areas of difficult access, and this is especially true of some tombs, may be thoroughly photographed even before complete opening. In certain situations such pre-excavation photography is the only record of materials which promptly disintegrate when exposed to the air after having been sealed up for centuries.

Another method similar to the periscope camera has been used with some success to secure stratigraphic "plugs." Long used by geologists and oceanographers, the device is like a large pipe with a sharpened end, its diameter dependent upon soil, stratigraphic needs, and available equipment. Forced into the soil by manual or mechanical means, the pipe becomes clogged with earth and other material directly in its path. When withdrawn, from the earth, the "plug" is carefully forced out. The various strata, occupational and otherwise, are quite visible and can be studied, measured and analyzed. Some small artifacts and sherds are also often included in the sample.

The chief drawback to this method, aside from the equipment necessary, is the distortion introduced into the measurement of individual strata by the relative smallness of the sample and by the force of compression necessitated in forcing the pipe into the soil. Nevertheless, the method allows a fast evaluation of a site's productivity for full-scale excavation.

Dating

Archaeology has not kept up with the vast strides in chronological measurement and analysis being made by the physical sciences today. The reasons for this lag are both technical (*i.e.* the need for specialized knowledge) and financial (*i.e.* the high cost of equipment and materials). On the other hand, physical scientists in education and in industry have done much to further archaeological research by devoting time and facilities to specific projects brought to their attention.

Probably the most spectacular advance in this area is the introduction of the Carbon 14 dating technique. This method of dating was originally developed by W. F. Libby and has been subsequently modified and refined. Basically the theory rests on the fact that radioactive isotopes of ordinary carbon are formed in the atmosphere through a bombardment of nitrogen by cosmic rays, with an atomic weight of 14 ("heavy carbon"). Ultimately these are absorbed, through plant life, by all animal forms at a stable rate and ratio. When the living organism dies, however, the absorption of Carbon 14 ceases, and the residual Carbon 14 within the organism starts to distintegrate. This disintegration takes place at a fixed rate which can be measured in the laboratory.

The "half life" of Carbon 14 is about 5,500 years, hence a scale may be established on the basis that the remaining amount of Carbon 14 has a definite relation to the elapsed time since the death of the organism. A Geiger-Counter arrangement is used—usually a circle of counters around the sample which is placed within a counting device. It was originally the practice to measure carbon or carbonized organic materials in a solid state by this method. Now, however, the organic materials are reduced to a gas and measured in that state.

Samples for Carbon 14 dating are more valuable from early periods because of instrumental errors which introduce a plus-minus variation of about five to ten percent, or somewhat less, depending on the material and the facilities. A sample run requires at least two ounces of charcoal, and about eight ounces of other organic material. The samples must be destroyed in testing, and this fact, along with the cost of testing, has sometimes proved to be a disadvantage.

Somewhat similar to Carbon 14 methods is the use of the thermoluminescent glow curve. This curve results from the measurement of a heated specimen (in powdered form), and is based on the principle that radiation displaces electrons in ceramic and stone objects, which when heated, emit a glow as they return to their "seats." A series of extremely complex treatments of the materials to be measured must be carried out, and the results, so far, are quite easily distorted. If finally perfected, this method may possibly serve for inorganic materials the same role the Carbon 14 process does for organic materials.

Another recent dating method involves the measurement of the fluourine content in bone. This is based on the absorption rate of fluourine from ground water by buried bones. The method is complicated by variations in the fluourine content of the ground water, itself, however, as well as by its limitation to buried bone alone. Chemical changes in soil levels, composition of soil levels and other applications of chemistry have also been made, with more or less success.

Dendrochronology has attracted a great deal of attention among some American archaeologists and anthropologists as a dating method. This technique is a scientific variation on the old "tree-ring counting" which used to be only a pastime. The theory behind the method is that the growth rings, added to a tree annually, may indeed be reduced to a chronological scale, on the basis of which an absolute scale may be based and comparisons made to it. The results of this method have been rewarding in certain cases, but again inherent errors within the system may preclude an absolute scale by this means alone.

Related to this are also geochronological systems which provide basic data, via geological "stratification." This information is helpful for the very ancient periods, but provides no help from the historical periods.

Analysis of Finds

The analysis of finds serves two main purposes: (1) to determine nature or composition and (2) to authenticate them. Often both ends are served by a single analysis. In this area of archaeological endeavor, the specialist must often be called in because of the highly technical nature of most of the work.

Perhaps the simplest analytical tools available are the magnifying glass and the microscope. By these devices not only the detail of fine artifacts (such as coins), the consistency of wares, the nature of finishes, but also actual nature and content (organic and mineral), surface conditions, and other minute distinctions can be made. The extent of the analysis by this means will be limited by the power of the instruments, and, to some extent, by the material. Detailed microscopic analysis is, of course, the field of the chemist, the geologist, the botanist, the zoologist or similar specialist, depending upon the material being investigated.

Related to this type of analysis is chemical analysis. Here, precise composition and information as to how that composition was achieved become the chief results. This is extremely important in terms of chronology in certain periods and in certain areas of art and archaeology. Generally, chemical analysis is costly, time-consuming, and uncertain in terms of specific results. However, very often industrial laboratories are interested in artifacts relating to their own products, or educational institutions will cooperate, so that an analysis may be secured without expense. Recent research has been done in regard to authentication of stone work (sculpture) by chemical means, and the techniques of the science have long been used for analysis of ancient (and forged) coins and other metal objects, pigments, ceramics and similar materials.

Certain simple "identification" reactions may be conducted by the amateur or layman, but usually even these may involve some degree of danger, either to the investigator or to the material being investigated. This is especially true, as was noted above, in the case of the use of acids and caustics. Consultation with an expert will generally be more profitable than trying to accomplish a chemical analysis alone.

Colorimetry, or color analysis, is one method in which even the most untrained member of a staff can learn to be proficient (providing he is not color-blind). There is, because of the demands of industry, a variety of color measurement or color standardization schemes on the market. Beginning with the "chips" put out by paint companies, one can progress to more "abstract" color standard books which involve the same technique—namely comparison of a color against a standard. On the highly technical level a spectroscopic colorimeter is employed for measuring exact wave lengths of light (hence "color"). These may be "opaque"—*i.e.* measure the color of a solid object, or require that the colored object be reduced to a solution (by grinding or dissolving). Such exact color measurement is generally unnecessary for the archaeologist, except in restoration, since both fixed colors (on pottery) and pigmented colors (*e.g.* on wall paintings) varied greatly in antiquity and were in no sense "standard."

Hardness tests are also of some value in analysis, and may even be linked to firing temperatures. These tests are generally done according to the standard range known as "Mohs' Scale." This is simply a collection of materials of known hardness, against which samples are compared by scratching. Rather than scratching sample against specimen, it is recommended that a small file be used, the same pressure being exerted in scratching both sample and specimens until comparable hardness is reached. The standard range goes from 1 to 10 in ascending order of hardness, generally represented by the range from talc (softest) to diamonds (hardest). A quick "field" test may be made of materials on the following rough basis:

Hardness 1—may be scratched with a fingernail
Hardness 3—may be scratched by a penny
Hardness 5—compare with glass
Hardness 7—compare with quartz
Hardness 10—compare with diamond

Kiln tests are also valuable for the insights they give into ancient techniques of firing and throwing. These may be done in any small kiln, preferably one with electric thermostatic controls to maintain even heat and permit exact temperature rises. Fragments are selected for testing, and inscribed with a small "target" for measurement. Each piece is measured in section with a micrometer prior to beginning the test. The pieces are placed in the kiln and the temperature brought to a specific level (*e.g.* 500° C / 932° F) which is maintained for a short time and then the kiln is allowed to cool. The pieces are again measured, and the process repeated at another, high level (*e.g.* 200° F higher).

When the fragments show a significant shrinkage in section the ancient firing point has been reached (actually passed, since the measured shrinkage would have already taken place had the piece been fired at the temperature which now produced it). If the steps in temperature rise are kept close enough, a very close approximation can be reached on the ancient kiln temperatures. Examination of color changes, core condition, and surface will also add to the information achieved by this means and permit a picture of the ancient kiln to be gained.

Finger prints to be obtained from ancient pottery vessels and figurines is an area of analysis just being explored in some areas. If enough such prints could be collected from the pottery of an area, it might be possible to trace movements of groups, or attribute artifacts to specific craftsmen. This has been undertaken with bronze statuary cast from clay originals, with some little success. Mold-made pieces (*e.g.* lamps, figurines, etc.) often bear the artisan's finger imprints. Regrettably, however, too few good specimens exist and no collections have yet been built up. Smudged prints are almost valueless, and some little technical skill is required to read and code prints at all.

Infra-red photography is a useful technique for the analysis and authentication of certain types of materials. Infra-red films and plates are available in a number of film sizes. No special camera is required, but a red filter (*e.g.* Wratten A) is used. Lighting may be daylight or photo-flood. This method is used is used in photographing paper and other similar material which has been charred or even fully burned, or has suffered deterioration due to mold or decay, discoloration, or deliberate alteration, or has been overwritten (a "palimpsest") or overprinted. The application of this technique for site photography is of possible value in terms of detecting vegetation changes over certain underground remains, depending upon the circumstances involved.

Ultra-violet photography is also a valuable technique for detecting restorations or changes and for "bringing out" faded or discolored writing, printing, or colors. Again, no special camera is needed, but an ultra-violet light source must be used. Pictures are taken in total darkness by the reflected ultra-violet light, or, using special filters, by the "glow" produced from certain objects when they are under this type of light. The film to be used depends on the method used, but is not a special variety. Ultra-violet light also makes a handy rapid visual analysis of certain materials possible, even without the photographic aspects. Alterations in documents and overpaintings will very often betray themselves by an obvious "glow" which is immediately visible under ultra-violet light. Often this saves considerable time and effort in delimiting the area or extent of alterations which must be removed or marked out.

X-Ray fluoroscopy and X-Ray photography are extremely valuable analytical tools, but their cost is great and they must be carried out only by skilled technicians. Both methods have been used to great advantage in determining shapes of corroded pieces, methods of construction, contents of core-cast sculpture, and similar data. This information is extremely valuable for reconstruction purposes.

Less restricted in use is the X-Ray Geiger-Counter Spectroscope, a geological instrument which has more than passing interest for pottery analysis, as well. This instrument provides a visual graph of mineral content of prepared samples by bombarding their surface with X-Rays and "reading" the reflected rays with a Geiger-Counter. A trained geologist must interpret the graphs, but preliminary visual comparison of pieces can be made by the layman. The drawbacks of this method lie in the scarcity of available machines, outside of industrial or educational institutions, the cost per "run," the necessity for destroying sample materials, and the complexity of the graphs. Further use of this technique may, however, prove of great interest in the future.

Another interesting, but very technical, development in archaeological analysis is the research being conducted in the field of paleoserology. This science deals with the problems of blood groupings of ancient peoples, as determined from mummified remains and human bones. By such means the entrance of specific type-groups can be traced, along with anthropological data. This line of analysis is generally limited to highly trained experts whose assistance must be sought in special cases.

Underwater Exploration

Underwater exploration is as old as the art of diving, but it has gained its present effectiveness from modern technological advances in breathing apparatus. The invention of diving "suits," either with external air supplies or self-contained units, permitted greater depths, increased mobility, and longer periods under water. The most modern developments have dispensed with most of the bulk and "skin-diving" has become widely popular.

As an archaeological method, underwater exploration assists, among other ways, in determining architectural features now covered by water or originally built in it (*e.g.* harbor facilities); in recovering artifacts lost, or deliberately thrown into water (*e.g.* into sacrificial pools, etc.); in salvaging materials lost in shipwrecks (*e.g.* in the ancient Mediterranean shipping lanes); and in similar recovery and salvage operations.

Unfortunately the popular attraction of skin diving has temporarily obscured the fact that it does not furnish, generally, a specific "provenance" or specific "strata" for its finds. A great deal of time has been lavished in devising submarine adaptations of "dust-

and-dirt" equipment for underwater work which are not all applicable. On the other hand, precise drawing and photographing of finds under water, relation of finds to context (*e.g.* ship types, ceramic typologies, etc.) careful recording, and proper evaluation are gradually making this new methodology more archaeologically scientific. Without a thorough archaeological awareness, however, the contributions of underwater operations are without meaning.

It must be noted too, that this type of exploration requires careful training, proper equipment, and preparation. Without all three, the method is extremely dangerous. Although not beyond the scope of the amateur, experience and trained supervision are absolute prerequisites.

EPILOGUE

Archaeology is not "the scientific study of ancient material remains" until those remains are studied, interpreted, and shared with other workers in the field through adequate publication. This may take the form of the many volumed work of the classical archaeologists, or may be simply a slim contribution to the "newsletter" of a local society. In any case, clear and adequate presentation of the site, the method, and the finds must be made. This is the responsibility imposed upon a digger, amateur or professional, once he sets spade and trowel to a given site.

Often a "preliminary report" of an excavation is made, prior to the complete study and publication of finds in the "final report." This is more in the nature of an announcement of work done, and must be followed by the complete story: the results of one "dig" are carefully presented and compared with the results of others, for purpose of chronology and typology. Ultimately, individual "type series" of pottery and other artifacts build up the local "index" so that individual specimens may be fitted into an over-all chronological scheme. The sequence of strata, made clear by the classing together of related "levels" into clear-cut "phases" finally takes shape, and the artifacts and customs of each individual culture or occupation are made clear.

Interpretation of results thus clothes the bare "bones" uncovered by excavation, with the "flesh" of significance, and what men call "history" is again made alive in a new age.

SECTION II

ARCHAEOLOGICAL ACTIVITY IN THE UNITED STATES AND CANADA

ARCHAEOLOGICAL
ACTIVITY IN
THE UNITED STATES

The material for this section was collected in a number of ways. An initial questionnaire was sent to the official state staff personnel, whenever possible, as well as to museums and academic institutions. The questionnaire data was supplemented with additional information sent along by those returning the forms, and with materials currently in print in the form of books, bulletins, newsletters and conference reports. Because of a number of factors, certain data could not be secured, or could not be included here for lack of space. It is felt, however, that the information contained in the following pages will at least form a basis for further inquiry on the part of those interested in the field. It is presented here by states as the most efficient form for reference. The bibliographical data, up to 1951, includes a variety of papers and articles from national, state, and local sources bearing upon work carried on in individual states up to that point. This material was largely based upon the extensive bibliography to be found, in greater detail, in *Archaeology of Eastern United States,* edited by James B. Griffin. The citations published since 1951 are restricted to those to be found in the major national publications in the field, with a few exceptions. This practice was adopted in order to call to the reader's attention some of the more significant earlier publications and sources, more current editions and copies of which will furnish further information. No attempt has been made to provide an exhaustive bibliography, even if that could be accomplished, but rather, it is the purpose here to draw attention to significant articles of the past, local, and state publications which will keep the reader informed of present progress and sources which are basic to an understanding of the field in general.

Particular appreciation is due to the following persons who assisted in gathering the material by returning questionnaire forms, by correspondence, and by furnishing other types of aid: James P. Bressler, Williamsport, Pennsylvania; David L. De Jarnette, University, Alabama; W. W. Wesley, State Archaeologist, Tucson, Arizona; Miss Hester A. Davis, Fayetteville, Arkansas; William Bascom and A. B. Elsasser, Berkeley, California; Willena D. Cartwright, Denver, Colorado; B. Robert Butler, Pocatello, Idaho; Thorne Deuel, Springfield, Illinois; Glenn A. Black, Angel Site, Newburgh, Indiana;

Marshall McKusick, State Archaeologist, Iowa City, Iowa; Thomas A. Witty, State Archaeologist, Topeka, Kansas; T. Latimer Ford, Ruxton, Maryland; Maurice Robbins, Attleboro, Massachusetts; Peter Jensen, St. Paul, Minnesota; Robert S. Neitzel, Jackson, Mississippi; Donald M. Johnson, Jefferson City, Missouri; Dale R. Henning, Columbia, Missouri; Kathryn B. Greywacz and Dorothy Cross, Trenton, New Jersey; Edward Weyer, Jr., Santa Fe, New Mexico; Fred Wendorf, Santa Fe, New Mexico; Erwin C. Zepp, Columbus, Ohio; W. Fred Kinsey, Harrisburg, Pennsylvania; Wesley R. Hurt, Vermillion, South Dakota; Thomas M. N. Lewis, Winter Haven, Florida; Lloyd M. Pierson, Shenandoah National Park, Virginia; Richard D. Wood, Montpelier, Vermont; Floyd E. Painter, Norfolk, Virginia; Joan Frieman, Madison, Wisconsin; and Miss Lola M. Homsher, Cheyenne, Wyoming.

Information included in this reference section is presented by states. Where information was available to the author, it is included; where there is none, it is so indicated; where it was not available, the item is left blank or the next item follows immediately.

STATE

A. Organization

This section relates to those organizations, state and amateur, and officials charged with control of archaeological activities within the state.

1. Official State Department and/or Controlling Body

2. Official(s) Charged With Preservation, Restoration, and Administration of State Historical and/or Archaeological Activities
Name, Address

3. State Archaeological Society or Related Organization
   Name, Address

B. Control
Legislation and Restrictions Concerning Excavation of Archaeological Sites Within the State.

Federal land in all states is subject to the federal antiquities law of 1906 entitled *An Act for the Preservation of American Antiquities*. It is based upon the principle that all federal lands and resources are held in trust for the people by the national government. It emphasizes the preservation of archaeological remains for exhibit and display in museums and for educational purposes. Section 3 of the Federal Act provides that "the examinations, excavations and gatherings are undertaken for the benefit of reputable museums, universities, colleges, or other recognized scientific or educational institutions, with a view to increasing the knowledge of such objects, and that the gathering shall be made for permanent preservation in public museums."

Many states have patterned their legislation after the federal antiquities law.

C. Sites

1. Main Ancient Cultures and/or Cultural Stages Represented in the State

   The cultures are indicated by names commonly used within that state.

2. Major Known Sites Reported
   Name of Site, Location, Culture Represented

   Some of these sites can no longer be located because of the advance of highways, dam projects, and housing developments.

D. Excavations
Major Excavations in the State—Past and Current

Name of Site, Location (Culture), Date, Excavator, Supporting Institution(s)

More than forty-two states are currently involved in "The Inter-Agency Archaeological Salvage Program." This program is a joint effort of federal and local agencies to salvage, preserve, and interpret archaeological, historical, and paleontological remains that are threatened with destruction by the United States water control program. Indians lived along stream banks, early pioneers settled there, and it is the remains of these settlements that are threatened.

As coordinating administrative agency, The National Park Service secures funds and arranges research contracts with State and local agencies. The Smithsonian Institution acts as research advisor for the various State Universities, Archaeological and Historical Societies involved in the salvage work.

E. Museums In State
   Name
   Address

F. Academic Institutions Within the State Offering Professional Archaeological Instruction
   Name, Address, Program(s) Offered

G. Bibliography
   In addition to the books and articles listed, other material will be found in the periodicals and special reports to which reference is made in citations of specific articles.

———————

ALABAMA

A. Organization
   1. University of Alabama Museums
   2. Curator of Anthropology, University of Alabama Museum, University Director, Department of Archives and History, Montgomery
   3. Alabama Archaeological Society
      Box 6126, University

B. Control
   Antiquities Act prohibits excavating except by State Agency.

C. Sites
   1. Paleo
      Archaic
      Woodland
      Mississippian
      Historic
   2. Moundville (Mound State Monument), Mississippian
      Shell Mound (Tennessee Valley), Archaic
      Burial Mounds (Tennessee Valley), Woodland
      Several thousand mounds have already been surveyed; Moundville with the group of Temple Mounds is best known.

D. Excavations
   Moundville, 1930—, D. L. DeJarnette, University of Alabama Museum

   Tennessee Valley, 1934–42, W. S. Webb and D. L. DeJarnette, RVA, WPA, University of Alabama Museum

   Coosa River Salvage, 1947–60, Webb and DeJarnette, Alabama Power Company and University of Alabama Museum

   Chattahoochee Salvage, 1960–61, DeJarnette, National Park Service and University of Alabama Museum

Stanfield Worley Shelter, 1960–61, DeJarnette, Alabama Archaeological Society, Archaeological Research Association of Alabama, and University of Alabama

Coosa Valley, 1962—

Chattahoochee Valley, 1962—

Excavations in Northern Alabama, 1962—, Alabama Archaeological Society

E. Museums

Archaeological Museum of Mound State
Box 66, Moundville

Alabama Museum of Natural History
P.O. Box Drawer "O," University

F. Academic Institutions
University of Alabama, University

G. Bibliography

DeJarnette, David L., and Steve B. Wimberley
The Bessemer Site: Excavation of Three Mounds and Surrounding Village Areas Near Bessemer, Alabama. Geological Survey of Alabama, Museum Paper 17, University, Alabama. 1941.

Griffin, James B.
"Report on the Ceramics of Wheeler Basin." In *An Archeological Survey of Wheeler Basin on the Tennessee River in Northern Alabama* by William S. Webb. 1939.

Haag, William G.
"Early Horizons in the Southeast." *American Antiquity,* Vol. 7, No. 3, pp. 209–222, Menasha. 1942.
"A Description and Analysis of the Pickwick Pottery." In *An Archeological Survey of Pickwick Basin in the Adjacent Portions of the States of Alabama, Mississippi and Tennessee* by William S. Webb and David L. DeJarnette, Bureau of American Ethnology, Bulletin 129, pp. 509–526, Washington. 1942.

Jones, Walter B.
"Geology of the Tennessee Valley Region of Alabama, with Notes on the Topographic Features of the Area, and the Effect of Geology and Topography Upon Aboriginal Occupation." In *An Archeological Survey of Wheeler Basin on the Tennessee River in Northern Alabama* by William S. Webb, Bureau of American Ethnology, Bulletin 122, pp. 9–20, Washington. 1939.

"Geology of the Pickwick Basin in Adjacent Parts of Tennessee, Mississippi and Alabama." In *An Archeological Survey of Pickwick Basin in the Adjacent Portions of the States of Alabama, Mississippi and Tennessee* by William S. Webb and David L. DeJarnette, Bureau of American Ethnology, Bulletin 129, pp. 327–335, Washington. 1942.

The Journal of Alabama Archaeology, University of Alabama.

Newman, Marshall T., and Charles E. Snow
"Preliminary Report on the Skeletal Material from Pickwick Basin, Alabama." In *An Archeological Survey of Pickwick Basin in the Adjacent Portions of the States of Alabama, Mississippi and Tennessee* by William S. Webb and David L. DeJarnette, Bureau of American Ethnology, Bulletin 129, pp. 393–507, Washington. 1942.

Webb, William S.
An Archeological Survey of Wheeler Basin on the Tennessee River in Northern Alabama. Bureau of American Ethnology, Bulletin 122, Washington. 1939.

Webb, William S. and David L. DeJarnette
An Archeological Survey of Pickwick Basin in the Adjacent Portions of the States of Alabama, Mississippi and Tennessee. Bureau of American Ethnology, Bulletin 129, Washington. 1942.

WIMBERLEY, STEVE B., and HARRY A. TOURTELOT
*The McQuorquodale Mound: A Manifestation of
the Hopewellian Phase in South Alabama.* Geological Survey of Alabama, Museum Paper No. 19, University, Alabama. 1941.

ARIZONA

A. Organization
   1. Arizona State Museum
   2. Director of the Arizona State Museum
      University of Arizona, Tucson
   3. Arizona Archaeological and Historical Society
      c/o Arizona State Museum, University of Arizona,
      Tucson

B. Control
   Arizona Antiquities Act of 1960 (Sections 41–771 to
   41–776) relates to Archaeological, Paleontological, and
   Historical Features of the State, providing for the preservation of antiquities within Arizona.

   No nonauthorized persons may excavate on lands controlled by the State of Arizona. Only educational institutions, public museums or nonprofit corporations organized for scientific research purposes may be authorized and then only after a permit is first secured from
   the Director of the Arizona State Museum.

C. Sites
   1. Llano, Early Man
      Cochise, Early Man
      Hohokam
      Anasazi
      Mogollon
   2. Snaketown
      Casa Grande National Monument
      Tonto National Monument
      Montezuma Castle National Monument

D. Excavations
   Snaketown, 1934–35, Gila Pueblo

Ventana Cave, 1941–42, Arizona State Museum and Department of Anthropology, University of Arizona

Winona and Ridge Ruin, 1935–39, Museum of Northern Arizona

Kinishaba, 1932–38, Arizona State Museum and Department of Anthropology, University of Arizona

Point of Pines, 1946–60, Arizona State Museum and Department of Anthropology, University of Arizona

Table Rock Pueblo, 1958, Chicago Natural History Museum

E. Museums

Arizona State Museum
University of Arizona, Tucson

Montezuma Castle National Monument
Camp Verde

Museum of Northern Arizona
Fort Valley Road, Flagstaff

Walnut Canyon National Monument
Flagstaff

Tonto National Monument
Roosevelt

F. Academic Institutions

University of Arizona, Tucson, Archaeology and Anthropology

G. Bibliography

Breternitz, David A.
Excavations at Nantack Village, Point of Pines, Arizona. Anthropological Papers, Number 1, University of Tucson. 1959.

Colton, Harold S.
Pottery Types of the Arizona Strip and Adjacent Areas in Utah and Nevada. Flagstaff. 1952.

Di Peso, Charles C.
The Sobaipuri Indians of The Upper San Pedro Valley. Southeastern Arizona. Dragoon. 1953.

DIXON, KEITH
Hidden House: A Cliff Ruin in Sycamore Canyon, Central Arizona. Flagstaff. 1956.

DOXIER, EDWARD P.
The Hopi-Tewa of Arizona. University of California Publications In American Archaeology and Ethnology, Vol. 44, Number 3. Berkeley and Los Angeles. 1954.

HAURY, EMIL W.
"An Alluvial Site on The San Carlos Indian Reservation, Arizona." *American Antiquity,* Vol. 23, pp. 2–27. Salt Lake City. 1957.

The Kiva, Arizona Archaeological and Historical Society, Tucson.

MARTIN, PAUL S. and J. B. RINALDO
Excavations in the Upper Little Colorado Drainage, Eastern Arizona. Chicago. 1960.

Museum of Northern Arizona Bulletin, Flagstaff.

Plateau, Museum of Northern Arizona, Flagstaff.

SMITH, WATSON
"Excavations in Big Hawk Valley." *Museum of Northern Arizona,* Bulletin 24. Flagstaff. 1952.

WOODBURY, RICHARD B.
Prehistoric Stone Implements of Northeastern Arizona. Papers of The Peabody Museum of American Archaeology and Ethnology, Vol. 34. Cambridge. 1954.

ARKANSAS

A. Organization
1. Laboratory of Archaeological Research
   University of Arkansas Museum, Fayetteville
2. Director of the University of Arkansas Museum
   Fayetteville

3. Arkansas Archaeological Society
   Central Office, University Museum
   University of Arkansas, Fayetteville

B. Control
   An Antiquities act will be introduced to the legislature at the 1963 session.

C. Sites
   1. Eastern Arkansas
      Mississippian Traditions
      Southwest Arkansas, Caddo
      Northwest Arkansas, Ozark Bluff Dwellers
   2. Ozark Bluff I, Archaic
      Williams Mound, Fourche-Maline, Caddoan
      Kirkham Place
      Crenshaw I
      Pachoha
      Menard
      Parkin Mound
      Rose Mound, Mississippian

D. Excavations
   Dardanelle Reservoir, Inter-Agency Archaeological Salvage Program

E. Museums
   University of Arkansas Museum
   Fayetteville

   Little Rock Museum of Natural History
   MacArthur Park, Little Rock

F. Academic Institutions
   University of Arkansas, Fayetteville

G. Bibliography
   BAERREIS, DAVID A.
      "The Archaic As Seen From The Ozark Region." *American Antiquity,* Vol. 24, pp. 270–275, Salt Lake City. 1959.

DELLINGER, S. C. and S. D. DICKINSON
"Possible Antecedents of the Middle Mississippian
Ceramic Complex in Northeastern Arkansas." *Amer-
ican Antiquity*, Vol. 6. No. 2, pp. 133–147, Menasha.
1940.
"Pottery from the Ozark Bluff Shelters." *American
Antiquity*, Vol. 7, No. 3, pp. 276–289, Menasha.
1942.

DICKINSON, S. D., and S. C. DELLINGER
"A Survey of the Historic Earthenware of the Lower
Arkansas Valley." *Bulletin of the Texas Archaeological and Paleontological Society*, Vol. 12, pp. 76–
97, Abilene. 1940.

DICKINSON, S. D., and H. J. LEMLEY
"Evidences of the Marksville and Coles Creek Complexes at the Kirkham Place, Clark County, Arkansas." *Bulletin of the Texas Archaeological and
Paleontological Society*, Vol. 11, pp. 139–189, Abilene. 1939.

GRIFFIN, JAMES B.
"The Archaeological Remains of the Chiwere Sioux."
American Antiquity, Vol. 2, No. 3, pp. 180–181,
Menasha. 1937.
"Culture Identity of the Ozark 'Top Layer'." *Amer-
ican Antiquity*, Vol. 2, No. 4, pp. 296–297, Menasha.
1937.

LEMLEY, H. J.
"Discoveries Indicating a Pre-Caddo Culture on
Red River in Arkansas." *Bulletin of the Texas Archaeological and Paleontological Society*, Vol. 8, pp.
25–55, Abilene. 1936.

LEWIS, T. H.
"The 'Old Fort' of Cross County, Arkansas." *The
Archaeologist*, Vol. 2, No. 11, pp. 319–325, Waterloo.
1896. "Mounds and Stone Cists at St. Paul, Minne-
sota." *The American Antiquarian and Oriental
Journal*, Vol. 18, No. 6, pp. 314–320, Chicago. 1894.

CALIFORNIA

A. Organization
   1. None
   2. University of California Archaeological Survey
      Los Angeles 24

      California State Division of Beaches and Parks
      P.O. Box 2390, Sacramento 11
   3. Archaeological Survey Association of Southern California
      Southwest Museum, Los Angeles 38

      Central California Archaeological Foundation
      Sacramento State College, Sacramento

      Archaeological Research Associates
      University of Southern California, Los Angeles 7

B. Control
   California State Penal Code of 1939 (Current Section 622 1/2) provides that every person, not the owner thereof, who willfully injures, disfigures, defaces, or destroys any object or thing of archaeological or historical interest or value, whether situated on private lands or within any public park or place, is guilty of a misdemeanor.
   More stringent legislation is being considered.

C. Sites
   1. Early Horizon
      Middle Horizon (Coastal Province and Interior Province)

      Late Horizon—Phase 1 and 2 (Marine Province, Alameda Province, Delta Province, Colusa Province)
      Historic
   2. Tommy Tucker Cave, Lassen County
      Emeryville Shell Mound
      Buena Vista Lake, Kern County
      Slick Rock Village Site

D. Excavations

Folsom Reservoir, Eldorado County, Inter-Agency Archaeological Salvage Program

Slick Rock Village Site, Terminus Reservoir, Inter-Agency Archaeological Salvage Program

Old Fort Charlotte (Historical), Inter-Agency Archaeological Salvage Program

E. Museums

Robert H. Lowie Museum of Anthropology
University of California, Berkeley 4

Southwest Museum
10 Highland Park, Los Angeles

Stanford University Museum
Stanford

San Diego Museum of Man
Balboa Park

Santa Barbara Museum of Natural History
Santa Barbara

F. Academic Institutions

University of California, Berkeley and Los Angeles, Archaeology, Anthropology, Paleontology

Stanford University, San Francisco, Anthropology

University of Southern California, Los Angeles, Archaeology

San Francisco State College, San Francisco, Anthropology

G. Bibliography

BELOUS, RUSSEL E.

"The Central California Chronological Sequence Reexamined." *American Antiquity,* Vol. 23, pp. 341–353, Salt Lake City. 1953.

CARTER, GEORGE F.

Pleistocene Man At San Diego. Baltimore. 1957.
"Pleistocene Man At San Diego: A Reply." *American Antiquity,* Vol. 24, pp. 319–320, Salt Lake City. 1959.

Harrington, Mark Raymond
A Pinto Site At Little Lake, California. Los Angeles. 1957.

Heizer, Robert F.
"The Archaeology of Central California I: Early Horizon." *Anthropological Records,* Vol. 12, No. 1. 1949.
"The Archaeology of The Napa Region." *University of California Archaeological Reports,* Vol. 12, No. 16. Berkeley. 1953.

Kroeber, Alfred L.
Native Cultures of the Southwest. University of California Publications in American Archaeology and Ethnology, Vol. 23, No. 9, Berkeley. 1928.

Kroeber, Alfred L. and M. J. Harner
Mohave Pottery. Anthropological Records, Vol. 16, No. 1. Berkeley. 1955.

Lathrop, Donald W., and Dick Shutler, Jr.
"An Archaeological Site in The High Sierra of California." *American Antiquity,* Vol. 20, pp. 226–239, Salt Lake City. 1954.

Masterkey, Southwest Museum, Los Angeles

McGeein, D. J. and W. C. Mueller
"A Shellmound in Marin County, California." *American Antiquity,* Vol. 21, pp. 52–62, Salt Lake City. 1955.

Meighan, Clement W.
"Californian Cultures and the Concept of An Archaic Stage." *American Antiquity,* Vol. 24, pp. 289–305, Salt Lake City. 1958.
"Little Harbor Site, Catalina Island." *American Antiquity,* Vol. No. 24, pp. 383–405, Salt Lake City. 1959.

Merriam, C. Hart
Studies of California Indians. Berkeley. 1955.

TRUE, D. L.
"An Early Complex in San Diego County, California." *American Antiquity,* Vol. 23, pp. 255–263, Salt Lake City. 1957.

WALLACE, WILLIAM JAMES and E. S. TAYLOR
"Archaeology of Wildrose Canyon, Death Valley National Monument." *American Antiquity,* Vol. 20, pp. 355–367, Salt Lake City. 1955.

COLORADO

A. Organization
    1. None
    2. Executive Director, The State Historical Society of Colorado
       State Museum Building, E. 14th Avenue and Sherman St.
       Denver 2
    3. Colorado Archaeological Society
       c/o University of Colorado, Boulder

B. Control
   A state antiquities law is being contemplated.

C. Sites
    1. Archaic
       Woodland
    2. Mesa Verde, Mesa Verde National Park

D. Excavations
   Mesa Verde National Park, National Park Service
   Western Slope of Colorado, University of Colorado with National Science Foundation
   Southwest Colorado, University of Colorado Museum

E. Museums
   University of Colorado Museum
   Boulder
   Colorado State Museum
   East 14th Avenue and Sherman St., Denver

Denver Museum of Natural History
Denver

F. Academic Institutions
University of Colorado, Boulder

G. Bibliography

BRYAN, KIRK, and LOUIS L. RAY
Geologic Antiquity of the Lindenmeier Site in Colorado. Smithsonian Miscellaneous Collections, Vol. 99, No. 2, Washington. 1940.

DICK, HERBERT W.
"The Status of Colorado Archaeology with a Bibliographic Guide." *Southwestern Lore,* Vol. 18, No. 4. 1953.

FOLMER, H.
"The Mallet Expedition." *Colorado Magazine,* Vol. 16, No. 5. 1939.

IRWIN, H. J. and C. C.
Excavations at the LoDaisKa Site in the Denver, Colorado, Area. Denver, 1959.

MORRIS, EARL H. and R. F. BURGH
Basket Maker II Sites Near Durango, Colorado. Washington, D.C. 1954.

ROBERTS, FRANK H. H., JR.
A Folsom Complex, Preliminary Report on Investigations at the Lindenmeier Site in Northern Colorado. Smithsonian Miscellaneous Collections, Vol. 94, No. 4, Washington. 1935.
Additional Information on the Folsom Complex, Report on the Second Season's Investigations at the Lindenmeier Site in Northern Colorado. Smithsonian Miscellaneous Collections, Vol. 95, No. 10, Washington. 1936.

CONNECTICUT

A. Organization
   1.
   2.

   3. Archeological Society of Connecticut
      c/o Mr. Frank Glynn, Secretary
      Box 2114, Yale Station, New Haven

B. Control

C. Sites
   1. Archaic
      Early Woodland
      Middle Woodland
      Late Woodland (Sebonac)
      Final Woodland (Niantic)
   2. Eagle Hill, Early and Middle Woodland
      Old Lynne, Sebonac
      Niantic Site, Niantic
      Indian River Site, Niantic

D. Excavations
   Southbury, Archeological Society of Connecticut
   Granniss Island, New Haven, Archeological Society of
   Connecticut

E. Museums
   Yale University Peabody Museum of Natural History
   170 Whitney Avenue, New Haven
   Fort Hill Indian Memorial Association
   Gallup Hill, Old Mystic
   Connecticut State Library Museum
   231 Capitol Avenue, Hartford

F. Academic Institutions
   Yale University, New Haven, Archaeology, Anthropology

G. Bibliography
   ASHLEY, MARGARET E.
      "A Study of the Ceramic Art of the Etowans." *Etowah Papers* (Warren K. Moorehead, ed.), No. 3, pp. 107–132, New Haven. 1932.

   BASTO, ARTHUR
      "The Second Summer's Field Work at the Village

Site at South Woodstock, Connecticut." *Bulletin of the Archaeological Society of Connecticut,* No. 8, pp. 27–44, New Haven. 1939.

Bulletin of the Archeological Society of Connecticut, New Haven.

Rouse, Irving B.
"Styles of Pottery in Connecticut." *Bulletin of the Massachusetts Archaeological Society,* Vol. 7, No. 1, pp. 1–8, Boston. 1945.
"Ceramic Traditions and Sequences in Connecticut." *Connecticut Archaeological Society Bulletin,* No. 21, pp. 10–25, New Haven. 1947.

DELAWARE

A. Organization
   1.
   2.
   3. Archaeological Society of Delaware
      c/o Mr. Charles F. Kier
      619 Broadway, Hammondton, N.J.
      Sussex Archeological Association
      Zwaanendael Museum, Lewes

B. Control
   Legislation relating to the preservation, ownership and excavation of archaeological sites is contained in Delaware Code Annotated, Title 7 c. 53, part 6, section 5301–5306.

C. Sites
   1. Archaic
      Early Woodland
      Middle Woodland
      Late Woodland
      Historic
   2. Tocks Island

D. Excavations
   St. Jones River Site near Dover

Tocks Island Reservoir Area, Upper Delaware River Valley

E. Museums
The Delaware State Museum
316 South Governors Avenue, Dover

Zwaanendael Museum
Lewes

F. Academic Institutions

G. Bibliography
Archeolog, Sussex Archeological Association
Bulletin, Archaeological Society of Delaware

FLORIDA

A. Organization
   1. Florida State Museum
   2. State Archeologist, Department of Conservation
   3. Florida Anthropological Society
      c/o Mrs. Alma J. Mattox, Secretary
      209 Beverly Rd., Cocoa

B. Control
   State legislation in 1961 created the position of State Archeologist.

C. Sites
   1. Paleo-Indian
      Archaic
      Early Woodland
      Middle Woodland
      Late Woodland
      Mississippian
   2. Mound Key
      Jungerman Site on Merritt Island
      Perico Island, Early Woodland
      Mt. Royal on St. Johns, Early to Late Woodland
      Weeden Island, Mississippian
      Safety Harbor, Mississippian

D. Excavations

Jungerman Site on Merritt Island, Florida State Museum and Florida Anthropological Society

Salvage archaeology along turnpike routes and at missile bases, Florida Anthropological Society

E. Museums

University of Florida, Florida State Museum
Gainesville

Museum of Science and Natural History
3280 S. Miami Avenue, Miami

Southeast Museum of the North American Indian
U.S. Highway 1, Marathon

Florida State University, University Museum
Tallahassee

F. Academic Institutions
University of Florida, Gainesville
Florida State University, Tallahassee

G. Bibliography

BOYD, MARK F., HALE G. SMITH, and JOHN W. GRIFFIN
Here They Once Stood. University of Florida Press.
Gainesville. 1951.

BULLEN, ADELAIDE K., and RIPLEY P. BULLEN
"The John's Island Site, Hernando County, Florida."
American Antiquity, Vol. 16, No. 1, pp. 23–45,
Menasha. 1950.

BULLEN, RIPLEY P.
"The Terra Ceia Site, Manatee County, Florida."
Florida Anthropological Society Publications, No. 3,
Gainesville. 1951.
n.d. "The Famous Crystal River Site." Manuscript
on file, Florida Park Service, Gainesville.

BULLEN, RIPLEY P. and ADELAIDE BULLEN
Excavations on Cape Haze Peninsula, Florida. Contributions of the Florida State Museum, Social Science, 1. Gainesville. 1956.

CHATELAIN, VERNE E.
The Defenses of Spanish Florida, 1565–1763. Carnegie Institution of Washington, Publication 511, Washington. 1941.

DYSON, ROBERT H., JR., and ELIZABETH TOOKER
The Palmer-Taylor Mound, Geneva, Florida. Anthropology Society, Peabody Museum (Hectographed). Cambridge, Massachusetts. 1949.

FERGUSON, VERA MASIUS
"Chronology at South Indian Field, Florida." *Yale University Publications in Anthropology,* No. 45, New Haven. 1951.

The Florida Anthropologist, Florida Anthropological Society, Gainesville.

GOGGIN, JOHN M.
"A Ceramic Sequence in South Florida." *New Mexico Anthropologist,* Vol. 3, pp. 36–40, Albuquerque. 1939.
"The Distribution of Pottery Wares in the Glades Archaeological Area of South Florida." *New Mexico Anthropologist,* Vol. 4, pp. 22–33, Albuquerque. 1940.
"Archaeological Investigations on the Upper Florida Keys." *Tequesta,* Vol. 4, No. 4, pp. 13–35, Coral Gables. 1944.
"A Preliminary Definition of Archaeological Areas and Periods in Florida." *American Antiquity,* Vol. 13, No. 2, pp. 114–127, Menasha. 1947.
"Some Pottery Types from Central Florida." *Bulletin No. 1,* Gainesville Anthropological Association. 1948.
"A Revised Temporal Chart of Florida Archaeology." *The Florida Anthropologist,* Vol. 1, Nos. 3–4, pp. 57–60, Gainesville. 1948.
"Cultural Traditions in Florida Prehistory." *The Florida Indian and His Neighbors,* pp. 13–44, Winter Park. 1949.

"Cultural Occupation at Goodland Point, Florida." *The Florida Anthropologist,* Vol. 2, Nos. 3–4, pp. 65–91, Gainesville. 1949.

"Stratigraphic Tests in the Everglades National Park." *American Antiquity,* Vol. 15, No. 3, pp. 228–246, Menasha. 1950.

"The Snapper Creek Site." *The Florida Anthropologist,* Vol. 3, Nos. 3–4, pp. 50–64, Gainesville. 1950.

GOGGIN, JOHN M., and FRANK H. SOMMER III
Excavations on Upper Matecumbe Key, Florida. Yale University Publications in Anthropology, No. 41, New Haven. 1949.

GREENMAN, EMERSON F.
"Hopewellian Traits in Florida." *American Antiquity,* Vol. 3, No. 4, pp. 327–332, Menasha. 1938.

GRIFFIN, JAMES B.
"The Significance of the Fiber-tempered Pottery of the St. Johns Area in Florida." *Journal of the Washington Academy of Science,* Vol. 35, No. 7, pp. 218–223, Menasha. 1945.

GRIFFIN, JOHN W.
"Toward Chronology in Coastal Volusia County." *The Florida Anthropologist,* Vol. 1, Nos. 3–4, pp. 49–56, Gainesville. 1948.

"Notes on the Archaeology of Useppa Island." *The Florida Anthropologist,* Vol. 2, Nos. 3–4, pp. 92–93, Gainesville. 1949.

"Test Excavations at the Lake Jackson Site." *American Antiquity,* Vol. 16, No. 2, pp. 99–112, Menasha. 1950.

GRIFFIN, JOHN W., and RIPLEY P. BULLEN
"The Safety Harbor Site, Pinellas County, Florida." *Florida Anthropological Society Publications,* No. 2. Gainesville. 1950.

Griffin, John W., and Hale G. Smith

The Goodnow Mound, Highlands County, Florida.
Contributions to the Archaeology of Florida, No. 1,
Florida Park Service, Tallahassee. 1948.

"Nocoroco: A Timucua Village of 1605 Now in
Tomoka State Park." *Florida Historical Quarterly,*
Vol. 27, No. 4, pp. 340–361, St. Augustine. 1949.

Higgs, Charles D.

"Spanish Contacts with the Ais (Indian River)
Country." *The Florida Historical Quarterly,* Vol. 21,
No. 1, pp. 25–39, St. Augustine. 1942.

Jenks, Albert E., and Mrs. H. H. Simpson, Sr.

"Beveled Artifacts in Florida of the Same Type as
Artifacts Found near Clovis, New Mexico." *American Antiquity,* Vol. 6, No. 4, pp. 314–319, Menasha.
1941.

Rainey, Froelich G.

"An Indian Burial Site at Crystal River, Florida."
The Florida Historical Society Quarterly, Vol. 13,
No. 4, pp. 185–192, Tallahassee. 1935.

Rouse, Irving B.

"Vero and Melbourne Man: A Cultural and Chronological Interpretation." *Transactions of the New
York Academy of Sciences,* Series 2, Vol. 12, No. 7,
pp. 220–224, New York. 1950.

"A Survey of Indian River Archaeology, Florida."
Yale University Publications in Anthropology, No.
44, New Haven. 1951.

Simpson, J. Clarence

"Folsom-like Points from Florida." *The Florida Anthropologist,* Vol. 1, Nos. 1–2, pp. 11–15, Gainesville. 1948.

Smith, Hale G.

"Two Historical Archaeological Periods in Florida."
American Antiquity, Vol. 13, No. 4, pp. 313–319,
Menasha. 1948.

"Results of an Archaeological Investigation of a Spanish Mission Site in Jefferson County, Florida." *The Florida Anthropologist,* Vol. 1, Nos. 1–2, pp. 1–10, Gainesville. 1948.

Two Archaeological Sites in Brevard County, Florida. Florida Anthropological Society Publications, No. 1, Gainesville. 1949.

"Crystal River, Revisited, Revisited, Revisited." *American Antiquity,* Vol. 17, No. 2, pp. 143–144, Salt Lake City. 1951.

Spoehr, Alexander

Camp, Clan, and Kin among the Cow Creek Seminole of Florida. Field Museum of Natural History, Anthropological Series, Vol. 33, No. 1, Chicago. 1941.

Kinship System of the Seminole. Field Museum of Natural History, Anthropological Series, Vol. 33, No. 2, Chicago. 1942.

The Florida Seminole Camp. Field Museum of Natural History, Anthropological Series, Vol. 33, No. 3, Chicago. 1944.

Changing Kinship Systems. Field Museum of Natural History, Anthropological Series, Vol. 33, No. 4, Chicago. 1947.

Steward, T. Dale

A Reexamination of the Fossil Human Skeletal Remains from Melbourne, Florida. Smithsonian Miscellaneous Collections, Vol. 106, No. 10, Washington. 1946.

Stirling, Matthew W.

"Florida Cultural Affiliations in Relation to Adjacent Areas." In *Essays in Anthropology Presented to A. L. Kroeber,* (Robert H. Lowie, ed.), pp. 351–357, Berkeley. 1936.

"The Historic Method as Applied to Southeastern Archeology." In *Essays in Historical Anthropology of North America,* Smithsonian Miscellaneous Collections, Vol. 100, pp. 117–123, Washington. 1940.

Trickey, E. Bruce
"A Chronological Framework for The Mobile Bay Region." *American Antiquity,* Vol. 23, pp. 388–396, Salt Lake City. 1958.

Willey, Gordon R.
"Culture Sequence in the Manatee Region of the Florida West Coast." *American Antiquity,* Vol. 13, No. 3, pp. 209–218, Menasha. 1948.
"The Cultural Context of the Crystal River Negative Painted Style." *American Antiquity,* Vol. 13, No. 4, pp. 325–328, Menasha. 1948.
Excavations in Southeast Florida. Yale University Publications in Anthropology, No. 42, New Haven.
Archaeology of the Florida Gulf Coast. Smithsonian Miscellaneous Collections, Vol. 113, Washington. 1949.

Willey, Gordon R., and Philip Phillips
"Negative Painted Pottery from Crystal River, Florida." *American Antiquity,* Vol. 10, No. 2, pp. 173–185, Menasha. 1944.

GEORGIA

A. Organization
    1.
    2.
    3. Society for the Preservation of Early Georgia History
       c/o Mr. Frank Schnell, Secretary
       Department of Archeology, University of Georgia
       Athens

B. Control

C. Sites
    1. Archaic
       Deptford Period (Early Woodland)
       Wilmington (Middle Woodland)
       Savannah I and II
       Irene Period (Mississippian)

2. Stallings Island, Late Archaic
   Deptford, Deptford, Wilmington and Savannah I
   The Haven Home Site, Savannah I
   Irene Site, Savannah II and Irene
   Etowah, Savannah II and Irene

D. Excavations
   Allatoona Reservoir, Inter-Agency Archaeological Salvage Program

   Survey of two mounds along the banks of the Oconee River, Oconee National Forest, University of Georgia, National Forest Service and local members of state society

E. Museums
   Emory University Museum,
   Bishops Hall, Atlanta

   Ocmulgee National Monument
   P.O. Box 936, Macon

F. Academic Institutions
   University of Georgia, Athens and Atlanta, Anthropology

G. Bibliography
   CLAFLIN, WILLIAM H., JR.
   The Stalling's Island Mound, Columbia County, Georgia. Papers of the Peabody Museum of American Archaeology and Ethnology, Harvard University, Vol. 14, No. 1, Cambridge. 1931.
   Early Georgia, Society for the Preservation of Early Georgia History, Athens.

   FAIRBANKS, CHARLES H.
   "The Taxonomic Position of Stalling's Island, Georgia." *American Antiquity,* Vol. 7, No. 3, pp. 223–231, Menasha. 1942.
   "The Kolomoki Mound Group, Early County, Georgia." *American Antiquity,* Vol. 11, No. 4, pp. 258–260, Menasha. 1946.

"The Macon Earth Lodge." *American Antiquity,* Vol. 12, No. 2, pp. 94–108, Menasha. 1946.
Archeology of the Funeral Mound, Ocmulgee National Monument, Georgia. Archeological Research Series, No. 3, National Park Service. Washington, D.C. 1956.

FAIRBANKS, CHARLES H., ARTHUR R. KELLY, GORDON R. WILLEY and PAT WOFFORD, JR.
"The Leake Mounds, Bartow County, Georgia." *American Antiquity,* Vol. 12, No. 2, pp. 126–127, Menasha. 1946.

HULSE, FREDERICK S.
"The People Who Lived at Irene: Physical Anthropology." In *Irene Mound Site, Chatham County, Georgia* by Joseph Caldwell and Catherine McCann, pp. 57–68, Athens. 1941.

JENNINGS, JESSE D.
"Recent Excavations at the Lamar Site, Ocmulgee National Monument, Macon, Georgia." *Proceedings of the Society for Georgia Archaeology,* Vol. 2, No. 2, pp. 45–55. 1939.

KELLY, A. R.
"The Macon Trading Post, an Historical Foundling." *American Antiquity,* Vol. 4, No. 4, pp. 328–333, Menasha. 1939.

LARSON, LEWIS H., JR.
"Southern Cult Manifestations on the Georgia Coast." *American Antiquity,* Vol. 23, pp. 426–430, Salt Lake City. 1958.

SEARS, WILLIAM H.
Excavations at Kolomoki, Final Report. Athens. 1956.

WARING, ANTONIO J., JR.
"The De Luna Expedition and Southeastern Cere-

monial." *American Antiquity,* Vol. 11, No. 1, pp. 57–58, Menasha. 1945.

"Hopewellian Elements in Northern Georgia." *American Antiquity,* Vol. 11, No. 2, pp. 119–120, Menasha. 1945.

Willey, Gordon R.

"Ceramic Stratigraphy in a Georgia Village Site." *American Antiquity,* Vol. 5. No. 2, pp. 140–147, Menasha. 1939.

"The Weeden Island Culture: A Preliminary Definition." *American Antiquity,* Vol. 10, No. 3, pp. 225–254, Menasha. 1945.

IDAHO

A. Organization
   1. None
   2. Director, Idaho Historical Society
      610 Parkway Drive, Boise

      Director, The Museum
      Idaho State College, Pocatello
   3. None

B. Control
   Antiquities Act to be presented to the 1963 legislature covering archeological, paleontological and certain geological materials occurring on state owned land.

C. Sites
   1. Old Cordilleran Culture
      Folsom
      Clovis
      Agate Basin
      Early forest hunting culture of Mesolithic period (unnamed)
   2. Fort Rock Cave
      Cougar Mt. Cave
      Kawaumkan Spring Midden

Indian Wells
Hot Creek
Olcott Site
Wilson Butte Cave on Snake River Plain
Birch Creek Valley

D. Excavations

Wilson Butte Cave, Snake River Plain, 1959–60, Ruth Gruhn Bryan, The Museum, Idaho State College

Birch Creek Valley, Eastern Idaho (Central Rockies), 1960–61, Earl H. Swanson, The Museum, Idaho State College

Upper Birch Creek Valley, 1961, Hind Sadek, The Museum, Idaho State College

Camas Prairie, North Central Idaho, 1961, B. Robert Butler, The Museum, Idaho State College

Brown's Bench, Southwest Idaho, 1957–59, Alfred Bowers, University of Idaho

Bruce's Eddy Reservoir, north fork of the Clearwater, 1962

E. Museums
Idaho State College Museum
Pocatello

F. Academic Institutions
Idaho State College, Pocatello

G. Bibliography
Occasional Papers of the Museum, Idaho State College, Pocatello

SWANSON, EARL H., JR., DONALD R. TUOHY, AND ALAN L. BRYAN
"Archaeological Explorations in Central and South Idaho—1958," *Occasional Papers of the Idaho State College Museum,* Number 2, Pocatello.

Tebiwa, The Journal of the Idaho State College Museum, Pocatello, Idaho.

ILLINOIS

A. Organization
1.
2. Director, Illinois State Museum
   Springfield
   Director, State Department of Conservation
   Springfield
3. Illinois State Archaeological Society
   Southern Illinois University Museum, Carbondale

   The Council of Illinois Archaeology
   c/o Illinois State Museum, Springfield

B. Control
   Senate Bill No. 552, adopted June 7, 1961, invokes pen-
   alties for unauthorized digging on State owned
   lands.

C. Sites
1. Archaic
   Early Woodland
   Hopewellian
   Late Woodland
   Mississipian
2. Modoc Rock Shelter, Archaic
   Baumer, Early Woodland
   Ogden-Fettie in Fulton County, Hopewellian
   Dillinger, Late Woodland
   Maple Mills, Late Woodland
   Cahokia, Mississippian
   Kincaid, Mississippian
   Starved Rock, Archaic

D. Excavations
   Cahokia, Warren K. Moorehead, University of Illinois

   Fulton and Massac Counties, Fay Cooper-Cole and
   Thorne Deuel, University of Chicago

   Starved Rock, Fay Cooper-Cole and Thorne Deuel,
   The University of Chicago, Illinois State Museum,
   and the Department of Public Works and Buildings

Modoc Rock Shelter, Randolph County, Melvin Fowler, Illinois State Museum

E. Museums

Illinois State Museum of Natural History and Art Springfield

University of Illinois Museum of Natural History Natural History Building, Springfield

Chicago Natural History Museum Roosevelt Road and Lake Shore Drive, Chicago

University of Chicago, Oriental Institute 1155 East 58 Street, Chicago

F. Academic Institutions

Northwestern University, Evanston and Chicago, Paleontology
Wheaton College, Wheaton, Anthropology
University of Chicago, Chicago, Archaeology, Anthropology, Paleontology
University of Illinois, Springfield
Southern Illinois University, Carbondale

G. Bibliography

BENNETT, JOHN W.

"Archaeological Horizons in the Southern Illinois Region." *American Antiquity,* Vol. 10, No. 1, pp. 12–22, Menasha. 1944.
Archaeological Explorations in Jo Daviess County Illinois. Chicago. 1945.

BENNETT, JOHN W., and MOREAU MAXWELL

"Archaeological Horizons in Southern Illinois." (Abstract) *Transactions of the Illinois State Academy of Science,* Vol. 35, No. 2, p. 50, Springfield. 1942.

BRIGHAM, WILLIAM B.

"The Arrowsmith Battlefield." *Transactions of the Illinois State Academy of Science,* Vol. 36, No. 2, pp. 71–72, Springfield. 1943.

Cole, Fay Cooper, *et al.*
Kincaid, A Prehistoric Illinois Metropolis. University of Chicago Press, Chicago. 1951.

Cole, Fay Cooper, and Thorne Deuel
Rediscovering Illinois: Archaeological Explorations In and Around Fulton County. Chicago. 1937.

Deuel, Thorne
"Illinois Records of 1000 A.D." *Journal of the Illinois State Historical Society,* Vol. 41, No. 3, pp. 219–230, Springfield. 1948.

Faye, S.
"The Foxes' Fort—1730." *Journal of the Illinois State Historical Society,* Vol. 28, No. 3, pp. 123–163, Springfield. 1935.

Fowler, Melvin L.
Rutherford Mound, Hardin County, Illinois. Scientific Papers, Vol. 7, No. 1, Illinois State Museum. Springfield. 1957.
Ferry Site, Hardin County, Illinois. Scientific Papers, Vol. 8, No. 1, Illinois State Museum. Springfield. 1957.
"Ware Groupings and Decorations of Woodland Ceramics in Illinois." *American Antiquity,* Vol. 20, pp. 213–225, Salt Lake City. 1954.
"Medoc Rock Shelter. An Early Archaic Site in Southern Illinois." *American Antiquity,* Vol. 24, pp. 257–270, Salt Lake City. 1958.

Griffin, James B., and Richard G. Morgan, editors
"Contributions to the Archaeology of the Illinois River Valley." *Transactions of the American Philosophical Society,* Vol. 32, Pt. 1, Philadelphia. 1941.

Griffin, John W., and Donald E. Wray
"Bison in Illinois Archaeology." *Transactions of the Illinois State Academy of Science,* Vol. 38, pp. 21–26, Springfield. 1946.

Grimm, R. E.
"Excavation of a Rock Shelter near Prairie du Rocker, Illinois." *Amateur Archeology Club,* Bulletin 1, pp. 16–23, St. Louis. 1947.

Grogan, Robert M.
"Beads of Meteoric Iron from an Indian Mound near Havana, Illinois." *American Antiquity,* Vol. 13, No. 4, pp. 302–305, Menasha. 1948.

Kelly, A. R.
"Some Problems of Recent Cahokia Archaeology." *Transactions of the Illinois State Academy of Science,* Vol. 25, No. 4, pp. 101–103, Springfield. 1933.

Langford, George
"The Kankakee River Refuse Heap." *American Anthropologist,* Vol. 21, No. 3, pp. 287–291, Lancaster. 1919.
"The Fisher Mound Group, Successive Aboriginal Occupations near the Mouth of the Illinois River." *American Anthropologist,* Vol. 29, No. 3, pp. 153x–206x, Menasha. 1927.
"Stratified Indian Mounds in Will County." *Transactions of the Illinois State Academy of Science,* Vol. 20, pp. 247–253, Springfield. 1928.
"The Fisher Mound and Village Site." *Transactions of the Illinois State Academy of Science,* Vol. 22, pp. 79–92, Springfield. 1930.

MacNeish, Richard S.
"Middle Woodland Cultures." *Transactions of the Illinois State Academy of Science,* Vol. 37, pp. 41–44, Springfield. 1944.
"The Pre-Pottery Faulkner Site of Southern Illinois." *American Antiquity,* Vol. 13, No. 3, pp. 232–243, Menasha. 1948.

Maxwell, Moreau S.
"A Summary of Illinois Archaeology." *The Wisconsin Archeologist,* Vol. 28, No. 2, pp. 19–33, Milwaukee. 1947.

Woodland Cultures of Southern Illinois: Archaeological Excavations in the Carbondale Area. Logan Museum Publications in Anthropology, Bulletin No. 7, Beloit College, Beloit. 1951.

McKern, W. C., Paul F. Titterington, and James B. Griffin

"Painted Pottery Figurines from Illinois." *American Antiquity,* Vol. 10, No. 3, pp. 295–302, Menasha. 1945.

Morgan, Richard G.

"Archaeology of the Chicago Area." *Transactions of the Illinois State Academy of Science,* Vol. 25, No. 4, pp. 91–92, Springfield. 1933.

Neumann, Georg K.

"Preliminary Notes on the Crania from Fulton County, Illinois." In *Rediscovering Illinois* by Fay Cooper Cole and Thorne Deuel, pp. 227–264, Chicago. 1937.

"The Crania from the Hagan Mound and Their Relationship to Those of Two Late-Prehistoric Populations of Central Illinois." *Transactions of the American Philosophical Society.* Vol. 32, Pt. 1, pp. 79–82, Philadelphia. 1941.

Schoenbeck, Ethel

"Discovery of a Buried Aboriginal Shellheap in the Illinois River Valley." *Transactions of the Illinois State Academy of Science,* Vol. 32, No. 2, pp. 61–62, Springfield. 1939.

"Cord-decorated Pottery in the General Peoria Region." *Transactions of the Illinois State Academy of Science,* Vol. 39, pp. 33–42, Springfield. 1946.

Smith, Hale G.

The Crable Site, Fulton County, Illinois. Anthropological Papers, No. 7, Museum of Anthropology, University of Michigan, Ann Arbor. 1951.

TEMPLE, WAYNE C.
Illinois Villages of the Illinois Country. Historic Tribes. Scientific Papers, Vol. 2, No. 2, Illinois State Museum. Springfield. 1958.

TITTERINGTON, PAUL F.
"The Cahokia Mound Group and Its Surface Material." *The Wisconsin Archeologist,* Vol. 13, No. 1, pp. 7–14, Milwaukee. 1933.
"Certain Bluff Mounds of Western Jersey County, Illinois." *American Antiquity,* Vol. 1, No. 1, pp. 6–46, Menasha. 1935.
The Cahokia Mound Group and Its Village Site Materials. St. Louis. 1938.
"Outline of Cultural Traits of the Jersey County, Illinois, Bluff Focus." *Bulletin of the Illinois State Archaeological Society,* Vol. 3, No. 1, pp. 15–22. 1940.
"The Jersey County, Illinois, Bluff Focus." *American Antiquity,* Vol. 9, No. 2, pp. 240–245, Menasha. 1942.

WRAY, DONALD E., and HALE G. SMITH
"An Hypothesis for the Identification of the Illinois Confederacy with the Middle Mississippi Culture in Illinois." *American Antiquity,* Vol. 10, No. 1, pp. 23–27, Menasha. 1944.

INDIANA

A. Organization
1. Indiana Historical Society
2. Director, Indiana Historical Society
State Library and Historical Building, Indianapolis 4
3. Indiana Historical Society
State Library and Historical Building, Indianapolis 4

B. Control
None

C. Sites
1. Paleo-Indian
Archaic
Early Woodland

    Adena
    Hopewell
    Middle Woodland
    Late Woodland, Fort Ancient
    Middle Mississippi
    Glacial Kame
  2. Angel Site, Classic Middle Mississippi
    Mann Site, Posey County
    Welborn Mound, Posey County
    "Albee Mound," Sullivan County

D. Excavations
  Angel Site, Vanderburgh County
  Indiana and Bowen Site, Marion County
  Highway Salvage Program, Indiana Historical Society
  Water impounding basin project, The Inter-Agency
    Archaeological Salvage Program

E. Museums
  Indiana Historical Society
  140 North Senate Avenue, Indianapolis 4
  Indiana State Museum, Indiana Department of Con-
    servation
  311 West Washington Street, Indianapolis 4

F. Academic Institutions
  Indiana University, Bloomington and Indianapolis, Anthropology, American Archaeology, Paleontology Field
  School at Angel Site in cooperation with Indiana University

G. Bibliography
  BLACK, GLENN A.
    *Archaeological Survey of Dearborn and Ohio Coun-
    ties.* Indiana History Bulletin, Vol. 11, No. 7, In-
    dianapolis. 1934.
    Excavation of a Blackford County Site. Indiana His-
    tory Bulletin, Vol. 12, No. 5, Indianapolis. 1935.
    Excavation of the Nowlin Mound. Indiana History
    Bulletin, Vol. 13, No. 7, Indianapolis. 1936.

"Cultural Complexities of Southwestern Indiana." *Proceedings of the Indiana Academy of Science,* Vol. 50, pp. 33–35, Indianapolis. 1941.

Clauser, Charles E.
"The Relationship Between a Coastal Angonkin and a Karankawa Cranial Series." *Proceedings of the Indiana Academy of Science,* Vol. 57, pp. 18–23, Indianapolis. 1948.

Guernsey, Elam Y.
"Relationships among the Various Clark County Sites." *Proceedings of the Indiana Academy of Science,* Vol. 48, pp. 27–32, Indianapolis. 1939.

Indiana History Bulletin, Indiana Historical Bureau, Indianapolis.

Lilly, Eli
Prehistoric Antiquities of Indiana. Indiana Historical Society, Indianapolis. 1937.
"A Cedar Point 'Glacial Kame' Burial." *Proceedings of the Indiana Academy of Science,* Vol. 51, pp. 31–33, Indianapolis. 1942.

McAllister, J. Gilbert
"The Archaeology of Porter County." *Indiana History Bulletin,* Vol. 10, No. 1, pp. 6–66, Indianapolis. 1932.

Miller, Rex K.
McCain Site, Dubois County, Indiana. Prehistory Research Series, Indiana Historical Society, Vol. 2, No. 1, Indianapolis.

Setzler, Frank M.
The Archaeology of the Whitewater Valley. Indiana History Bulletin, Vol. 7, No. 12, Indianapolis. 1930.
The Archaeology of Randolph County and the Fudge Mound. Indiana History Bulletin, Vol. 9, No. 1, Indianapolis. 1931.

IOWA

A. Organization
   1. State Archeologist
   2. State Archeologist
      State University of Iowa, Iowa City
   3. Iowa Archeological Society
      State University of Iowa, Iowa City

B. Control
   The State Archeologist has the primary responsibility for the discovery, location, and excavation of archeological sites and for the recovery, restoration, and preservation of archeological remains in and for the state of Iowa. It is not legal to excavate on state land unless one is a professional archaeologist and the specimens are retained in an approved museum. Permission from the State Archeologist is required in order to dig.

C. Sites
   1. Paleo-Indian
      Archaic
      Woodland including Hopewell
      Mill Creek, intensive agriculturalists
      Glenwood, intensive agriculturalists
      Oneonta, intensive agriculturalists
      Mississippian
   2. Effigy Mounds
      Mill Creek, Mississippian
      Oneonta, Mississippian
      Simonsen Mound, Archaic
      Turin Mound, Archaic
      Hill Lane Farm Mound, Archaic

D. Excavations
   Effigy Mounds, State Archeologist and National Park Service

   Red Rock Reservoir, Marshall McKusick, State Archeologist and National Park Service

   Coralville Reservoir, Smithsonian Institution with the Inter-Agency Salvage Program

E. Museums
Effigy Mounds National Monuments, Visitor Center
McGregor

Sanford Museum and Planetarium
117 East Willow Street, Cherokee

F. Academic Institutions
State University of Iowa, Iowa City

G. Bibliography
BEAUBIEN, PAUL L.
"Cultural Variation Within Two Woodland Mound Groups of Northeastern Iowa." *American Antiquity,* Vol. 19, pp. 56–66, Salt Lake City. 1953.

Journal of the Iowa Archeological Society, Iowa City

KEYES, CHARLES
"An Outline of Iowa Archeology." *Minnesota Archeologist,* Vol. 8, No. 1, pp. 4–7, Minneapolis. 1942.

MOTT, MILDRED
"The Relation of Historic Indian Tribes to Archaeological Manifestations in Iowa." *Iowa Journal of History and Politics,* Vol. 36, No. 3, pp. 227–314, Iowa City. 1938.

ORR, ELLISON
"Indian Pottery of the Oneonta or Upper Iowa Valley in Northeastern Iowa," *Proceedings of the Iowa Academy of Science,* Vol. 21, pp. 231–239, Des Moines. 1914.

KANSAS

A. Organization
1. Kansas State Historical Society
2. State Archeologist, Kansas State Historical Society
10th and Jackson Streets, Topeka
3. Kansas Anthropological Society
c/o Kansas State Historical Society
10th and Jackson Streets, Topeka

B. Control
   None

C. Sites
   1. Archaic
      Plains Woodland
      Central Plains Phase
      Coalescent Traditions (protohistoric)
      Historic
   2. Griffing, Minneapolis, Salina (Smokey Hill Aspect)
      Tobias, Saxman, Malone, Paint Creek, Thompson
      (Great Bend Aspect)
      Scott County Park (Dismal River Aspect)
      Fanning Site (Oneonta Aspect)
      Glen Elder Site (White Rock Aspect)

D. Excavations
   Reservoir Salvage Program: Pomona, Wilson, Milford,
      Council Grove, Melvern, John Redmond Reservoirs,
      National Park Service
   Elk City Reservoir, Kansas State Historical Society
   Cheney Reservoir, 1962, National Park Service
   John Redmond Reservoir, 1963, National Park Service

E. Museums
   Kansas State Historical Society
   Memorial Building, 10th and Jackson Streets, Topeka
   Fort Hays Kansas State College Museum
   Hays
   Museum of Natural History, University of Kansas
   Lawrence

F. Academic Institutions
   University of Kansas, Lawrence, Anthropology and
   Field work in Alaska and Panama

G. Bibliography
   WEDEL, WALDO R.
      An Introduction to Kansas Archaeology, Bureau of
      American Ethnology, Bulletin 174. Washington.
      1959.

n.a. *Archeological Remains in Central Kansas and Their Possible Bearing on the Location of Quivira.* Smithsonian Miscellaneous Collections, Vol. 101, No. 7, Washington. 1942.

KENTUCKY

A. Organization
   1.
   2.
   3.

B. Control
   None

C. Sites
   1. Paleo-Indian
      Archaic
      Early Woodland
      Middle Woodland
      Middle Mississippi
   2. Parish Site, Hopkins County, Paleo-Indian
      Green River Valley, Archaic
      Mt. Horeb Site, Archaic
      Baumer, Archaic
      Drab Orchard, Archaic
      King Site
      Major Site, Henderson
      Indian Knoll

D. Excavations

E. Museums
   Behringer Museum of Natural History
   Devow Park, Covington
   University of Kentucky, Museum of Anthropology
   Lexington

F. Academic Institutions
   University of Kentucky, Lexington, Anthropology, Archaeology

G. Bibliography

HAAG, WILLIAM G.

"The Pottery from the C. and O. Mounds at Paintsville." In *The C. and O. Mounds at Paintsville, Sites JO 2 and JO 9, Johnson County, Kentucky* by William S. Webb, University of Kentucky Reports in Anthropology and Archaeology, Vol. 5, No. 4, pp. 341–349, Lexington. 1942.

FUNKHOUSER, W. D., and W. S. WEBB

The Chilton Site in Henry County, Kentucky. University of Kentucky Reports in Archaeology and Anthropology, Vol. 3, No. 5, Lexington. 1937.

GRIFFIN, JAMES B.

"Comments on the Bintz Site." *American Antiquity,* Vol. 18, p. 262, Salt Lake City. 1952.

MACCORD, HOWARD A.

"The Bintz Site." *American Antiquity,* Vol. 18, pp. 239–244, Salt Lake City. 1952.

SKARLAND, IVAR

"The Skeletal Material." In *The Chiggerville Site, Site 1, Ohio County, Kentucky* by William S. Webb and William G. Haag, University of Kentucky Reports in Anthropology and Archaeology, Vol. 4, No. 1, pp. 28–49, Lexington. 1939.

SNOW, CHARLES E.

Indian Knoll Skeletons of Site Oh2, Ohio County, Kentucky. The University of Kentucky Reports in Anthropology, Vol. 4, No. 3, Pt. 2, Lexington. 1948.

WEBB, WILLIAM S.

The Wright Mounds: Sites 6 and 7, Montgomery County, Kentucky. The University of Kentucky Reports in Anthropology, Vol. 5, No. 1, Lexington. 1940.

Mt. Horeb Earthworks, Site I, and the Drake Mound, Site II, Fayette County, Kentucky. The University of Kentucky Reports in Anthropology and Archaeology, Vol. 5, No. 2, Lexington. 1941.

The C. and O. Mounds at Paintsville, Sites JO 2 and JO 9, Johnson County, Kentucky. The University of Kentucky Reports in Anthropology and Archaeology, Vol. 5, No. 4, Lexington. 1942.

Indian Knoll, Site Oh 2, Ohio County, Kentucky. The University of Kentucky Reports in Anthropology and Archaeology, Vol. 4, No. 3, Pt. 1, Lexington. 1946.

The Carlson Annis Mound, Site 5, Butler County, Kentucky. University of Kentucky Reports in Anthropology, Vol. 7, No. 4, Lexington. 1950.

The Jonathan Creek Village, Site 4, Marshall County, Kentucky, Lexington. 1952.

WEBB, WILLIAM S., and W. D. FUNKHOUSER
The McLeod Bluff Site in Hickman County, Kentucky. The University of Kentucky Reports in Archaeology and Anthropology, Vol. 3, No. 1, Lexington. 1933.

WEBB, WILLIAM S., and WILLIAM G. HAAG
The Chiggerville Site, Site 1, Ohio County, Kentucky. The University of Kentucky Reports in Anthropology, Vol. 4, No. 1, Lexington. 1939.

Cypress Creek Village Sites 11 and 12, McLean County, Kentucky. The University of Kentucky Reports in Anthropology, Vol. 4, No. 2, Lexington. 1940.

Archaic Sites in McLean County, Kentucky. The University of Kentucky Reports in Anthropology, Vol. 7, No. 1, Lexington. 1947.

The Fisher Site, Fayette County, Kentucky. The University of Kentucky Reports in Anthropology, Vol. 7, No. 2, Lexington. 1947.

WEBB, WILLIAM S., and CHARLES E. SNOW
The Adena People. The University of Kentucky Reports in Anthropology and Archaeology, Vol. 6, Lexington. 1945.

LOUISIANA

A. Organization
   1.
   2.
   3.

B. Control
   None

C. Sites
   1. Archaic
      Early Woodland
      Middle Woodland
      Early Mississippi
      Middle Mississippi
      Historical Decline
   2. Little Woods, Archaic
      Big Oak, Archaic
      Tchefuncte, Archaic
      Copell, Archaic
      Poverty Point, Archaic
      Lafayette Mound, Early Woodland
      Vermillion River, Early Woodland
      Marksville Mounds, Middle Woodland
      Crooks, Middle Woodland
      McQuorquodale, Middle Woodland

D. Excavations
   Bellevue Mound (Burial Mound Site), The Inter-
   Agency Archaeological Salvage Program

E. Museums
   Marksville Prehistoric Indian Museum
   Marksville

   Tulane University of Louisiana Museum
   6823 St. Charles Avenue, New Orleans

F. Academic Institutions
   Tulane University, New Orleans, Anthropology
   Louisiana State University, Baton Rouge, Geology

G. Bibliography

FORD, JAMES A.

Ceramic Decoration Sequence at an Old Indian Village Site Near Sicily Island Louisiana. Anthropological Study No. 1, Department of Conservation, Louisiana Geological Survey, New Orleans. 1935.

Analysis of Indian Village Site Collections from Louisiana and Mississippi. Anthropological Study No. 2, Department of Conservation, Louisiana Geological Survey, New Orleans. 1936.

Excavations in the Vicinity of Cali, Columbia. Yale University Publications in Anthropology, No. 31, New Haven. 1944.

FORD, JAMES B. and C. H. WEBB

Poverty Point: A Late Archaic Site in Louisiana. Anthropological Papers of the American Museum of Natural History, Vol. 46, 1, New York. 1956.

FORD, JAMES A., and GORDON R. WILLEY

Crooks Site: A Marksville Period Burial Mound in La Salle Parish, Louisiana. Anthropological Study No. 3, Department of Conservation, Louisiana Geological Survey, New Orleans. 1940.

FOWKE, GERARD

"Archeological Investigations—II: Explorations in the Red River Valley in Louisiana." *Forty-fourth Annual Report, Bureau of American Ethnology, 1926–1927,* pp. 495–548, Washington. 1928.

QUIMBY, GEORGE I.

The Bayou Goula Site, Iberville Parish, Louisiana. Chicago. 1957.

WALKER, WINSLOW M.

A Caddo Burial at Natchitoches, Louisiana. Smithsonian Miscellaneous Collections, Vol. 94, No. 14, Washington. 1935.

The Troyville Mounds, Catahoula Parish, Louisiana. Bureau of American Ethnology, Bulletin 113, Washington. 1936.

WEBB, CLARENCE H.

"Stone Vessels from a Northeast Louisiana Site." *American Antiquity,* Vol. 9, No. 4, pp. 386–394, Menasha. 1944.

"A Second Historic Caddo Site at Natchitoches, Louisiana." *Bulletin of the Texas Archaeological and Paleontological Society,* Vol. 16, pp. 52–83, Abilene. 1945.

"Two Unusual Types of Chipped Stone Artifacts from Northwest Louisiana." *Bulletin of the Texas Archaeological and Paleontological Society,* Vol. 17, pp. 9–17, Abilene. 1946.

"Evidences of Pre-Pottery Cultures in Louisiana." *American Antiquity,* Vol. 13, No. 3, pp. 227–231, Menasha. 1948.

The Belcher Mound. Memoirs of the Society for American Archaeology, Number 16, Salt Lake City. 1959.

MAINE

A. Organization
  1.
  2.
  3. The Archeological Society
     Robert Abbe Museum of Stone Age Antiquities
     Sieur de Mont Spring, Bar Harbor

B. Control
   None at present, but persons interested in Maine archaeology are trying to interest the public in the establishment of an antiquities law.

C. Sites
  1. Archaic
     Early Woodland
     Middle Woodland
     Late Woodland
  2. Taft's Point Shell Mound, West Gouldsboro, Archaic to Late Woodland

Waterside Shell Heap, Frenchman's Bay, Middle Woodland

Nevin's Shell Heap

D. Excavations

Taft's Point Shell Mound, Wendell S. Hadlock

Waterside Shell Heap, John H. Rowe

Nevin's Shell Heap, Douglas S. Byers

Preliminary Survey of St. George River Area, Wendell S. Hadlock

Aroostook Region Survey

E. Museums

Robert Abbe Museum of Stone Age Antiquities

Sieur de Mont Spring, Bar Harbor

F. Academic Institutions

G. Bibliography

HADLOCK, WENDELL S.

The Taft's Point Shell Mound at West Gouldsboro, Maine. Bulletin of the Robert Abbe Museum, No. 5, Bar Harbor. 1939.

ROWE, JOHN H.

"Excavations in the Waterside Shell Heap, Frenchman's Bay, Maine." *Papers of the Excavators' Club,* Vol. 1, No. 3, Cambridge. 1940.

MARYLAND

A. Organization

1. None
2. None
3. Archeological Society of Maryland
   c/o Maryland Academy of Sciences
   400 Cathedral Street, Baltimore

B. Control

None.

C. Sites
  1. Early Archaic
     Late Archaic
     Early Woodland
     Middle Woodland
     Late Woodland
     Historic
  2. West River, Adena
     Sandy Hill, Adena
     Shepard Sites, Middle to Late Woodland
     Winslow, Early to Late Woodland
     Bluemont—Soapstone Quarry
     Ballard Rock Shelter

D. Excavations
   West River

   Sandy Hill

   Shepard Sites

   Winslow

   Bluemont

   Ballard Rock Shelter

   Crompton Site

   Most of these sites have been excavated by the Archeological Society of Maryland

E. Museums
   Maryland Academy of Sciences
   400 Cathedral Street, Baltimore

   Baltimore Museum of Art
   Wyman Park, Baltimore

F. Academic Institutions
   Johns Hopkins University, Baltimore, Archaeology,
   Anthropology, Paleontology

G. Bibliography
   GRAHAM, WILLIAM J.
   *The Indians of Port Tobacco River, Maryland, and
   Their Burial Places*. Washington. 1935.

SLATTERY, RICHARD G.
"A Prehistoric Indian Site on Selden Island, Montgomery County, Maryland." *Journal of the Washington Academy of Sciences,* Vol. 36, No. 8, pp. 262–266, Menasha. 1946.

STEARNS, RICHARD E.
The Hughes Site. Proceedings of the Natural History Society of Maryland, No. 6, Baltimore. 1940.

MASSACHUSETTS

A. Organization
1. None
2. None
3. Massachusetts Archaeological Society, Inc.
c/o Bronson Museum, Attleboro

B. Control
None.

C. Sites
1. Paleolithic
Archaic
Early Woodland
Middle Woodland
Late Woodland
2. Peake Hill
Ford
Grassy Island
Clarks Pond
Bull Brook Site, Archaic
Titicum
Clark Pond, Woodland
Wapanucket Site, Middleboro

D. Excavations
Wapanucket Site, Middleboro (Archaic Village)
Middleboro (Paleo Site), Cohannet Chapter of the Massachusetts Archaeological Society

E. Museums
  Bronson Museum
  8 North Main Street, Attleboro
  Peabody Museum of Archaeology and Ethnology, Harvard University
  11 Divinity Avenue, Boston
  Robert S. Peabody Foundation for Archaeology
  Phillips Academy, Andover

F. Academic Institutions
  Harvard University, Cambridge, Anthropology and Archaeology
  Radcliffe College, Cambridge, Anthropology and Archaeology

G. Bibliography
BULLEN, RIPLEY P.
  "Culture Dynamics in Eastern Massachusetts." *American Antiquity,* Vol. 14, No. 1, pp. 36–48, Menasha. 1948.
  Excavations in Northeastern Massachusetts. Papers of the Robert S. Peabody Foundation for Archaeology, Vol. 1, No. 3, Andover. 1949.

BULLEN, RIPLEY P., and EDWARD BROOKS
  "The Squam Pond Indian Site, Nantucket, Massachusetts." *Bulletin of the Massachusetts Archaeological Society,* Vol. 8, No. 4, pp. 56–59, Boston. 1947.

Bulletin of the Massachusetts Archaeological Society, Attleboro

BYERS, DOUGLAS S., and FREDERICK JOHNSON
  Two Sites on Martha's Vineyard. Papers of the Robert S. Peabody Foundation for Archaeology, Vol. 1, No. 1, Andover. 1940.

COMPTON, CARL B.
  "Amateur and Professional Relations." *Bulletin of the Massachusetts Archaeological Society,* Vol. 23, No. 2, pp. 36–37, Attleboro. 1962.

JOHNSON, FREDERICK, *et al.*

The Boylston Street Fishweir. Papers of the Robert S. Peabody Foundation for Archaeology, Vol. 2, Andover. 1949. *The Boylston Street Fishweir, II.* Papers of the Robert S. Peabody Foundation for Archaeology, Vol. 4, No. 1, Andover. 1942.

JOHNSON, FREDERICK, and HUGH M. RAUP

Grassy Island. Papers of the Robert S. Peabody Foundation for Archaeology, Vol. 1, No. 2, Andover. 1947.

MOFFETT, ROSS

"Some Shell Heaps in Truro, Massachusetts." *Bulletin of the Massachusetts Archaeological Society,* Vol. 7, No. 2, pp. 17–23, Boston. 1946.

ROBBINS, MAURICE

The Faulkner Spring Site. Papers of the Attleboro Museum of Art and History, No. 1. 1944.

"The Ford Site, a Prehistoric Station in Norton, Massachusetts." *American Antiquity,* Vol. 12, No. 2, pp. 80–94, Menasha. 1946.

n.a. *Wapanucket No. 6, An Archaic Village in Middleboro, Massachusetts*. Cohannet Chapter, Massachusetts Archaeological Society. Cohannet. 1959.

MICHIGAN

A. Organization
1.
2.
3. Aboriginal Research Club
828 Clay St., Algonac

Michigan Archaeological Society
c/o Museum of Anthropology
University of Michigan, Ann Arbor

B. Control
Control of excavation and survey as per Compiled Laws of Michigan, 1948, Vol. 2c. 399.4

C. Sites
  1. Archaic
     Early Woodland
     Middle Woodland
     Late Woodland
     Iroquoian Complex
     Upper Mississippi Complex
  2. Copper Pits on Isle Royal
     Wolfe Site, Early-Middle Woodland

D. Excavations
  Riviere au Vase Site, Macomb County, The Inter-Agency Archaeological Salvage Program

E. Museums
  University of Michigan, Museum of Anthropology
  Ann Arbor

  Michigan State University Museum
  East Lansing

  Muskegon County Museum
  1259 Marquette Avenue, Muskegon

F. Academic Institutions
  University of Michigan, Ann Arbor, Archaeology and Anthropology

  Michigan State University, East Lansing, Archaeology and Anthropology

G. Bibliography
CUNNINGHAM, WILBUR M.
  A Study of the Glacial Kame Culture in Michigan, Ohio, and Indiana. Occasional Contributions from the Museum of Anthropology of the University of Michigan, No. 12, Ann Arbor. 1948.

GREENMAN, EMERSON F.
  "Michigan Mounds, with Special Reference to Two in Missaukee County." *Papers of the Michigan Academy of Science, Arts, and Letters,* Vol. 7, pp. 1–9, Ann Arbor. 1927.
  "Cultural Relationships of Archaeological Sites in

the Upper Great Lakes Region." *Papers of the Michigan Academy of Science, Arts, and Letters,* Vol. 24, Pt. 4, pp. 1–10, Ann Arbor. 1939.

The Wolf and Furton Sites, Macomb County, Michigan. Occasional Contributions from the Museum of Anthropology of the University of Michigan, No. 8, Ann Arbor. 1939.

"An Early Industry on a Raised Beach near Killarney, Ontario." *American Antiquity,* Vol. 8, No. 3, pp. 260–265, Menasha. 1943.

"The Hopewellian in the Detroit-Windsor Area." *Papers of the Michigan Academy of Science, Arts, and Letters,* Vol. 30, pp. 457–464, Ann Arbor. 1945.

HINSDALE, W. B.

"The Missaukee Preserve and Rifle River Forts." *Papers of the Michigan Academy of Science, Arts, and Letters,* Vol. 4, Pt. 1, pp. 1–11, New York. 1925.

"Indian Mounds, West Twin Lake, Montmorency County, Michigan." *Papers of the Michigan Academy of Science, Arts, and Letters,* Vol. 10, pp. 91–101, Ann Arbor. 1929.

"Reports of Archaeological Field Work in the Summer of 1928 in Montmorency, Newaygo and Lake Counties, Michigan." *Papers of the Michigan Academy of Science, Arts, and Letters,* Vol. 12, pp. 127–135, Ann Arbor. 1930.

Archaeological Atlas of Michigan. Michigan Handbook Series, No. 4, University Museums, University of Michigan, Ann Arbor. 1931.

MANSON, CARL, HOWARD A. MACCORD, and JAMES B. GRIFFIN

"The Culture of the Keyser Farm Site." *Papers of the Michigan Academy of Science, Arts, and Letters,* Vol. 29, pp. 375–418, Ann Arbor. 1944.

MASON, RONALD J.

Late Pleistocene Geochronology and the Paleo-Indian Penetration into the Lower Michigan Peninsula. Ann Arbor. 1958.

QUIMBY, GEORGE I., JR.

"Dated Indian Burials in Michigan." *Papers of the Michigan Academy of Science, Arts, and Letters,* Vol. 23, pp. 63–72, Ann Arbor. 1938.

"Aboriginal Camp Sites on Isle Royale, Michigan." *American Antiquity,* Vol. 4, No. 3, pp. 215–223, Menasha. 1939.

"European Trade Articles as Chronological Indicators for the Archaeology of the Historic Period in Michigan." *Papers of the Michigan Academy of Science, Arts, and Letters,* Vol. 24, Pt. 4, pp. 25–31, Ann Arbor. 1939.

"Hopewellian Pottery Types in Michigan." *Papers of the Michigan Academy of Science, Arts, and Letters,* Vol. 26, pp. 489–494, Ann Arbor. 1941.

The Goodall Focus: An Analysis of Ten Hopewellian Components in Michigan and Indiana. Prehistory Research Series, Indiana Historical Society, Vol. 2, No. 2, Indianapolis. 1941.

"The Natchezan Culture Type." *American Antiquity,* Vol. 7, No. 3, pp. 255–275, Menasha. 1942.

"The Ceramic Sequence within the Goodall Focus." *Papers of the Michigan Academy of Science, Arts, and Letters,* Vol. 28, pp. 543–548, Ann Arbor. 1943.

"Some New Data on the Goodall Focus." *Papers of the Michigan Academy of Science, Arts, and Letters,* Vol. 29, pp. 419–423, Ann Arbor. 1944.

"The Possibility of an Independent Agricultural Complex in the Southeastern United States." In *Human Origins, Selected Readings,* Series II, No. 19, pp. 206–210, Chicago. 1946.

"Fluted Points and Geochronology of the Lake Michigan Basin." *American Antiquity,* Vol. 23, pp. 247–254, Salt Lake City. 1957.

MINNESOTA

A. Organization

   1. State Archeologist and Conservation Department of Minnesota

   2. State Archeologist
      University of Minnesota, Minneapolis
   3. Minnesota Archaeological Society
      2303 Third Avenue South, Minneapolis 4

B. Control
A permit from the Conservation Department or permission from the State Archeologist is required before excavation or survey on either private or state property.

C. Sites
   1. Early Man
      Archaic
      Woodland (North Minnesota)
      Mississippian (South Minnesota)
   2. Browns Valley
      Oconto, Mississippi Valley
      Schelling
      Grey Cloud Island
      Forrest Lake
      Bryan
      Red Wing
      Over 10,000 burial mounds surveyed
      Pipestone National Monument

D. Excavations
   1. Spring Lake Project, 1954–59, Eldon Johnson, The Science Museum

      Red River Valley, 1960—, Eldon Johnson, University of Minnesota

      "Fort Sweney," 1962, Peter Jenson, The Science Museum

      Field sessions in archaeology, Wilford and Johnson, University of Minnesota

E. Museums
University of Minnesota, Anthropology Museum
325 Ford Hall, Minneapolis

The Science Museum
51 University Avenue, St. Paul 3

Pipestone National Monument
Pipestone

F. Academic Institutions
University of Minnesota, Minneapolis, St. Paul and
Duluth, Anthropology and Archaeology

G. Bibliography
Barrett, Samuel A.
Ancient Aztalan. Bulletin of the Public Museum of
the City of Milwaukee, Vol. 13. 1953.

Bennett, John W.
"Hopewellian in Minnesota." *American Antiquity,*
Vol. 9, No. 3, p. 336, Menasha. 1944.

Bryan, Kirk
"Minnesota Man: A Discussion of the Site." *Science,*
Vol. 82, No. 2121, pp. 170–171, Lancaster, Garrison.
1935.

Bryan, Kirk, Henry Retzek, and Franklin T. Mc-
Cann
"Discovery of Saulk Valley Man of Minnesota, with
an Account of the Geology." *Bulletin of the Texas
Archaeological and Paleontological Society,* Vol. 10,
pp. 114–135, Abilene. 1938.

Flaskerd, George A.
"Some Folsom and Yuma Type Points from Minnesota." *Minnesota Archeologist,* Vol. 11, No. 2, pp.
32–33, Minneapolis. 1945.

Griffin, James B.
"An Unusual Oneonta Vessel from Minnesota."
American Antiquity, Vol. 11, No. 2, pp. 120–121,
Menasha. 1945.

Jenks, Albert E.
"The Problem of the Culture from the Arvilla
Gravel Pit." *American Anthropologist,* Vol. 34, No.
3, pp. 455–466, Menasha. 1932.
"Recent Discoveries in Minnesota Prehistory." *Min-*

nesota History: A Quarterly Magazine, Vol. 16, No. 1, pp. 1–21, St. Paul. 1935.

Pleistocene Man in Minnesota. Minneapolis. 1936.

Minnesota's Browns Valley Man and Associated Burial Objects. American Anthropological Association, Memoir 49, Menasha. 1937.

POWELL, LOUIS H.

Spring Lake Archeology—Point Profiles. St. Louis. 1955.

SMITH, G. HUBERT

"Excavating the Site of Old Fort Ridgely." *Minnesota History: A Quarterly Magazine,* Vol. 20, No. 2, pp. 146–155, St. Paul. 1939.

WILFORD, LLOYD A.

"A Tentative Classification of the Prehistoric Cultures of Minnesota." *American Antiquity,* Vol. 6, No. 3, pp. 231–249, Menasha. 1941.

"Minnesota Archaeology: Current Explorations and Concepts." *Proceedings of the Minnesota Academy of Science,* Vol. 10, pp. 20–26. 1942.

"The Prehistoric Indians of Minnesota: The Mille Lacs Aspect." *Minnesota History: A Quarterly Magazine,* Vol. 25, No. 4, pp. 329–341, St. Paul. 1944.

"The Prehistoric Indians of Minnesota: The Headwaters Lakes Aspect." *Minnesota History: A Quarterly Magazine,* Vol. 26, No. 4, pp. 312–329, St. Paul. 1945.

"Three Villages of the Mississippi Pattern in Minnesota." *American Antiquity,* Vol. 11, No. 1, pp. 32–40. Menasha. 1945.

"A Revised Classification of the Prehistoric Cultures of Minnesota." *American Antiquity,* Vol. 21, pp. 130–142, Salt Lake City. 1955.

MISSISSIPPI

A. Organization

    1. Mississippi Department of Archives and History Museum Division

    2. Director of Department of Archives and History
Chief Curator, Mississippi Historical Museum
(State)

    P.O. Box 571, Jackson 5

    3. None in Mississippi
The Mississippi Valley Historical Association (area
wide)

B. Control

General Laws of the State of Mississippi, 1938, Chapter 161, pp. 362–363.

Permits to examine, excavate or gather objects of antiquity on an archaeological site may be granted by the director of archives and history to institutions or persons for the benefit of reputable museums, universities, and colleges, etc. Failure to do so shall constitute a misdemeanor.

C. Sites

    1. Aboriginal, Archaic through Poverty Point
Tchefuncte
Marksville
Troyville and/or Issaquene
Coles Creek and/or Baytown
Plaquemine
Mississippian
Historic, Choctaw, Chickasaw, Natchez, Tunica

    2. Jaketown, Poverty Point and Mississippian
Lower Yazoo Basin Site, Poverty Point through Historic
Big Black River Burial Mounds, Plaquemine
Emeral Mound and Gordon Site, Plaquemine
Bynum Mounds, Marksville and Chickasaw
Fatherland Site, Historic Natchez
Winterville Mounds, Mississippian

D. Excavations

Fatherland Site, 1930, J. A. Ford, Department of Archives and History

Big Black River, 1927–32, Department of Archives and History

Jaketown, 1951 and 1958, Ford, Phillips and Haag, Lower Mississippi Valley Archaeological Survey

Northeast Mississippi, 1941, Bynum, Emeral and Gordon, National Park Service

Northwest Mississippi Archeological Survey, 1940–47, Lower Mississippi Valley Archaeological Survey

Grand Village of the Natchez and temple plaza, 1962, Department of Archives and History

E. Museums
State Historical Museum
State Street at East Capitol, Box 571, Jackson 5
University of Mississippi Museum
Box 603, University

F. Academic Institutions
University of Mississippi, University

G. Bibliography

COLLINS, HENRY B., JR.
"Potsherds from Choctaw Village Sites in Mississippi." *Journal of the Washington Academy of Science,* Vol. 17, No. 10, pp. 259–263, Menasha. 1927.
"Excavations at a Prehistoric Indian Village Site in Mississippi." *Proceedings of the U. S. National Museum,* Vol. 79, Art. 32, Washington. 1932.

COTTER, JOHN L.
"The Gordon Site in Southern Mississippi." *American Antiquity,* Vol. 18, pp. 110–126, Salt Lake City. 1952.

CROSWELL, C.
"Mound Explorations in Southeastern Missouri." *Transactions of the Academy of Science of St. Louis,* Vol. 3, pp. 531–538. 1878.

DEUEL, THORNE
"Basic Cultures of the Mississippi Valley." *American Anthropologist,* Vol. 37, No. 3, pp. 429–445, Menasha. 1935.

FORD, JAMES A., and GEORGE I. QUIMBY, JR.
The Tchefuncte Culture, An Early Occupation of the Lower Mississippi Valley. Society for American Archaeology. Memoir No. 2, Menasha. 1945.

FORD, JAMES A., P. PHILLIPS and W. G. HAAG
The Jaketown Site in West Central Mississippi. Anthropological Papers of the American Museum of Natural History, Vol. 45, 1, New York. 1955.

GRIFFIN, JAMES B.
"The Central Mississippi Valley Archaeological Survey." *News Letter,* Southeastern Archaeological Conference, Vol. 2, No. 4, pp. 17–19. Mimeographed. 1941.
The Fort Ancient Aspect, Its Cultural and Chronological Position in Mississippi Valley Archaeology. Ann Arbor. 1943.

JENNINGS, JESSE D.
"Chickasaw and Earlier Indian Cultures of Northeast Mississippi." *The Journal of Mississippi History,* Vol. 3, No. 3, pp. 155–226. 1941.
"The Archaeological Survey of the Natchez Trace." *American Antiquity,* Vol. 9, No. 4, pp. 408–414, Menasha. 1941.
"Hopewell-Copena Sites Near Nashville." *American Antiquity,* Vol. 12, No. 2, p. 126, Menasha. 1946.

MISSOURI

A. Organization
   1. University of Missouri
   2. Archaeological Interpreter
      Archaeological Research Center, Miami

      Director of American Archaeology
      15 Switzler Hall
      University of Missouri, Columbia

      Historian, State Parks
      Jefferson City

Director, Museum of Anthropology
15 Switzler Hall
University of Missouri, Columbia
3. Missouri Archaeological Society
15 Switzler Hall
University of Missouri, Columbia

B. Control
Strict control and preservation of archaeological remains located on State property.

C. Sites
1. Paleo-Indian, Clovis fluted tradition
Archaic
Woodland, some Hopewellian
Late Woodland
Mississippian
Historic
2. Graham Cave
Campbell Site
Utz Site, Historic
Rice Site

D. Excavations
Bull Shoals Reservoir
Table Rock Reservoir
Pomme de Terre Reservoir
Joanna Reservoir
Kansas City area
St. Louis area
Exploration Cave
Kemna Cave
White River

E. Museums
University of Missouri Museum of Anthropology
15 Switzler Hall, Columbia
Missouri State Museum
Capitol Building, Jefferson

University of Missouri Archaeological Research Center
Van Meter State Park, Miami

Museum of Science and Natural History
2 Oak Knoll Park, St. Louis

Kansas City Museum
3218 Gladstone Boulevard, Kansas City

F. Academic Institutions
University of Missouri, Columbia, American Archaeology and Anthropology

G. Bibliography

Adams, Robert McCormick
"Archaeological Investigations in Jefferson County, Missouri, 1939–40." *Transactions of the Academy of Science of St. Louis,* Vol. 30, No. 5, pp. 151–221. 1941.

Adams, Robert McCormick, and Winslow M. Walker
"Archaeological Surface Survey of New Madrid County, Missouri." *The Missouri Archaeologist,* Vol. 8, No. 2, pp. 3–23, Columbia. 1942.

Berry, Brewton, and Carl Chapman
"An Oneota Site in Missouri." *American Antiquity,* Vol. 7, No. 3, pp. 290–305, Menasha. 1942.

Berry, Brewton, J. E. Wrench, Carl Chapman, and Wilber Seitz
"Archaeological Investigations in Boone County, Missouri." *The Missouri Archaeologist,* Vol. 4, No. 3, pp. 2–36, Columbia. 1938.

Blake, Leonard W.
"A Hopewell-like Site Near St. Louis." *The Missouri Archaeologist,* Vol. 8, No. 1, pp. 2–7, Columbia, 1942.

Brownlee, Richard
"Mounds on Chariton River in Macon County." *The Missouri Archaeologist,* Vol. 2, No. 2, pp. 7–8, Columbia. 1936.

CHAPMAN, CARL

"A Preliminary Survey of Missouri Archaeology: Part I, Historic Indian Tribes." *The Missouri Archaeologist,* Vol. 10, Pt. 1, Bulletin No. 20, pp. 1–55, Columbia. 1946.

"A Preliminary Survey of Missouri Archaeology: Part II, Middle Mississippi and Hopewellian Cultures." *The Missouri Archaeologist,* Vol. 10, Pt. 2, Bulletin No. 21, pp. 60–94, Columbia. 1947.

"A Preliminary Survey of Missouri Archaeology: Part III, Woodland Cultures and the Ozark Bluff Dwellers." *The Missouri Archaeologist,* Vol. 10, Pt. 3, Bulletin No. 22, pp. 98–132, Columbia. 1948.

"A Preliminary Survey of Missouri Archaeology: Part IV, Ancient Cultures and Sequence." *The Missouri Archaeologist,* Vol. 10, Pt. 4, Bulletin No. 23, pp. 136–164, Columbia. 1948.

EICHENBERGER, J. ALLEN

"Investigations of the Marion-Ralls Archaeological Society in Northeast Missouri." *The Missouri Archaeologist,* No. 19, pp. 3–69, Columbia. 1944.

EVERS, EDWARD

"Ancient Pottery of Southeastern Missouri." *Contributions to the Archaeology of Missouri,* Archaeological Section of the St. Louis Academy of Science, Part 1, pp. 21–30. 1880.

FAIRBANKS, CHARLES H.

"The Kirksville Site." *The Missouri Archaeologist,* Vol. 4, No. 2, pp. 2–4, Columbia. 1938.

FENENGA, FRANKLIN

"Pottery Types from Pulaski County." *The Missouri Archaeologist,* Vol. 4, No. 2, pp. 5–7, Columbia. 1938.

FOWKE, GERARD, N. D. MCEVERS, JOHN WULFING, and DAVID I. BUSHNELL, JR.

"The Montezuma Mounds." *Missouri Historical Society Collections,* Vol. 2, No. 5, St. Louis. 1905.

Harrington, J. C.
"Report on the Excavation of Mound Bo1:1." *The Missouri Archaeologist,* Vol. 4, No. 1, pp. 1–11, Columbia. 1938.

Hoebel, E. Adamson
The Archaeology of Bone Cave, Miller County, Missouri. Anthropological Papers of the American Museum of Natural History, Vol. 40, Pt. 2, New York. 1946.

Logan, Wilfred D.
Graham Cave, An Archaic Site in Montgomery County, Missouri. Columbia. 1952.

MacCurdy, George Grant
"Shell Gorgets from Missouri." *American Anthropologist,* Vol. 15., No. 3, pp. 395–414. Lancaster. 1913.

Mack, John
"Archaeological Work at the University of Missouri." *The Missouri Archaeologist,* Vol. 8, No. 1, pp. 19–20, Columbia. 1942.

McKinney, Joe J.
Hopewell Sites in the Big Bend Area of Central Missouri. Columbia. 1954.
Memoirs of the Missouri Archaeological Society, Missouri Archaeological Society, University of Missouri, Columbia.
The Missouri Archeologist, Missouri Archaeological Society, University of Missouri, Columbia.

Ruwwe, J. W.
"Primitive Man in Phelps County." *The Missouri Magazine,* Vol. 8, No. 9, pp. 8–9, Jefferson City. 1936.

Shippee, J. M.
"Hopewellian and Middle Mississippi Remains from the Kansas City Area." *The Missouri Archaeologist,* Vol. 7, No. 2, pp. 28–32, Columbia. 1941.

"Nebo Hill, a Lithic Complex in Western Missouri." *American Antiquity,* Vol. 14, No. 1, pp. 29–32, Menasha. 1948.

Titterington, Paul F.
"Some Non-pottery Sites in St. Louis Area." *Illinois State Archaeological Society,* n.s., Vol. 1, No. 1, pp. 19–30. 1950.

Tong, Marvin E., Jr.
"Cox, An Archaic Site in the Ozarks." *American Antiquity,* Vol. 20, pp. 124–129, Salt Lake City. 1954.

Walker, Winslow M., and Robert McCormick Adams
"Excavations in the Matthews Site, New Madrid County, Missouri." *Transactions of the Academy of Science of St. Louis,* Vol. 31, No. 4, pp. 75–120.

Wedel, Waldo R.
Archaeological Investigations of Platte and Clay Counties, Missouri. United States National Museum Bulletin 183, pp. 245–273. Washington, D.C. 1943.

MONTANA

A. Organization
   1.
   2.
   3.

B. Control
   Legislation relating to the preservation, ownership, and excavation of archaeological sites is contained in Montana Revised Codes, 1947, replacement Vol. 4, Allen Smith Col. 1953 c., 12, Sec. 75–1201–1206, and Montana Revised Codes, Vol. 4, 1957 Cumulative Pocket Supplement c.3, Sec. 62–301–314.

C. Sites
   1. Early Period, Folsom, Yuma Focus
      Middle Period

> Late Period, Mandan, Hidatsa, Crow, Arikara, Cheyenne

2. Pictograph Cave, Billings, Early to Late
   Lewis Site, Glendive, Early
   Hagen Site, Glendive, Late Crow
   Ash Coulee Site, Terry, Late Crow
   Little Cayuse Mountain, east of Melville, Late
   Tipi Pole Spring, Late
   Thirty Mile Mesa Site, Billings, Late Crow

D. Excavations
   Pictograph Cave, Billings, 1937–41, Montana Archaeological Survey

   Tiber Reservoir, The Inter-Agency Archaeological Salvage Program

E. Museums
   Museum of the Plains Indian
   Browning
   Montana State University
   McGill Museum
   Carter County Museum
   County High School, Carter County

F. Academic Institutions
   Montana State University, Bozeman

G. Bibliography
   Kehoe, Thomas F.

   > *Stone Tipi Rings in North Central Montana and the Adjacent Portion of Alberta, Canada: Their Historical, Ethnological and Archaeological Aspects,* Bureau of American Ethnology, Anthropological Paper No. 62. Washington. 1960.

   Mulloy, William

   > *The Hagen Site: A Prehistoric Village on the Lower Yellowstone.* University of Montana Publications in the Social Sciences, No. 1, Missoula. 1942.
   > "A Prehistoric Campsite Near Redlodge, Mon-

tana." *American Antiquity,* Vol. 9, No. 2, pp. 170–179, Menasha. 1942.

MULLOY, WILLIAM, and OSCAR LEWIS
"Some Early Types of Points from the Lower Yellowstone Country." *American Antiquity,* Vol. 8, No. 3, pp. 298–299, Menasha. 1943.

NEBRASKA

A. Organization
   1.
   2.
   3. Nebraska State Historical Society
      1500 R. Street, Lincoln

B. Control
   Legislation relating to the preservation, ownership, and excavation of archaeological sites is contained in Resolution, Nebraska House of Representatives, May 14, 1935, Nebraska Senate, May 24, 1935; Nebraska, Revised Statutes, Vol. 2, Crimes and Punishments Sec. 28–1032–1034.

C. Sites
   1. Early Period, Folsom, Yuma Focus
      Middle Period

      Late Period, Mandan, Hidatsa, Crow, Arikara, Cheyenne

   2. Signal Butte, Scottsbluff County, Early to Late
      Ash Hollow Cave, Ogalalla, Early to Late

D. Excavations
   Signal Butte, 1932, Strong

   Lime Creek Site, Medicine Creek Reservoir, The Inter-Agency Archaeological Salvage Program

E. Museums
   Nebraska State Historical Society
   1500 R. Street, Lincoln

University of Nebraska State Museum
101 Merrill Hall, 14th and U Street
Lincoln 8

F. Academic Institutions
University of Nebraska, Lincoln, Archaeology, Anthropology

G. Bibliography

CHAMPE, JOHN L.
Ash Hollow Cave. University of Nebraska Studies, New Series, No. 1, Lincoln. 1946.

GUNNERSON, JAMES H.
An Introduction to Plains Apache Archeology and the Dismal River Aspect, Bulletin of American Ethnology, Anthropological Papers No. 58. Washington. 1960.

HILL, A. T., and GEORGE METCALF
"A Site of the Dismal River Aspect in Chase County, Nebraska." *Nebraska History,* Vol. 22, No. 2, pp. 158–215, Lincoln. 1941.

KIVETT, MARVIN F.
"Woodland Sites in Nebraska." *Publications in Anthropology, No. 1, Nebraska State Historical Society,* Lincoln. 1952.

KIVETT, MARVIN F. and A. T. HILL
"Archeological Investigations Along Medicine Creek." *Notebook No. 1, Laboratory of Anthropology, University of Nebraska,* pp. 25–26, Lincoln. 1949.

STRONG, W. DUNCAN
An Introduction to Nebraska Archeology. Smithsonian Miscellaneous Collections, Vol. 93, No. 10, Washington. 1935.

NEVADA

A. Organization
1. Nevada State Museum

2. Board of Directors
   Nevada State Museum, Carson City
3.

B. Control
   No person may investigate, explore, or excavate an historic or prehistoric site on federal or state lands or remove any object therefrom unless he is the holder of a valid and current permit issued by the Board of Directors of the Nevada State Museum, and then only by qualified personnel for educational purposes. (Nevada Revised Statutes, Chapter 381.)

C. Sites
   1.
   2.

D. Excavations

E. Museums
   Nevada State Museum
   Carson City
   Lake Mead National Recreation Area
   601 Nevada Highway, Boulder City

F. Academic Institutions

G. Bibliography
   COLTON, HAROLD S.
      Pottery Types of the Arizona Strip and Adjacent Areas in Utah and Nevada. Flagstaff. 1952.
   HEIZER, ROBERT F. and A. D. KRIEGER
      Archaeology of Humboldt Cave, Churchill County, Nevada. Berkeley. 1956.

NEW HAMPSHIRE

A. Organization
   1.
   2.
   3. New Hampshire Archeological Society
      c/o Mr. Paul Holmes
      Hale Spring Road, Box 382, Plaistow

B. Control
None

C. Sites
   1. Archaic
      Early Woodland
      Middle Woodland
      Late Woodland
   2. Litchfield

D. Excavations
   Survey of Cartagena Island in the Merrimack River Basin

   Brackett's Point Site at Greenland

   Litchfield Site

   Clarks Island

E. Museums
   Dartmouth College Museum
   Hanover

F. Academic Institutions
   Dartmouth College, Hanover

G. Bibliography
   Archeologist, New Hampshire Archeological Society

NEW JERSEY

A. Organization
   1. New Jersey State Museum Archeological Laboratory
   2. Archeological Adviser
      New Jersey State Museum, Trenton
   3. Archeological Society of New Jersey
      State House Annex, Trenton

B. Control
None

C. Sites
   1. Paleo-Indian
      Archaic
      Early Woodland

Middle Woodland
Late Woodland
2. Abbott Farm, Archaic and Early Woodland
   Riggins Site
   Bell-Philhower Site
   Koens-Crispin Site, Archaic and Early Woodland
   Salisbury, Middle Woodland
   Goose Island, Middle Woodland

D. Excavations
   Abbott Farm, 1936–41, Dorothy Cross, W.P.A. and New Jersey State Museum

   Test excavations: Beisler site near Wallpack Center, Brace Site at Montague, Miller Site at Calno, National Park Service, New Jersey State Museum and Archeological Society of New Jersey

   Tocks Island Reservoir Area, Warren and Sussex Counties, Charles W. Ward

E. Museums
   Archeological Society of New Jersey
   New Jersey State Museum
   State House Annex, West State Street, Trenton
   Princeton University
   Museum of Natural History
   Guyot Hall, Princeton

F. Academic Institutions
   Princeton University, Princeton, Archaeology

G. Bibliography
   Bulletin, Archeological Society of New Jersey, Trenton.

   CROSS, DOROTHY
   Archaeology of New Jersey, Vol. 1, Trenton, 1941.
   Archaeology of New Jersey; The Abbott Farm, Vol. 2, Trenton, 1956.

   HAWKES, E. W., and RALPH LINTON
   A Pre-Lenape Site in New Jersey. Anthropological Publications, University of Pennsylvania, Vol. 6, No. 3, Philadelphia. 1916.

HEYE, GEORGE G., and GEORGE H. PEPPER
Exploration of a Munsee Cemetery near Montague, New Jersey. Contributions from the Museum of the American Indian, Heye Foundation, Vol. 4, No. 3, New York. 1915.

News Letters, Archeological Society of New Jersey, Trenton.

NEW MEXICO

A. Organization
1. New Mexico Science Commission
   State Land Office
2. Commissioner of the State Land Office
   Commissioner of Public Lands
3. Archaeological Society of New Mexico
   c/o Regional Headquarters, National Park Service
   Old Pecos Road, Santa Fe

B. Control
No person may excavate, appropriate, injure, or destroy any object of historical, archaeological, or scientific value without the recommendation of the Science Commission and the consent of the State Land Office. Permits for such activities may be granted to those deemed properly qualified to conduct such activities. (Laws of New Mexico, 1931, Chapter 42, Page 81)

C. Sites
1. Early Period
   Middle Period
   Late Period
2. Folsom Site, Early Period
   Sandia Cave, Early Period
   Blackwater Draw Loc. 1, Early Period
   Abo
   Coronado State Monument
   Frijoles and Bandelier National Monument, Pueblo
   Mesa Verde
   Mimbres-Mogollon
   Puye

D. Excavations

Abo, 1938–40, 1944, 1946, 1957, The School of American Research

Blackwater Draw, The School of American Research

Coronado State Monument, 1935–39, 1944, 1952, 1957–58

Navajo Dam Salvage, 1946, The School of American Research

Quarai, 1934–36, 1938–40, 1950, 1957–58, The School of American Research

Yunqe-Yunqe, 1944–49, The School of American Research

Pecos, 1938–40, 1950, 1957–58, The School of American Research and later the Phillips Andover Academy

Hidalgo County, 1960—, The School of American Research and The Museum of New Mexico

E. Museums

Museum of New Mexico
Palace Avenue, Santa Fe

School of American Research
Santa Fe

F. Academic Institutions

School of American Research, Santa Fe, Anthropology, Archaeology

University of New Mexico, Albuquerque, Anthropology and Archaeology

G. Bibliography

El Palacio, Museum of New Mexico, Santa Fe.

AGOGINO, GEORGE and F. C. HIBBEN

"Central New Mexico Paleo-Indian Cultures." *American Antiquity,* Vol. 23, pp. 422–425, Salt Lake City. 1958.

ALLEN, J. W. and C. H. McNUTT

"A Pit House Site Near Santa Ana Pueblo, New Mexico." *American Antiquity,* Vol. 20, pp. 241–255, Salt Lake City. 1954.

Bluhm, Elaine A.
The Sawmill Site, A Reserve Phase Village, Pine Lawn Valley, Western New Mexico. Chicago. 1957.

Danson, Edward B.
An Archaeological Survey of West Central New Mexico and East Central Arizona. Papers of the Peabody Museum of Archaeology and Ethnology, Cambridge, Mass. 1957.

Hebben, Frank C.
"Excavations at Pottery Mound, New Mexico." *American Antiquity,* Vol. 21, pp. 179–185, Salt Lake City. 1955.

Judd, Neil M., *et al.*
The Material Culture of Pueblo Bonito. Washington, D.C. 1954.

Hewett, Edgar L. (Revised by B. P. Dutton)
Pajarito Plateau and its Ancient People. Albuquerque. 1953.

Kidder, A. V., H. S. and C. B. Cosgrove
"The Pendleton Ruin, Hidalgo County, New Mexico." *Contributions to American Anthropology and History,* Vol. 10, Carnegie Institution of Washington, Washington. 1949.

Martin, Paul S., J. B. Rinaldo and E. Bluhm
Caves of the Reserve Area. Chicago. 1954

Martin, Paul S., J. B. Rinaldo, E. A. Bluhm and H. C. Cutler
Higgins Flat Pueblo, Western New Mexico. Chicago. 1956.

Martin, Paul S., *et. al.*
Late Mogollon Communities. Four Sites of the Tularosa Phase, Western New Mexico. Chicago. 1957.

Roosa, William B.
"The Lucy Site in Central New Mexico." *American*

Antiquity, Vol. 21, pp. 310–311, Salt Lake City. 1956.

SELLARDS, E. H.
"Fossil Bison and Associated Artifacts from Milnesand, New Mexico." *American Antiquity,* Vol. 20, pp. 336–344, Salt Lake City. 1955.

STUBBS, STANLEY A. and W. S. STALLINGS, JR.
The Excavation of Pindi Pueblo, New Mexico. Santa Fe. 1953.

WENDORF, FRED (assembler)
Salvage Archaeology in the Chama Valley, New Mexico. Santa Fe. 1953.

NEW YORK

A. Organization
  1.
  2.
  3. New York State Archeological Association
     State Museum Education Building
     Rochester

B. Control
  Strict control of archaeological survey and excavation as proscribed in New York *Laws,* 1922, *Laws,* 1923, c. 90, and *Laws* 1958 (Public Works Bill 15r, amending sec. 233 of the education laws.)

C. Sites
  1. Archaic
     Early Woodland
     Middle Woodland
     Late Woodland
     Final Woodland
  2. Ripley Site, Chautauqua County, Archaic
     Lamoka Lake Site, Archaic
     Finch Site, Archaic
     Matinecock Point, Early Woodland
     Burial Site, Cuylerville, Early Woodland

Vinette Site, Point Peninsula, Early and Middle
Woodland
Kane, Middle Woodland
Liddyke, Middle Woodland
Kipp Island, West Rush, Middle Woodland
Wickham, Middle and Late Woodland
Sackett Farm
Owasco Lake
Snell Site, Montgomery County
Bowmans Brook State Island
Weaver Lake Site near Cooperstown
Chance Site, Schoharie, Final Woodland

D. Excavations

Menands Site and Bent Site, 1961, Van Epps-Hartley
Chapter, New York State Archeological Association

The Saugerties Rock Shelter, 1961, Mid-Hudson Chapter, NYSAA

Owasco culture, Whites Site and Thurston Site, 1961,
Chenango Chapter, NYSAA

Moses Kill and Harris Sites and South Bay Site, 1961,
Auringer-Seelye Chapter, NYSAA

E. Museums

Museum of the American Indian Heye Foundation
Broadway and 155 St., New York City

State Museum
State Museum Educational Building
657 East Ave., Rochester

Natural History Museum
New York City

Buffalo Museum of Science
Humboldt Park, Buffalo

Blue Mountain Lake Museum
Blue Mountain Lake

F. Academic Institutions
Cornell University, Ithaca, Anthropology
Barnard College, New York City, Anthropology

New York University, New York City, Anthropology
and Archaeology
Brooklyn College, Brooklyn, Anthropology
Queens College, Queens, Anthropology
Hunter College, New York City, Anthropology
Columbia University, New York City, Anthropology

G. Bibliography

PARKER, ARTHUR C.

*Excavations in an Erie Indian Village and Burial
Site at Ripley, Chautauqua County, New York.* New
York State Museum Bulletin, No. 117, Albany. 1907.
The Archeological History of New York. Parts 1
and 2. New York State Museum Bulletin, Nos.
235–238, Albany. 1922.

*Researches and Transactions of the New York State
Archeological Association,* Rochester.

RITCHIE, WILLIAM A.

*The Lamoka Lake Site: The Type Station of the
Archaic Algonkin Period in New York.* Researches
and Transactions of the New York State Archaeo-
logical Association, Vol. 7, No. 4, Rochester. 1932.
*New Evidence Relating to the Archaic Occupation of
New York.* Researches and Transactions of the New
York State Archaeological Association, Vol. 8, No. 1,
Rochester. 1936.
"Culture Influences from Ohio in New York Ar-
chaeology." *American Antiquity,* Vol. 2, No. 3, pp.
182–194, Menasha. 1937.
*Certain Recently Explored New York Mounds and
Their Probable Relation to the Hopewell Culture.*
Research Records of the Rochester Museum of Arts
and Sciences, No. 4. 1938.
"A Perspective of Northeastern Archaeology." *Amer-
ican Antiquity,* Vol. 4, No. 2, pp. 94–112, Menasha.
1938.
*Two Prehistoric Village Sites at Brewerton, New
York, Type Components of the Brewerton Focus,*

Laurentian Aspect. Research Records of the Rochester Museum of Arts and Sciences, No. 5. 1940.

The Pre-Iroquoian Occupations of New York State. Rochester Museum of Arts and Sciences, Memoir No. 1. 1944.

An Early Site in Cayuga County, New York; Type Component of the Frontenac Focus, Archaic Pattern. Researches and Transactions of the New York State Archaeological Association, Vol. 10, No. 1, Rochester. 1945.

A Stratified Prehistoric Site at Brewerton, New York. Research Records of the Rochester Museum of Arts and Sciences, No. 8. 1946.

Dutch Hollow, An Early Historic Period Seneca Site in Livingston County, New York. Albany. 1954.

Traces of Early Man in The Northeast. Albany. 1957.

Ritchie, William A., and Richard S. MacNeish
"The Pre-Iroquoian Pottery of New York State." *American Antiquity,* Vol. 15, No. 2, pp. 97–124, Menasha. 1949.

Smith, Carlyle S.
The Archaeology of Coastal New York. Anthropological Papers of the American Museum of Natural History, Vol. 43, Pt. 2, New York. 1950.

NORTH CAROLINA

A. Organization
   1.
   2.
   3. North Carolina Archeological Society
      Box 301, Chapel Hill

B. Control
   Strict control of excavation, survey, and preservation of archaeological sites as set forth in North Carolina General Statutes, 1955, c. 121, and Public Laws, 1935, Session c. 198 (S.B. 304).

C. Sites
  1. Paleo
     Archaic Woodland
     Mississippian
  2. Indian Mound in Cumberland City
     Old Tuscarora
     Contentnea Creek, Network of Tuscarora
     Gaston Reservoir
     Wilkesboro Reservoir
     Town Creek Indian Mound
     Peachtree Mound

D. Excavations
   Salvage Program in North Carolina River Basins:
   Gaston, Cowan Ford, and Wilkesboro Reservoirs

E. Museums
   University of North Carolina Research Laboratory of
   Anthropology
   Person Hall, Chapel Hill
   Brunswick Town State Historic Site
   225 Pine Grove Drive, Wilmington

F. Academic Institutions
   University of North Carolina, Chapel Hill, Anthropology

G. Bibliography
   HAAG, WILLIAM G.
   The Archaeology of Coastal North Carolina. Baton
   Rouge. 1958.

   PORTER, CHARLES W., III
   "Fort Raleigh National Historic Site, North Caro-
   lina: Part of the Settlement Sites of Sir Walter
   Raleigh's Colonies of 1585–1586 and 1587." *The
   North Carolina Historical Review*, Vol. 20, No. 1,
   pp. 22–42. 1943.

   SETZLER, FRANK M., and JESSE D. JENNINGS
   Peachtree Mound and Village Site, Cherokee County,

North Carolina. Bureau of American Ethnology, Bulletin 131, Washington. 1941.

NORTH DAKOTA

A. Organization
   1.
   2.
   3. North Dakota State Historical Society
      Bismarck

B. Control
   Legislation relating to the preservation, ownership and excavation of archaeological sites is contained in North Dakota, Laws 1915. c. 160, p. 3, North Dakota, Laws 1939 (S.B. 130)

C. Sites
   1. Early Period
      Middle Period
      Late Period
   2. Sheyenne-Cheyenne, southeast of Lisbon, Late

D. Excavations
   Rock Village at Garrison Reservoir, The Inter-Agency Archaeological Salvage Program

E. Museums
   State Historical Society Museum
   Bismarck

   Theodore Roosevelt National Memorial Park
   Medora

F. Academic Institutions

G. Bibliography
   Will, George F.
      "A Resumé of North Dakota Archaeology." *North Dakota Historical Quarterly,* Vol. 7, Nos. 2–3, pp. 150–161, Bismarck. 1933.

   Will, George F., and Thad C. Hecker
      "Upper Missouri River Valley Aboriginal Culture in

North Dakota." *North Dakota Historical Quarterly,*
Vol. 11, Nos. 1–2, pp. 5–126, Bismarck. 1944.

OHIO

A. Organization
   1. The Ohio Historical Society
   2. Curator of Archaeology
      The Ohio Historical Society
      Ohio State Museum, Columbus 10
   3. Archaeological Society of Ohio
      65 N. Foster St., Norwalk

B. Control
   A permissive act administered by the Ohio Historical
   Society requiring that all records relative to non-
   museum archaeological activities be placed in the permanent files of The Ohio Historical Society is being
   contemplated.

C. Sites
   1. Paleo-Indian
      Archaic
      Glacial Kame
      Adena
      Hopewell
      Late Woodland
      Fort Ancient
      Erie
   2. Seip Mound
      Newark Earthworks
      Serpent Mound
      Fort Ancient
      Fort Hill
      Miamisburg Mound

D. Excavations
   The Ohio Historical Society has carried out at least one
   major site excavation during each summer season,
   under the general direction of the Curator of Archaeology, since its establishment some 77 years ago.

Major emphasis in the future will be placed on the investigation of prehistoric sites in six reservoir areas in central and south-central Ohio.

E. Museums

Mound City Group National Monument
Chillicothe

Ohio State Museum
Columbus 10

Cincinnati Museum of Natural History
Cincinnati

Cleveland Museum of Natural History
Cleveland

F. Academic Institutions
University of Miami, Oxford, Anthropology

G. Bibliography

GOSLIN, ROBERT
"A Bone Atlatl Hook from Ohio." *American Antiquity,* Vol. 10, No. 2, pp. 204–205, Menasha. 1944.

GREENMAN, EMERSON F.
"Excavation of the Coon Mound and an Analysis of the Adena Culture." *Ohio Archaeological and Historical Quarterly,* Vol. 41, No. 3, pp. 369–410, Columbus. 1932.
"Excavation of the Reeve Village Site, Lake County, Ohio." *The Ohio State Archaeological and Historical Quarterly,* Vol. 44, No. 1, pp. 2–64, Columbus. 1935.
"Seven Prehistoric Sites in Northern Ohio." *The Ohio State Archaeological and Historical Quarterly,* Vol. 44, No. 2, pp. 220–237, Columbus. 1935.
"Two Prehistoric Villages near Cleveland, Ohio." *The Ohio State Archaeological and Historical Quarterly,* Vol. 46, No. 4, pp. 305–366, Columbus. 1937.

GRIFFIN, JAMES B.
"The Ceramic Affiliations of the Ohio Valley Adena Culture." In *The Adena People* by William S. Webb

and Charles E. Snow, University of Kentucky Reports in Anthropology and Archaeology, Vol. 6, pp. 220–246, Lexington. 1945.

HOOTON, EARNEST A., and CHARLES C. WILLOUGHBY
Indian Village Site and Cemetery near Madisonville, Ohio. Papers of the Peabody Museum of American Archaeology and Ethnology, Vol. 8, No. 1, Cambridge. 1920.

MILLS, WILLIAM C.
"Archaeological Remains of Jackson County." *Ohio Archaeological and Historical Quarterly,* Vol. 21, pp. 175–214, Columbus. 1912.
"Exploration of the Tremper Mound." *Ohio Archaeological and Historical Quarterly,* Vol. 25, No. 3, pp. 262–398, Columbus. 1916.
"Exploration of the Mound City Group." *Ohio Archaeological and Historical Quarterly,* Vol. 31, No. 4, pp. 423–584, Columbus. 1922.
"Exploration of the Mound City Group." In *Certain Mounds and Village Sites in Ohio,* Vol. 3, No. 4, pp. 245–406, Columbus. 1922.

MOFFAT, ROSS
"The Raisch-Smith Site: An Early Indian Occupation in Preble County, Ohio." *The Ohio State Archaeological and Historical Quarterly,* Vol. 58, No. 4, Columbus. 1949.

MOOREHEAD, WARREN K.
"The Hopewell Mound Group of Ohio." *Field Museum of Natural History, Publication* 211, *Anthropological Series,* Vol. 6, No. 5, Chicago. 1922.
The Cahokia Mounds. University of Illinois Bulletin, Vol. 26, No. 4, Urbana. 1928.

MORGAN, RICHARD G., and H. H. ELLIS
"The Fairport Harbor Village Site." *The Ohio State Archaeological and Historical Quarterly,* Vol. 52, No. 1, pp. 3–64, Columbus. 1943.

MORGAN, RICHARD G.
   Review of *The Adena People* by William S. Webb
   and Charles E. Snow. *American Antiquity,* Vol. 12,
   No. 1, pp. 54–58, Menasha. 1946.
   "Fort Ancient." *The Ohio State Archaeological and
   Historical Quarterly,* Columbus. 1946.

OEHLER, CHARLES M.
   Turpin Indians. Cincinnati Museum of Natural
   History, Popular Publication Series No. 1. 1950.

SHETRONE, HENRY C.
   "Exploration of the Wright Group of Prehistoric
   Earthworks." *Ohio Archaeological and Historical
   Quarterly,* Vol. 33, pp. 341–358, Columbus. 1924.
   "Explorations of the Hopewell Group of Prehistoric
   Earthworks." *Ohio Archaeological and Historical
   Quarterly,* Vol. 35, No. 1, pp. 1–227, Columbus.
   1926.
   "Some Ohio Caves and Rock Shelters Bearing Evi-
   dences of Human Occupancy." *Ohio Archaeological
   and Historical Quarterly,* Vol. 37, No. 1, pp. 1–34,
   Columbus. 1928.
   The Mound Builders. New York. 1930.
   "The Folsom Phenomena as Seen from Ohio." *The
   Ohio State Archaeological and Historical Quarterly,*
   Vol. 45, No. 3, pp. 240–256, Columbus. 1936.

SHETRONE, HENRY C., and EMERSON F. GREENMAN
   "Explorations of the Seip Group of Prehistoric
   Earthworks." *Ohio Archaeological and Historical
   Quarterly,* Vol. 40, No. 3, pp. 343–509, Columbus.
   1931.

WILLOUGHBY, CHARLES C., and EARNEST A. HOOTON
   *The Turner Group of Earthworks, Hamilton
   County, Ohio.* Papers of the Peabody Museum of
   Archaeology and Ethnology, Vol. 8, No. 3, Cam-
   bridge. 1922.

OKLAHOMA

A. Organization
   1.
   2.
   3. Oklahoma Anthropological Society
      University of Oklahoma, Norman

B. Control
   Preservation, ownership and excavation of archaeological sites are strictly regulated by legislation as set forth in Oklahoma Laws 1935, c. 34, art. 19, pp. 165–67. Statutes Annotated, title 53, sec. 1–19.

C. Sites
   1.
   2. Spiro Mound
      Eufaula Mound
      Black Mound
      William's Mound, Le Flore County
      Norman Site Excavations, near Wagoner
      Brackett Site

D. Excavations

E. Museums
   The Gilcrease Institute of American History and Art
   2401 Newton Street, Tulsa

F. Academic Institutions
   University of Oklahoma, Norman and Oklahoma City, Anthropology, Archaeology

G. Bibliography
   BARREIS, DAVID A.
      "Two New Cultures in Delaware County, Oklahoma." *Oklahoma Prehistorian,* Vol. 2, No. 1, pp. 2–5, Tulsa. 1939.
      Preceramic Horizons of Northeastern Oklahoma. Anthropological Paper No. 6, Museum of Anthropology, University of Michigan, Ann Arbor. 1951.

BELL, ROBERT E.
"The Scott Site, Le Flore County, Oklahoma."
American Antiquity, Vol. 18, pp. 314–331, Salt Lake
City. 1953.
Bulletin, Oklahoma Anthropological Society, Nor-
man.

BURNETT, E. K.
The Spiro Mound Collection in the Museum. Contributions from the Museum of the American Indian, Heye Foundation, Vol. 14, New York. 1945.

FINKLESTEIN, J. JOE
"The Norman Site Excavations Near Wagoner,
Oklahoma." *Oklahoma Prehistorian,* Vol. 3, No. 3,
pp. 2–15, Tulsa. 1940.

HOWARD, LYNN E.
"Preliminary Report on Cherokee County, Oklahoma, Archaeology." *Oklahoma Prehistorian,* Vol.
3, No. 1, pp. 2–11, Tulsa. 1940.

NEWKUMET, PHIL J.
"Preliminary Report on Excavation of the William's Mound, Le Flore County, Oklahoma." *Oklahoma Prehistorian,* Vol. 3, No. 2, pp. 2–10, Tulsa.
1940.

ORR, KENNETH G.
"Field Report on the Excavations of Indian Villages
in the Vicinity of the Spiro Mound, Le Flore
County." *Oklahoma Prehistorian,* Vol. 2, No. 2, pp.
8–15, Tulsa. 1939.
"The Eufaula Mound: Contributions to the Spiro
Focus." *Oklahoma Prehistorian,* Vol. 4, No. 1, pp.
2–15, Tulsa. 1941.
"The Archaeological Situation at Spiro, Oklahoma;
A Preliminary Report." *American Antiquity,* Vol.
11, No. 4, pp. 228–256, Menasha. 1946.

OREGON

A. Organization
   1.
   2.
   3. Oregon Archaeological Society

B. Control
   Regulations relating to preservation, ownership, and excavation of archaeological sites are set forth in Oregon Revised Statutes, sec. 273.250, 273.260. (Laws 135, c. 380).

   The State Land Board on recommendation of the President of the University of Oregon may issue permits for work on State land.

   Oregon State Museum of Anthropology in Museum of Natural History, University of Oregon, is official state depository for anthropological collections belonging to the state.

C. Sites
   1. Early Man
      "Desert Culture"
      Columbia River—Salmon Subsistence Plateau
      Coastal Maritime
   2. Roaring Springs Cave
      Fort Rock Cave
      The Dalles—WS
      Kawumkan Springs

D. Excavations
   Archaeological research in the Northern Great Basin, L. S. Cressman, Carnegie Institution of Washington
   Klamath Prehistory, 1956, L. S. Cressman, American Philosophical Society
   Cultural Sequences at The Dalles, 1960, L. S. Cressman, American Philosophical Society
   John Day Dam Site on the Columbia River, 1962
   Salt Caves Dam Site on the Klamath River, 1962

Round Butte Dam on the Deschutes-Crooked-Metolioes River, 1962

E. Museums

University of Oregon, Museum of Natural History Eugene

Klamath County Museum
Klamath Falls

Oregon Historical Society
235 S.W. Market, Portland

F. Academic Institutions
University of Oregon, Eugene, Anthropology

G. Bibliography

CARLSON, ROY L.

"Klamath Henwas and Other Stone Sculpture." *American Anthropologist,* Vol. 61, No. 1, pp. 88–96, Menasha. 1959.

CRESSMAN, L.S.

Klamath Prehistory. The Prehistory of the Culture of the Klamath Lake Area, Oregon. Transactions of the American Philosophical Society, Vol. 46, 4, Philadelphia. 1956.

OSBORNE, DOUGLAS

Excavations in the McNary Reservoir Basin Near Umatilla, Oregon. Bureau of American Ethnology, Bulletin 166. Washington, D.C. 1957.

PENNSYLVANIA

A. Organization
1. Pennsylvania Historical and Museum Commission
2. Executive Director
   Pennsylvania Historical and Museum Commission
   Director of the Bureau of Museum and Historic Sites
   Chief Curator, State Museum

State Archaeologist
Chief, Historic Sites and Properties
3. Society for Pennsylvania Archaeology
   c/o Vincent R. Mrozoski, Secretary-Treasurer
   Box 368, Aliquippa

B. Control
   None

C. Sites
   1. Paleo-Indian
      Early Woodland
      Middle Woodland
      Late Woodland
      Historic
   2. Poplar Island, Archaic
      Sugar Run Mound Cluster, Early Woodland
      Crall Mound, Early Woodland
      Wolves Den Rock Shelter, Early Woodland
      Montague, Late Woodland
      Troutman, Late Woodland
      Strickler, Late Woodland
      Schultz Farm, Late Woodland
      Valley Forge, Historic

D. Excavations
   Sheep Rock, Huntingdon County
   Graeme Park, Horsham
   Valley Forge
   Ibaugh Site

E. Museums
   Pennsylvania State Museum
   Harrisburg
   University of Pennsylvania, University Museum
   Philadelphia
   Carnegie Institute, Carnegie Museum
   Pittsburgh

F. Academic Institutions

Bryn Mawr College, Bryn Mawr, Anthropology and Archaeology

University of Pennsylvania, Philadelphia, Anthropology

Carnegie Institute, Pittsburgh

G. Bibliography

Augustine, Edgar E.

"Recent Discoveries in Somerset County." *The Pennsylvania Archaeologist,* Vol. 8, No. 1, pp. 6–12, Milton.

"Indian Fortifications in Somerset County." *The Pennsylvania Archaeologist,* Vol. 8, No. 2, pp. 41–45, Milton. 1938.

"Somerset County Excavations: The Powell Sites." *The Pennsylvania Archaeologist,* Vol. 8, No. 3, pp. 60–63, Milton. 1938.

"Important Research on Peck and Martz Rock Shelter Sites in Somerset County." *The Pennsylvania Archaeologist,* Vol. 8, No. 4, pp. 83–88, Milton. 1938.

Bliss, Wesley

"Archaeological Field Activity of the Pennsylvania Historical Commission in 1941. IV: The Sugar Run Mound Cluster." *The Pennsylvania Archaeologist,* Vol. 12, No. 2, pp. 35–38, Milton. 1942.

Butler, Mary

Three Archaeological Sites in Somerset County, Pennsylvania. Bulletin of the Pennsylvania Historical Commission, No. 753, Harrisburg. 1939.

"Two Lenape Rock Shelters near Philadelphia." *American Antiquity,* Vol. 12, No. 4, pp. 246–255, Menasha. 1947.

Cadzow, Donald A.

"Mr. George Fisher's Discoveries in Western Pennsylvania." *The Pennsylvania Archaeologist,* Vol. 3, No. 3, pp. 3–5, Harrisburg. 1933.

Archaeological Studies of the Susquehannock Indi-

ans of Pennsylvania. Publications of Pennsylvania Historical Commission, Vol. 3, Safe Harbor Report No. 2, Harrisburg. 1936.

CLAUSEN, CARL
"The Wolves' Den Shelter." *The Pennsylvania Archaeologist,* Vol. 3, No. 2, pp. 7–9, 19, Harrisburg. 1932.

ENGBERG, ROBERT M.
"Archaeological Report," in "Archaeological Work in Westmoreland and Fayette Counties, 1929." *Western Pennsylvania Historical Magazine,* Vol. 13, No. 2, pp. 71–103, Pittsburg. 1930.
"Algonkian Sites of Westmoreland and Fayette Counties, Pennsylvania." *Western Pennsylvania Historical Magazine,* Vol. 14, No. 3, pp. 143–184, Pittsburgh. 1931.

GODCHARLES, FREDERIC A.
"Rich Variety of Andaste Indian Material Yielded by Excavating Long House Sites in Clinton County, Pennsylvania." *Pennsylvania Archaeologist,* Vol. 4, No. 3, pp. 13–15, Milton. 1934.

JONES, ROBERT W.
"The Clemson Mound." *Annual Report of the Pennsylvania Historical Commission,* No. 5, pp. 89–111, Harrisburg. 1931.

The Pennsylvania Archaeologist, Society for Pennsylvania Archaeology, Gettysburg.

RHODE ISLAND

A. Organization
   1.
   2.
   3. Narrangansett Archaeological Society of Rhode Island
      c/o Miss Elisabeth G. Weeks, Secretary
      277 Brooks St., Providence 6

B. Control

C. Sites
1. Archaic
   Early Woodland
   Middle Woodland
   Late Woodland
2. Locust Spring Site
   Greenwood
   Green Point on Narragansett Bay

D. Excavations
   Locust Spring Cite, Greenwood, 1957–61, Dr. Wm.
   Fowler

E. Museums
   Tomaquag Indian Memorial Museum
   Burdickville Rd., Ashaway

   Roger Williams, Park Museum
   Providence

F. Academic Institutions

G. Bibliography

SOUTH CAROLINA

A. Organization
   1.
   2.
   3. South Carolina Archaeological Society
      c/o Mr. James E. Livingston
      1461 Ilex St., Columbia

B. Control

C. Sites
1. Archaic
   Early Woodland
   Middle Woodland
   Late Woodland
   Mississippian
   Historic

   2. Thom's Creek, Beaufort District
      Chester Field, Beaufort District
      Little Island, Beaufort District
      Union Land, Jasper District
      McCollum Site, Chester District
      Greenville Mound
      McDowell Mound

D. Excavations

E. Museums
   Charleston Museum
   125 Rutledge Avenue
   Charleston

F. Academic Institutions

G. Bibliography

FLANNERY, REGINA

An Analysis of Coastal Algonquian Culture. The Catholic University of America, Anthropological Series, No. 7, Washington. 1939.

"Some Notes on a Few Sites in Beaufort County, South Carolina." *Anthropological Papers,* No. 21, *Bureau of American Ethnology Bulletin* 133, pp. 143–153, Washington. 1943.

GRIFFIN, JAMES B.

"Ceramic Collections from Two South Carolina Sites." *Papers of the Michigan Academy of Science, Arts, and Letters,* Vol. 30, pp. 465–478, Ann Arbor. 1945.

"An Analysis and Interpretation of the Ceramic Remains from Two Sites Near Beaufort, South Carolina." *Anthropological Papers,* No. 22, *Bureau of American Ethnology Bulletin* 133, pp. 155–168, Washington. 1943.

"The De Luna Expedition and the 'Buzzard Cult' in the Southeast." *Journal of the Washington Academy of Science,* Vol. 34, No. 9, pp. 299–303, Menasha. 1944.

"The Iroquois in American Prehistory." *Papers of the Michigan Academy of Science, Arts, and Letters,* Vol. 29, pp. 357–374, Ann Arbor. 1944.

WAUCHOPE, ROBERT
"Fluted Points from South Carolina." *American Antiquity,* Vol. 4, No. 4, pp. 344–346, Menasha. 1939.

SOUTH DAKOTA

A. Organization
  1. South Dakota Archaeological Commission
     W. H. Over Museum of the State University of South Dakota
     Vermillion
  2. Chairman of the South Dakota Archaeological Commission
     c/o W. H. Over Museum of the State University of South Dakota
     Vermillion
  3. None

B. Control
  Archaeological Commission was created by Chapter 255, Sessions Laws 1947, to conduct archaeological excavations. In addition, the Commission is given the power to issue permits for excavations on State Land. Excavations on State Land without permit are strictly forbidden by this act.

C. Sites
  1. Folsom
     Yuma
     Early foraging cultures
     Woodland
     Arikara (Prehistoric)
     Mandan (Prehistoric)
  2. Ludlow Cave, Late Crow
     Leavenworth, Late Arikara
     Mitchell Site, Protohistoric

D. Excavations
   Thomas Riggs Village Site
   Rock Shelters in Fall River County
   Mitchell Indian Village
   Brandon Village Site
   Split Rock Creek Mounds
   La Roche Site
   Robinson Site
   Meyer Site
   Swanson Site
   Scalp Creek Site
   Spotted Bear Site
   These excavations since 1938 have been variously supported by the W.P.A., W. H. Over Museum, and the South Dakota Archaeological Commission and the National Park Service
   Site in the vicinity of Chamberlain, 1962, W. H. Over Museum, South Dakota Archaeological Commission and National Park Service

E. Museums
   South Dakota State Historical Museum
   Memorial Building, Pierre
   Pettigrew Museum
   Sioux Falls
   University of South Dakota, W. H. Over Museum
   Vermillion

F. Academic Institutions
   University of South Dakota, Vermillion, Archaeology, Anthropology

G. Bibliography
   Lehmer, Donald J., *et al.*
   Archaeological Investigations in the Oahe Dam Area, South Dakota, 1950–51. Bureau of American Ethnology, Bulletin 158, Washington, D.C. 1954.

MELEEN, ELMER E.
A Preliminary Report of the Mitchell Indian Village Site and Burial Mounds. Archaeological Studies, Circular 2, Pt. 1, University of South Dakota Museum, Vermillion. 1938.

METCALF, GEORGE
"Additional Data From the Dodd and Phillips Ranch Sites, South Dakota." *American Antiquity,* Vol. 21, pp. 305–309, Salt Lake City. 1956.

MONTGOMERY, HENRY
"Remains of Prehistoric Man in the Dakotas." *American Anthropologist,* Vol. 8, No. 4, pp. 640–651, Lancaster. 1906.

Museum News, W. H. Over Museum, State University of South Dakota, Vermillion.

OVER, W. H.
"The Archaeology of Ludlow Cave and Its Significance." *American Antiquity,* Vol. 2, No. 2, pp. 126–129, Menasha. 1936.

SPAULDING, ALBERT C.
The Arzberger Site, Hughes County, South Dakota. Ann Arbor. 1956.

WEDEL, WALDO R.
Archeological Materials from the Vicinity of Mobridge, Bureau of American Ethnology, Bulletin # 157, Washington. 1955.

TENNESSEE

A. Organization
1. Department of Anthropology, The Frank H. McClung Museum
   University of Tennessee, Knoxville
2. Director of The Frank H. McClung Museum
3. The Tennessee Archaeological Society
   c/o The Frank H. McClung Museum, Knoxville

B. Control

No legislation. Tennessee Archaeological Society was organized in 1944 and through the medium of its periodicals, meetings, and correspondence, effective control has been exerted.

C. Sites

1. Paleo-Indian
   Archaic
   Early Woodland
   Middle Woodland
   Early and Late Temple Mound
   Historic Yuchi
   Creek and Cherokee
2. Hiwassee Island
   Gray Site
   Mouse Creek
   Candy Creek
   Watts Bar
   Lenoir Island
   Dallas Site

D. Excavations

All major excavations were sponsored by the University of Tennessee under the direction of Thomas M. N. Lewis, along the following rivers:

Tennessee

Clinch

Powell

French Broad

Hiwassee

Little Tennessee

Obion

Cumberland

E. Museums

The University of Tennessee, The Frank M. McClung Museum
Knoxville

The Memphis Museum
Memphis

F. Academic Institutions
The University of Tennessee, Knoxville, Anthropology

G. Bibliography

GRIFFIN, JAMES B.
"The Ceramic Remains from Norris Basin, Tennessee." In *An Archeological Survey of the Norris Basin in Eastern Tennessee* by William S. Webb, Bureau of American Ethnology, Bulletin 118, pp. 253–358, Washington. 1938.

LEWIS, T. M. N.
"Late Horizons in the Southeast." In *Recent Advances in American Archaeology,* Proceedings of the American Philosophical Society, Vol. 86, No. 2, pp. 304–312, Philadelphia. 1943.
"The Duck River Cache." *Tennessee Archaeologist,* Vol. 3, No. 4, pp. 54–57. 1947.

LEWIS, T. M. N., and MADELINE KNEBERG
The Prehistory of the Chicamauga Basin in Tennessee. Tennessee Anthropology Papers No. 1, Knoxville. 1941.
Hiwassee Island: An Archaeological Account of Four Tennessee Indian Peoples. Knoxville. 1946.
The Archaic Horizon in Western Tennessee. Tennessee Anthropology Papers No. 2, The University of Tennessee Record, Extension Series, Vol. 23, No. 4, Knoxville. 1947.

MacCURDY, GEORGE GRANT
"Some Mounds of Eastern Tennessee." *Proceedings of the Nineteenth International Congress of Americanists,* pp. 59–74, Washington. 1917.

The Tennessee Archaeologist, Knoxville.

WEBB, WILLIAM S.
An Archeological Survey of the Norris Basin in Eastern Tennessee. Bureau of American Ethnology, Bulletin 118, Washington. 1938.

TEXAS

A. Organization
   1.
   2.
   3. Texas Archeological Society
      c/o Department of Anthropology
      University of Texas, Austin 12

      Dallas Archaeological Society
      Dallas

B. Control
   Preservation, ownership, and excavation of archaeological sites are strictly regulated by legislation as set forth in Texas. Penal Code vol. 1, 1952, art. 1472 (Acts, 1931, 42 Leg. 1st C. S., c. 32, p. 7) and art. 147b (Acts, 1939 46th Leg., p. 60).

C. Sites
   1.
   2. Gahagan Mound
      Belcher Mound
      George C. Davis Site, Cherokee County

D. Excavations
   Whitney Reservoir on Brozas River, Smithsonian

E. Museums
   University of Texas Anthropology Museum
   Pearce Hall, Austin

   Panhandle Plains Historical Museum
   2401 11th Avenue, Canyon

   Texas Western College, El Paso Centennial Museum
   El Paso

F. Academic Institutions
   University of Texas, Austin, Anthropology
   Texas Western College, El Paso, Anthropology

G. Bibliography
   Bulletin of the Texas Archeological Society. Texas Archeological Society. Austin.

CROOK, WILSON W. J. and R. K. HARRIS
"A Pleistocene Campsite Near Lewisville, Texas."
American Antiquity, Vol. 23, pp. 233–246, Salt Lake
City. 1957.

DICKINSON, S. D.
"Certain Vessels from the Clements Place: An Historic Caddo Site." *Bulletin of the Texas Archaeological and Paleontological Society,* Vol. 13, pp. 117–132,
Abilene. 1941.

HODGES, MR. and MRS. T. L.
"Suggestion for Identification of Certain Mid-
Ouachita Pottery as Cahinnio Caddo." *Bulletin of the
Texas Archaeological and Paleontological Society,*
Vol. 16, pp. 98–116, Abilene. 1945.

JACKSON, A. T.
"A 'Perpetual Fire' Site." *Bulletin of the Texas Archaeological and Paleontological Society,* Vol. 8, pp.
134–173, Abilene. 1936.

JENKS, ALBERT E., and LLOYD A. WILFORD
"The Sauk Valley Skeleton." *Bulletin of the Texas
Archaeological and Paleontological Society,* No. 10,
pp. 136–168, Abilene. 1938.

KELLEY, J. CHARLES
"The Desert Cultures and the Balcones Phase: Ar-
chaic Manifestations in the Southwest and Texas."
American Antiquity, Vol. 24, pp. 276–288, Salt Lake
City. 1958.

KRIEGER, ALEX D.
*Culture Complexes and Chronology in Northern
Texas.* University of Texas Publication, No. 4640,
Austin. 1946.
"The Eastward Extension of Puebloan Datings
Toward Cultures of the Mississippi Valley." *Ameri-
can Antiquity,* Vol. 12, No. 3, pp. 141–148, Menasha.
1947.
"The First Symposium on the Caddoan Archaeologi-

cal Area." *American Antiquity,* Vol. 12, No. 3, pp. 198–207, Menasha. 1947.

NEWELL, H. PERRY, and ALEX D. KRIEGER
The George C. Davis Site, Cherokee County, Texas. Society for American Archaeology Memoir No. 5, Menasha. 1947.

SHACKELFORD, WILLIAM J.
"Excavations at the Polvo Site in Western Texas." *American Antiquity,* Vol. 20, pp. 256–262, Salt Lake City. 1954.

SUHM, DEE A., *et al.*
"An Introductory Handbook of Texas Archaeology." *Bulletin,* Texas Archaeological Society, Vol. 25, Austin. 1954.

WATT, FRANK H. (editor)
Central Texas Archeologist. Waco. 1953.

WEBB, CLARENCE H., and MONROE DODD, JR.
"Further Excavations of the Gahagan Mound; Connections with a Florida Culture." *Bulletin of the Texas Archaeological and Paleontological Society,* Vol. 11, pp. 92–127, Abilene. 1939.
"Pottery Types from the Belcher Mound Site." *Bulletin of the Texas Archaeological and Paleontological Society,* Vol. 13, pp. 89–116, Abilene. 1941.

WOODBURY, GEORGE
Notes on Some Skeletal Remains of Texas. The University of Texas Bulletin, No. 3734, Austin. 1937.

UTAH

A. Organization
   1. Utah State Park and Recreation Commission
   2. Director, Utah State Park and Recreation Commission
      Salt Lake City

3. Utah Statewide Archaeological Society
c/o Anthropology Museum, University of Utah
Salt Lake City

B. Control
Rules and Regulations of the Utah State Park and Recreation Commission and the county in which the excavation is to be undertaken must both issue permits for excavation on state land.

C. Sites
1. Great Basin
Pueblo
Desert Culture, Ancient
2. Danger Cave, Desert
Alkali Ridge in Southeastern Utah, Developmental
Pueblo
Hovenweep National Monument, Classic Pueblo
Paragonah, Virgin Branch, Pueblo
Dead Man's Cave
Promontory
Blackrock

D. Excavations
Danger Cave, 1950, J. D. Jennings
Alkali Ridge, 1930, J. O. Brew
Paragonah, 1950's, Clement Meighan
Yampa Canyon area, 1940's, Robert Lister
Glen Canyon area, University of Utah and the National
Park Service

E. Museums
Moab Museum
Moab
Anthropology Museum, University of Utah
Salt Lake City

F. Academic Institutions
University of Utah, Salt Lake City, Archaeology and
Anthropology

G. Bibliography

BREW, JOHN OTIS
Archaeology of Alkali Ridge, Southeastern Utah.
Papers of the Peabody Museum of American Archaeology and Ethnology, Vol. 21, Cambridge. 1946.

COLTON, HAROLD S.
Pottery Types of the Arizona Strip and Adjacent Areas in Utah and Nevada. Flagstaff. 1952.

GUNNERSON, JAMES H.
"A Fluted Point Site in Utah." *American Antiquity,*
Vol. 21, pp. 412–414, Salt Lake City. 1956.
An Archaeological Survey of the Fremont Area. Salt Lake City. 1957.

JENNINGS, JESSE D.
Danger Cave. Memoirs of the Society for American Archaeology, Number 14, Salt Lake City. 1957.

LISTER, ROBERT H.
The Glen Canyon Survey in 1957. Salt Lake City. 1958.

MEIGHEN, CLEMENT W., *et al.*
Archeological Investigations in Iron City, Utah. Salt Lake City. 1956.

RUDY, JACK R.
Archeological Survey of Western Utah. Salt Lake City. 1953.
Pine Park Shelter, Washington County, Utah. Salt Lake City. 1954.

SMITH, ELMER R.
The Archaeology of Deadman Cave, Utah. Bulletin of the University of Utah, Vol. 32, No. 4, Salt Lake City. 1941.

TAYLOR, DEE C.
Two Fremont Sites and Their Positions in Southwestern Prehistory. University of Utah Anthropological Papers, No. 29, Salt Lake City. n.d.

Wormington, H. M.
A Reappraisal of the Fremont Culture, With a Summary of the Archaeology of the Northern Periphery. Denver. 1955.

VERMONT

A. Organization
1. Vermont Historical Society
2. Vermont Board of Historic Sites
3. None

B. Control
New York–Vermont Interstate Commission on the Lake Champlain Basin has urged the States of New York and Vermont to pass appropriate legislation to reserve to their States all the archaeological and historical artifacts of recognized antiquity and thus aid in preserving the historical heritage of these two states.

C. Sites
1. Pre-historic
Pre-Algonkian
Old Algonkian
Abnaki
Iroquoian
Historic
2. Orwell
Vergennes
Isle La Motte
Newbury
Hubbardton
Champlain Valley

D. Excavations
Orwell, 1934, Museum of the American Indian, Heye Foundation
Vergennes, Champlain Valley Archaeological Society (now defunct)
Champlain Valley Sites, 1933–51, Vermont Historical Society

Highgate, William Ross and William A. Ritchie

Mount Independence, historical excavation, Fort Ticonderoga Association

E. Museums
Vermont Historical Society
State Administration Building
Montpelier

F. Academic Institutions

G. Bibliography
BAILEY, JOHN H.
"A Stratified Rock Shelter in Vermont." *Proceedings of the Vermont Historical Society,* Vol. 8, No. 1, pp. 3–30, Brattleboro. 1940.

RITCHIE, WILLIAM A.
Traces of Early Man in the Northeast. Albany. 1957.

VIRGINIA

A. Organization
1. None
2. None
3. Archeological Society of Virginia
c/o Mrs. G. Alexander Robertson, Corresponding Secretary
3718 Brookside Road, Richmond 25

B. Control
No restrictions as to work done on private land. The Archeological Society of Virginia can by law hold state highway construction long enough to salvage archaeological material threatened by destruction.

C. Sites
1. Williamson, Paleo
Occoneechee, Late Prehistoric Siouan
Waratan, Late Archaic, Early Woodland Shell Heap Culture
Powhatan, Late Prehistoric—Historic

Dismal Swamp, Archaic
Nottoway, Late Prehistoric—Historic Iroquoian
Greensville, Historic Siouan
Chilhowee, Historic Cherokee

2. Clover Cree
Highland County
Battle Mound
Rockbridge County
James River
Botetourt
Linville Mound
Patawomeke

D. Excavations

Early Jamestown, John L. Cotter, National Park Service

Occoneechee, Clarksville Area, Carl F. Miller, Smithsonian Institution

Potts Site, Chicahominy River, Ben C. McCarey

Chesopean Site, Lynnhaven Inlet, Floyd E. Painter

Helmet Site, James River, Floyd E. Painter

Conners Midden, Halifax County, Col. Robert P. Carroll

Greensville Site, William Moseley

Mons Site, Bedorford County

E. Museums
Smithsonian Institution
Washington, D.C.

Vallentine Museum
Richmond

Jamestown Museum
Jamestown

Virginia Military Institute
Lexington

F. Academic Institutions

G. Bibliography

ATWOOD, ALBERT W.
"Tidewater Virginia, Where History Lives." *National Geographic Magazine,* Vol. 81, No. 5, pp. 617–656, Washington.

Bulletin of the Archaeological Society of Virginia, Staunton

BUSHNELL, DAVID I., JR.
Villages of the Algonquian, Siouan, and Caddoan Tribes West of the Mississippi. Bureau of American Ethnology, Bulletin 77, Washington. 1922.
Burials of the Algonquian, Siouan, and Caddoan Tribes West of the Mississippi. Bureau of American Ethnology, Bulletin 83, Washington. 1927.
The Manahoac Tibes in Virginia, 1608. Smithsonian Miscellaneous Collections, Vol. 94, No. 8, Washington. 1935.
Indian Sites Below the Falls of the Rappahannock, Virginia. Smithsonian Miscellaneous Collections, Vol. 96, No. 4, Washington. 1937.

EVANS, CLIFFORD
A Ceramic Study of Virginia Archaeology, Bureau of American Ethnology Bulletin 160, Washington. 1955.

HOLLAND, C. G.
Preceramic and Ceramic Cultural Patterns in Northwest Virginia, Bureau of American Ethnology, Anthropological Papers 57, Washington. 1960.

MANSON, CARL
"Marcey Creek Site: An Early Manifestation in the Potomac Valley." *American Antiquity,* Vol. 13, No. 3, pp. 223–227, Menasha. 1948.

STEWART, T. DALE
"Excavating the Indian Village of Patawomeke (Potomac)." *Explorations and Field-Work of the Smith-*

sonian Institution in 1938, pp. 87–90, Washington. 1939.

"The Finding of an Indian Ossuary on the York River in Virginia." *Journal of the Washington Academy of Science,* Vol. 30, No. 8, pp. 356–364, Menasha. 1940.

WASHINGTON

A. Organization
   1.
   2.
   3. Washington Archaeological Society
      Seattle

B. Control
   Preservation, ownership and excavation of archaeological sites are strictly regulated by legislation as set forth in Washington, Laws 1941, c. 216; Laws, 1943, pp. 37–38, c. 19; Reminaton's Revised Statutes, Supplement of 1949, sec. 27.52.010–27.52.020.

C. Sites
   1.
   2. Ash Cave
      Meyer Caves

D. Excavations

E. Museums
   University of Washington
   Washington State Museum
   4037 15th North East
   Seattle

   Yakima Valley Museum
   2105 Tieton Drive
   Yakima

   Seattle Art Museum
   Volunteer Park
   Seattle

F. Academic Institutions
   University of Washington, Seattle, Anthropology
   State College of Washington, Pullman, Anthropology

G. Bibliography

BRYAN, ALAN L.
   "Archaeology of the Yale Reservoir, Lewis River,
   Washington." *American Antiquity,* Vol. 20, pp. 281–
   283, Salt Lake City. 1954.
   "Excavations at Meyer Caves in East Central Wash-
   ington." *Davidson Journal of Anthropology,* Vol. 1,
   Seattle. 1955.
   "Results and Interpretations of Recent Archaeologi-
   cal Research in Western Washington with Circum-
   Boreal Implications," *Davidson Journal of Anthro-
   pology,* Vol. 3, Seattle. 1957.

BUTLER, B. R.
   "Ash Cave (45 WW 61): A Preliminary Report,"
   The Washington Archaeologist, Vol. 2, Seattle. 1958.

CARLSON, ROY L.
   "Chronology and Culture Change in the San Juan
   Islands, Washington." *American Antiquity,* Vol. 25,
   Salt Lake City. 1960.

DAUGHERTY, RICHARD D.
   Archaeology of the Lind Coulee Site, Washington.
   Proceedings of the American Philosophical Society,
   Vol. 100, 3, Philadelphia. 1956.
   Northwest Archaeology Number. Research Studies
   of the State College of Washington, Vol. 24, 1, Pull-
   man. 1956.
   "Early Man in Washington." *Information Circular
   No. 32,* State of Washington, Division of Mines and
   Geology. 1959.

Davidson Journal of Anthropology, Seattle.

n.a. *New Interpretations of Aboriginal American Cultural History.* 75th Anniversary Volume of the Anthropological Society of Washington. 1955.

Swanson, Earl H.
"The Schaake Village Site in Central Washington."
American Antiquity, Vol. 24, pp. 161–171, Salt Lake
City. 1958.

Swanson, Earl H. and W. T. Lee
"A Small Rock Shelter in Eastern Washington."
American Antiquity, Vol. 24, pp. 430–431, Salt Lake
City. 1959.

The Washington Archaeologist, Washington Archaeological Society. Seattle.

WEST VIRGINIA

A. Organization
   1.
   2. State Archeologist
   3. West Virginia Archeological Society
      c/o Mr. Charles R. Lally
      314 Garfield St., McMechen

B. Control

C. Sites
   1. Paleo-Indian
      Archaic
      Early Woodland
      Middle Woodland
      Late Woodland
      Historic
   2. Moundsville
      Cresap Mound
      Orchard Site
      Mount Carbon-village site

D. Excavations

E. Museums
   The Mound Museum
   Moundsville

F. Academic Institutions

G. Bibliography

Solecki, Ralph S.

Exploration of an Adena Mound at Natrium, West Virginia. Bureau of American Ethnology, Bulletin 151. Washington, D.C. 1953.

The West Virginia Archeologist, West Virginia Archeological Society. Moundsville

WISCONSIN

A. Organization
   1. Conservation Department
   2.
   3. Wisconsin Archeological Society
      c/o Phil H. Weigan
      1276 North 63rd Court
      Wauwatosa 13

      State Historical Society of Wisconsin
      Madison

B. Control
   Destruction of Indian Mounds of any type or any prehistoric or historic Indian remains located on public lands is forbidden. The Conservation Commission is authorized to grant permission to remove or destroy such remains for educational or scientific purposes. Wisconsin Statute 27.012

C. Sites
   1. Archaic, Old Copper
      Woodland, Hopewell, Effigy Mound
      Late Woodland
      Middle Mississippi
      Upper Mississippi, Oneota
   2. Raddatz and Durst rockshelters, Archaic
      Trempealeau, Red Cedar, Highsmith, Price, Archaic
      Neale and McClaughry groups, Effigy Mound
      Kletzien and Nitschke groups, Effigy Mound
      Kolterman group, Effigy Mound
      Hahn village site, Late Woodland

Aztalan site, Middle Mississippi
Walker Hooper, Shrake-Gillies, Midway, McCauley, White Karow, and Carcajou, Upper Mississippi

D. Excavations
Oconto Site, Oconto
Reigh Site, Oshkosh
Raddatz Rockshelter, Leland, 1957, Warren L. Wittry
Trempealeau Mounds, 1928, Will McKern
Aztalan, Wisconsin Archeological Survey

E. Museums
Milwaukee Public Museum
818 W. Wisconsin Avenue, Milwaukee
State Historical Society of Wisconsin Museum
Madison
Douglas County Historical Museum
Superior
Oshkosh Public Museum
Oshkosh

F. Academic Institutions
Beloit College, Beloit
University of Wisconsin, Madison, Archaeology
Lawrence College, Appleton, Anthropology

G. Bibliography
Barrett, Samuel A., and Alanson B. Skinner
Certain Mounds and Village Sites of Shawano and Oconto Counties, Wisconsin. Bulletin of the Public Museum of the City of Milwaukee, Vol. 10, No. 5. 1932.

Byers, Douglas S.
"Fluted Points from Wisconsin." *American Antiquity,* Vol. 7, No. 4, p. 400, Menasha. 1942.

Bulletin of the Public Museum of the City of Milwaukee.

COOPER, L. R.
Red Cedar Variant of the Wisconsin Hopewell Culture. Bulletin of the Public Museum of the City of Milwaukee, Vol. 16, No. 2. 1933.

HALL, ROBERT L.
"A Style Analysis of Wisconsin Woodland Pottery." *Wisconsin Archeologist,* Vol. 31, No. 1, Milwaukee. 1950.

McKERN, W. C.
A Wisconsin Variant of the Hopewell Culture. Bulletin of the Public Museum of the City of Milwaukee, Vol. 10, No. 2. 1931.
"An Hypothesis for the Asiatic Origin of the Woodland Pattern." *American Antiquity,* Vol. 3, No. 2, pp. 138–143, Menasha. 1937.
"The Midwestern Taxonomic Method as an Aid to Archaeological Culture Study." *American Antiquity,* Vol. 4, No. 4, pp. 301–313, Menasha. 1939.
"Wisconsin Archaeology in the Light of Recent Finds in Other Areas." *The Wisconsin Archeologist,* Vol. 20, No. 1, pp. 1–5, Milwaukee. 1939.
"The First Settlers of Wisconsin." *Wisconsin Magazine of History,* Vol. 26, No. 2, pp. 153–169, Madison. 1942.
Preliminary Report on the Upper Mississippi Phase in Wisconsin. Bulletin of the Public Museum of the City of Milwaukee, Vol. 16, No. 3. 1945.
"Aztalan." *The Wisconsin Archeologist,* Vol. 27, No. 2, pp. 41–52, Milwaukee. 1946.

McKERN, W. C., and ROBERT RITZENTHALER
"Trait List of the Prehistoric Wisconsin Cultures: The Woodland Peoples." *The Wisconsin Archeologist,* Vol. 26, No. 4, pp. 66–79, Milwaukee. 1945.

QUIMBY, GEORGE I.
"Fluted Points and Geochronology of the Lake Michigan Basin." *American Antiquity,* Vol. 23, pp. 247–254, Salt Lake City. 1957.

RITZENTHALER, ROBERT
"The Osceola Site: An 'Old Copper' Site near Potosi, Wisconsin." *The Wisconsin Archeologist*, Vol. 27, No. 3, pp. 53–70, Milwaukee. 1946.
Prehistoric Indians of Wisconsin. Milwaukee. 1953.

ROWE, CHANDLER W.
The Effigy Mound Culture of Wisconsin. Milwaukee. 1956.

The Wisconsin Archeologist, Wisconsin Archeological Society, Milwaukee.

WITTRY, WARREN L., and R. E. RITZENTHALER
"The Old Copper Complex: An Archaic Manifestation in Wisconsin." *American Antiquity*, Vol. 21, pp. 244–254, Salt Lake City. 1955.

WOOD, E. F.
"A Central Basin Manifestation in Eastern Wisconsin." *American Antiquity*, Vol. 1, No. 3, pp. 215–219, Menasha. 1936.

WYOMING

A. Organization
   1. State Land Board for Archaeological Work
      State Archive and Historical Department
   2. State Geologist, University of Wyoming, Laramie
      Director, State Archive and Historical Department, Cheyenne
   3. Wyoming Archaeological Society
      c/o Richard Eklund, President
      Box 1787, Casper

B. Control
   Legislation is being contemplated by Wyoming State Historical Society, Wyoming Archaeological Society and State Archives and Historical Department

C. Sites
   1. Early Period
      Middle Period

Late Period: Mandan, Hidatsa, Crow, Arikara,
Cheyenne
2. Finley Site, Early
Teepee Creek, Late
Birdshead Cave, Owl Creek Mts., All

D. Excavations
Birdshead Cave Site

E. Museums
Wyoming State Museum
State Office Building
Cheyenne

F. Academic Institutions

G. Bibliography
BLISS, WESLEY
"Birdshead Cave, A Stratified Site in Wind River
Basin, Wyoming." *American Antiquity,* Vol. 15, No.
3, pp. 187–196, Menasha. 1950.

COE, MICHAEL D.
"The Edgar Site, Northwestern Wyoming." *American Antiquity,* Vol. 24, pp. 431–433, Salt Lake City.
1959.

DAVIS, E. MOTT
*Archaeological Survey of the Big Sandy Reservoir
Area, Southwestern Wyoming.* Lincoln. 1956.

HOWARD, EDGAR B.
"The Finley Site: Discovery of Yuma Points in Situ
near Eden, Wyoming." *American Antiquity,* Vol. 8,
No. 3, pp. 224–234, Menasha. 1943.

HOWELLS, WILLIAM W.
"Crania from Wyoming Resembling 'Minnesota
Man'." *American Antiquity,* Vol. 3, No. 4, pp. 318–
326, Menasha. 1938.

SATTERTHWAITE, LINTON
*Stone Artifacts At and Near the Finley Site, Near
Eden, Wyoming.* Philadelphia. 1957.

ARCHAEOLOGICAL
ACTIVITY IN
CANADA

In view of the extent of archaeological and anthropological activities being carried on in the various provinces of Canada, it was felt that a brief summary of organizations, museums, academic institutions and bibliographical sources should be included for the benefit of both Canadian and United States readers. As a consequence, the following information is presented as an introduction to that work. Obviously, it is again impossible to include all the data which might be assembled. This is particularly true in the case of the bibliographies. However, selected articles and larger works, along with sources for further investigation, have been included as a sample of the types of work and specific interests over the course of a considerable span of years in Canada. In individual provinces, local societies and local governmental offices can also supply additional information and re-sources.

Archaeological and related organizations, museums, and academic institutions have been grouped together for purposes of convenience. Bibliographical data have been selected and organized by provinces, with a general bibliography following.

ORGANIZATIONS

Custody of national monuments is intrusted to the National Parks Service of the Department of Northern Affairs and National Resources, formerly the Department of Resources and Development (to 1950), under the Minister of Northern Affairs and National Resources, Ottawa. Of major importance, in this respect, is the work of the National Museum of Canada, along with the provincial and other museums of Canada.

Local historical archives are the responsibility of the Provincial Archivists (Department of Education).

Antiquities, prior to January 1, 1847 in origin, may be imported into Canada without customs duty, when for deposit in certain educational institutions, under such regulations as may be prescribed by the Ministry.

GENERAL ORGANIZATIONS

Canadian Historical Association
N. Fee, Secretary
Public Archives of Canada
Ottawa

Canadian Research Council for Anthropology
University of Ottawa
Ottawa

Canadian Social Science Research Council
166 Marlborough Avenue
Ottawa

LOCAL ORGANIZATIONS (See also: MUSEUMS)

ALBERTA

Historical Society of Alberta
Mr. W. E. Edmonds, Secretary
11146 91st Avenue
Edmonton, Alberta

BRITISH COLUMBIA

British Columbia Historical Association
Miss Helen Boutilier, Secretary
976 West 13th Avenue
Vancouver, British Columbia

Art, Historical and Scientific Association
Mr. T. P. O. Menzies, City Museum
Vancouver, British Columbia

MANITOBA

Historical and Scientific Society of Manitoba
J. A. Jackson, Secretary, Provincial Library
Winnipeg, Manitoba

NOVA SCOTIA

Nova Scotia Historical Society
Dr. W. L. Payzant, K.C.
92 Granville Street
Halifax, Nova Scotia

Cape Sable Historical Society
Mrs. Sarah H. Richan, Secretary
Barrington Passage
Barrington, Nova Scotia

Queens City Historical Society
Miss Anne Hendry, Secretary
Main Street
Liverpool, Nova Scotia

ONTARIO

Ontario Archaeological Society
Miss Lyn Soucy, Secretary
71 Boulton Drive
Toronto 5, Ontario

Ontario Historical Society
Dr. J. J. Talman, Secretary
Library, University of Western Ontario
London, Ontario

Kent Historical Society
Chatham, Ontario

Kingston Historical Society
Kingston, Ontario

Victoria County Historical Society
Lindsay, Ontario

Niagara Historical Society
Castlereagh Street
Ontario, Ontario

Oakville Historical Society
Oakville, Ontario

Historical Society of the City and County of Peterborough
Peterborough, Ontario

Thunder Bay Historical Society
Port William, Ontario

QUEBEC

Archaeological Association of Quebec
Miss Elizabeth Weldon, Secretary
4216 Western Avenue, Apt 6
Westmount, Quebec

SASKATCHEWAN

Saskatchewan Historical Society
608 McCallum Hill Building
Regina, Saskatchewan

MUSEUMS

Luxton Museum, Banff, Alberta

Glenbow Foundation Museum, Calgary, Alberta

Drumheller and District Museum, Drumheller, Alberta

Historical Museum of Medicine Hat, Medicine Hat, Alberta

Western Canadian Pioneer Museum, Wetaskiwin, Alberta

Museum of Geology, Palaeontology and Archaeology, University of Alberta, Edmonton, Alberta

Alert Bay Public Library and Museum, Alert Bay, British Columbia

Ashcroft Museum, Ashcroft, British Columbia

Campbell River and District Museum, Campbell River, British Columbia

Chilliwack and District Museum, Chilliwack, British Columbia

South Cariboo Historical Museum, Clinton, British Columbia

Langley Centennial Museum, Fort Langley, British Columbia

Skeena Treasure House, Hazelton, British Columbia

Kamloops Museum Association Museum, Kamloops, British Columbia

Okanagan Museum and Archives Association Museum, Kelowna, British Columbia

Museum of Northern British Columbia, Prince Rupert, British Columbia

Saanich Pioneer Society Museum, Saanichton, British Columbia

City Archives, History Museum, Vancouver, British Columbia

Lipsett Museum, Vancouver, British Columbia

Pacific National Exhibition, Vancouver, British Columbia

Vancouver City Museum, Vancouver, British Columbia

Vernon Board of Museum and Archives, Vernon, British Columbia

Provincial Museum of Natural History and Anthropology, Victoria, British Columbia

Thunderbird Park Museum, Victoria, British Columbia

Provincial Museum of Natural History and Anthropology, Victoria, British Columbia

City Museum, Vancouver, British Columbia

Museum of Anthropology, University of British Columbia, Vancouver, British Columbia

The Hudson's Bay Company's Museum, Winnipeg, Manitoba

The New Brunswick Museum, St. John, New Brunswick

Miramichi Natural History Museum, Chatham, New Brunswick

York-Sunbury Historical Society Museum, Fredericton, New Brunswick

Dalhousie University Museum, Halifax, Nova Scotia

Queens County Historical Society Museum, Liverpool, Nova Scotia

Newfoundland Museum, St. John's, Newfoundland

Fort Malden National Historic Park Museum, Amhersburg, Ontario

Simcoe County Museum, Barrie, Ontario

Fairfield Village Museum, Brantford, Ontario

The Norwich Pioneers Society Museum, Burgessville, Ontario

Haldimand County Historical Society Museum, Cayuga, Ontario

Chatham-Kent Museum, Chatham, Ontario

Dundas Historical Society Museum, Dundas, Ontario

Quetico Provincial Park Museum, Fort Frances, Ontario

Jordan Historical Museum of The Twenty, Jordan, Ontario

Waterloo Historical Society Museum, Kitchener, Ontario

Assiginack Museum, Manitowaning, Manitoulin Island, Ontario

Sainte Marie Museum, Midland, Ontario

Lennox and Addington County Museum, Napanee, Ontario

McLaughlin Public Library, Oshawa, Ontario

Champlain Trail Museum, Pembroke, Ontario

Bruce County Historical Museum, Southampton, Ontario

Algonquin Provincial Park Museum, Whitney, Ontario

The National Museum of Canada, Ottawa, Ontario

Royal Ontario Museum, University of Toronto, Toronto, Ontario

Museum of Indian Archaeology, University of Western Ontario, London, Ontario

Abbey Dawn Museum, Kingston, Ontario

Huronia House, Midland, Ontario

Bruce County Historical Museum, Southampton, Ontario

Geological, Mineralogical and Ethnological Museum, Queen's University, Kingston, Ontario

Public Library and Art Museum, London, Ontario

McCord Museum, McGill University, Montreal, Quebec

Musée Saguenéen, Chicoutimi, Quebec

Chauvin House, Tadoussac, Quebec

University of Saskatchewan Museum, Saskatoon, Saskatchewan

Prince Albert Historical Museum, Prince Albert, Saskatchewan

Provincial Museum of Natural History, Regina, Saskatchewan

W. D. MacBride Museum, Whitehorse, Yukon

ACADEMIC INSTITUTIONS

Offering first degree, honors, M.A., or doctoral programs in Archaeology, Anthropology, or Sociology.

University of Alberta
Edmonton, Alberta

University of British Columbia
Vancouver, British Columbia

University of Manitoba
Winnipeg, Manitoba

University of New Brunswick
Fredericton, New Brunswick

Dalhousie University
Halifax, Nova Scotia

Acadia University
Wolfville, Nova Scotia

University of Ottawa
Ottawa, Ontario

University of Toronto
Toronto, Ontario

Careleton University
Ottawa, Ontario

McMaster University
Hamilton, Ontario

University of Montreal
Montreal, Quebec

Laval University
Quebec, Quebec

McGill University
Montreal, Quebec

University of Saskatchewan
Saskatoon, Saskatchewan

SELECTED PROVINCIAL BIBLIOGRAPHY

ALBERTA

Ewers, John C.
  The Blackfeet . . . Norman. University of Oklahoma
  Press. 1958.

Jenness, Diamond
  "The Sarcee Indians of Alberta." National Museum of
  Canada, *Bulletin* # 90, *Anthropological Series* # 23,
  Ottawa. 1939.

Kehoe, Thomas F.
  "Stone Tipi Rings . . ." Smithsonian Institution, Bureau
  of American Ethnology, *Bulletin* 173, # 62, Washington, D.C. 1960.

BRITISH COLUMBIA

Borden, Charles E.
"DjRi3, An Early Site in the Fraser Canyon, B.C.".
National Museum of Canada, *Bulletin* # 112, pp. 101–118, Ottawa. 1960.

Borden, Charles E.
"Preliminary Report on Archaeological Investigations in the Fraser Delta Region." *Anthropology in British Columbia,* No. 1, pp. 13–27, Victoria. 1950.

Borden, Charles E.
"Results of Archaeological Investigations in Central British Columbia." *Anthropology in British Columbia,* No. 3, pp. 31–41, Victoria. 1952.

Caldwell, W. W.
"An Archaeological Survey of the Okanagan and Similkameen Valleys of British Columbia." *Anthropology in British Columbia,* No. 4, pp. 10–25, Victoria. 1954.

Duff, Wilson
"Prehistoric Stone Sculpture of the Fraser River and Gulf of Georgia." *Anthropology in British Columbia,* No. 5, pp. 15–151, Victoria. 1956.

Duff, Wilson and Charles E. Borden
"A Scollsbluff-Eden Point From British Columbia." *Anthropology in British Columbia,* No. 4, pp. 33–34, Victoria. 1954.

Hill-Tout, Charles
"Later Prehistoric Man in British Columbia." *Transactions,* Royal Society of Canada, Sec. Series 1895–1896, Vols. I, II, pp. 103–122.

Hill-Tout, Charles
"Notes of the Prehistoric Races of British Columbia and Their Monuments." *The British Columbia University Record,* Christmas, 1899, Victoria & Vancouver.

Smith, Harlan I.
"Archaeology of Lytton, British Columbia." *Memoirs of the American Museum of Natural History,* Pt. III, II, New York. 1899.

SMITH, HARLAN I.
"Archaeology of the Thompson River Region, British Columbia." *Memoirs of the American Museum of Natural History,* Pt. VI, II, New York. 1900.

SMITH, HARLAN I.
"Archaeology of the Gulf of Georgia and Puget Sound." *Memoirs of the American Museum of Natural History,* Pt. VI, IV, New York. 1907.

SMITH, HARLAN I.
"Kitchen-Middens of The Pacific Coast of Canada." National Museum of Canada, *Bulletin* # 56. Ottawa. 1929.

"The Archaeological Collection from the Southern Interior of British Columbia." Canada, Department of Mines, *Geological Survey,* Ottawa. 1913.

British Columbia Historical Quarterly, Provincial Archives, Victoria.

MANITOBA

GIDDINGS, J. L., JR.
"A Flint Site in Northernmost Manitoba." *American Antiquity,* 21, pp. 255–268, Salt Lake City. 1956.

LEE, T. E.
"The Stott Mound and Village, Near Brandon, Manitoba." National Museum of Canada, *Annual Report . . . 1952–1953,* Ottawa. 1954.

MACNEISH, R.
"An Introduction to the Archaeology of Southeast Manitoba." National Museum of Canada, *Bulletin* # 157, *Anthropological Series* # 44, Ottawa. 1958.

NEW BRUNSWICK

WALLIS, WILSON D. and R. S. WILSON
"Malecite Indians of New Brunswick." National Museum of Canada, *Bulletin* # 148, *Anthropological Series* # 40, Ottawa. 1957.

See also:

Publications of the New Brunswick Museum, Monograph Series. St. John, New Brunswick.

NORTHWEST TERRITORIES

COLLINS, H. B.

"Excavations at Frobisher Bay, Baffin Island, Northwest Territories (Preliminary Report)." National Museum of Canada, *Annual Report . . . 1948–1949, Bulletin* # 118, pp. 18–43, Ottawa. 1950.

KING, ARDEN R.

"Cattle Point: A Stratified Site in The Southern Northwest Coast Region." *Memoir No. 7,* Society for American Archaeology, Menasha. 1950.

MACDONALD, S. D.

"Report on Investigations at Mould Bay, Prince Patrick Island, Northwest Territories," National Museum of Canada, *Annual Report . . . 1952–1953,* Ottawa. 1954.

MACNEISH, R. S.

"An Archaeological Reconnaissance in the Northwest Territories." National Museum of Canada, *Bulletin* # 123, Ottawa. 1951.

MACNEISH, R. S.

"Archaeological Reconnaissance in the Mackenzie River Drainage." National Museum of Canada, *Annual Report . . . 1951–1952, Bulletin* # 128, Ottawa. 1953.

MACNEISH, R. S.

"The Pointed Mountain Site Near Ft. Liard, Northwest Territories, Canada." *American Antiquity,* 19, pp. 234–253. Salt Lake City. 1954.

MANNING, T. H.

"A Mixed Cape Dorset-Thule Site on Smith Island, East Hudson Bay." National Museum of Canada, *Annual Report . . . 1949–1950, Bulletin* # 123, pp. 64–71, Ottawa. 1951.

MAXWELL, M. S.

"An Archaeological Analysis of Eastern Grant Land, Ellesmere Island, Northwest Territories." National

Museum of Canada, *Bulletin* # 170, *Anthropological Series* # 49, Ottawa. 1960.

O'BRYAN, DERIC
"Excavation of a Cape Dorset House Site, Mill Island, West Hudson Strait." National Museum of Canada, *Annual Report . . . 1951–1952, Bulletin* # 128, pp. 40–57, Ottawa. 1953.

NOVA SCOTIA

SMITH, H. I. and W. J. WINTEMBERG
"Some Shell Heaps in Nova Scotia." National Museum of Canada, *Bulletin* # 47, *Anthropological Series* # 9, Ottawa. 1929.

See also:
Proceeding and Transactions of the Nova Scotia Institute of Science.

ONTARIO

EMERSON, J. N.
"Preliminary Report on the Excavations of the Kant Site, Renfrew County, Ontario." National Museum of Canada, *Annual Report . . . 1947–1948,* Ottawa. 1949.

EMERSON, J. N. and R. E. POPHAM
"Comments on 'The Huron and Lalonde Occupations of Ontario'." *American Antiquity,* 18, pp. 162–164, Salt Lake City. October 1952.

GREENMAN, E. F.
"An Early Industry on a Raised Beach Near Killarney, Ontario." *American Antiquity,* Salt Lake City. 1943.

GREENMAN, E. F. and G. M. STANLEY
"The Archaeology and Geology of Two Early Sites Near Killarney, Ontario." *Papers of the Michigan Academy of Science, Arts and Letters,* Vol. 28, pp. 505–531, Ann Arbor. 1943.

HUNTER, A. F.
"Sites of Huron Villages in the Township of Medonte." *Appendix To The Report of The Minister of Education,* Ontario. 1902.

JURY, WILFRED
"The Alway Prehistoric Site . . ." Museum of Indian
Archaeology, *Bulletin of the Museums, University of
Western Ontario*, No. 1, London. 1937.

JURY, WILFRED
"Fairfield on the Thames." Museum of Indian Archae-
ology, *Bulletin of the Museums, University of Western
Ontario*, No. 5, London. 1945.

JURY, WILFRED and ELSIE JURY
"The Burley Site." Museum of Indian Archaeology,
*Bulletin of the Museums, University of Western On-
tario*, No. 9, pp. 57–75, London. 1952.

JURY, WILFRED
"Saint Louis . . ." Museum of Indian Archaeology,
*Bulletin of the Museums, University of Western On-
tario*, No. 10, pp. 1–76, London. 1955.

KENYON, WALTER
The Inverhuron Site, Bruce Co., Ontario, 1957. Toronto. 1959.

KIDD, K. E.
The Excavation of Ste. Marie I. Toronto. 1949.

LAIDLAW, GEORGE E.
"North Victoria County, New Sites. "*Archaeological
Report, 1899* (Minister of Education), Toronto. 1900.

LAIDLAW, GEORGE E.
"List of Village Sites in Victoria County." *Archaeological Report* (Minister of Education), Ontario. 1912.

LEE, T. E.
"A Preliminary Report on an Archaeological Survey of
Southwestern Ontario for 1950." National Museum of
Canada, *Annual Report . . . 1950–1951, Bulletin* # 126,
pp. 64–75, Ottawa. 1952.

LEE, T. E.
"A Preliminary Report on the Sheguiandah Site, Mani-
toulin Island." National Museum of Canada, *Annual
Report . . . 1951–1952, Bulletin* # 128, pp. 58–67,
Ottawa. 1953.

LEE, T. E.
"The Giant Site, Manitoulin Island, 1951." National Museum of Canada, *Annual Report . . . 1952–1953, Bulletin* # 132, pp. 66–71, Ottawa. 1954.

LEE, T. E.
"The First Sheguiandah Expedition, Manitoulin Island, Ontario." *American Antiquity,* 20, pp. 101–111, Salt Lake City. 1954.

LEE, T. E.
"The Second Sheguiandah Expedition, Manitoulin, Ontario." American Antiquity, 21, pp. 63–71, Salt Lake City, 1955.

LEE, T. E.
"Position and Meaning of a Radiocarbon Sample from the Sheguiandah Site, Ontario." *American Antiquity,* 22, p. 79, Salt Lake City. 1956.

LEECHMAN, D. and F. DE LAGUNA
"An Archaeological Survey of the North Bank of the St. Lawrence . . . Ontario." National Museum of Canada, *Annual Report . . . 1947–1948,* Ottawa. 1949.

MACNEISH, R. S.
"A Possible Early Site in the Thunder Bay District, Ontario." National Museum of Canada, *Bulletin* # 125, Ottawa. 1952.

POPHAM, ROBERT E.
"Late Huron Occupations of Ontario: An Archaeological Survey of Innisfil Township." *Ontario History,* 42, pp. 81–90, Toronto. 1950.

RIDLEY, FRANK
"The Huron and Lalonde Occupations of Ontario." *American Antiquity,* 17, pp. 197–210, Salt Lake City. 1952.

RIDLEY, FRANK
"The Fallis Site, Ontario." *American Antiquity,* 18, pp. 7–14, Salt Lake City. 1952.

WINTEMBERG, W. J.
"Artifacts from Ancient Graves and Mounds in Ontario." *Transactions, Royal Society, Canada,* 3rd series, Vol. XXII, Ottawa. 1928.

WINTEMBERG, W. J.
"Uren Prehistoric Village Site, Oxford County, Ontario." National Museum of Canada, *Bulletin* # 51, *Anthropological Series* # 10, Ottawa. 1928.

WINTEMBERG, W. J.
"Roebuck Prehistoric Village, Grenville County, Ontario." National Museum of Canada, *Bulletin No.* 83, *Anthropological Series* # 19, Ottawa. 1937.

WINTEMBERG, W. J.
"Lawson Prehistoric Village Site, Middlesex County, Ontario." National Museum of Canada, *Bulletin* # 94, *Anthropological Series* # 25, Ottawa. 1939.

See also:
University Bulletin, Museum of Indian Archaeology, University of Western Ontario, London.
Annual, Royal Ontario Museum, Division of Art and Archaeology, Toronto.

QUEBEC

RODGERS, EDWARD S. and MURREY, H.
"Archaeological Investigations in the Region About Lakes Mistassini and Albanel, Province of Quebec, 1948." *American Antiquity,* 15, pp. 322–337, Salt Lake City. 1950.

RODGERS, EDWARD and ROGER A. BRADLEY
"An Archaeological Reconnaissance in South-Central Quebec, 1950." *American Antiquity,* 19, pp. 138–144, Salt Lake City. 1953.

SASKATCHEWAN

HARP, ELMER, JR.
"The Moffatt Archaeological Collection from the Dubawnt Country, Canada." *American Antiquity,* 24, pp. 412–422, Salt Lake City. 1959.

HARP, ELMER, JR.
"Prehistoric Man in Manitoba and Saskatchewan." *American Anthropologist,* n.s., 10, pp. 33–40, Lancaster. 1908.

GENERAL BIBLIOGRAPHY

GENERAL BIBLIOGRAPHY

The material in the following entries was selected from a number of sources. The major ones include the bibliography already noted in *Archaeology of Eastern United States,* edited by James B. Griffin, the wonderfully annotated *Abstracts of Technical Studies In Art And Archaeology* (1943–1952), compiled by Rutherford J. Gettens and Bertha M. Usilton for the Freer Gallery of Art, and numerous scientific books and periodicals available to the author. Again, no attempt has been made to collect more than a sample of the material, and each category is intended to serve as a guide to the types of bibliographical sources one may consult, as well as to furnish a few basic references in each case.

American Archaeology: General

AGOGINO, GEORGE A. and SALLY SACHS
   "The Failure of State and Federal Legislation to Protect Archaeological Resources." *Tebiwa, The Journal of the*

Idaho State College Museum, Vol. 3, Nos. 1 and 2, pp. 43–46, Pocatello. 1960.

BENNETT, JOHN W.
"Recent Developments in the Functional Interpretation of Archaeological Data." *American Antiquity,* Vol. 9, No. 2, pp. 208–219, Menasha. 1943.

BENNETT, WENDELL C.
"Area Archeology." *American Anthropologist,* Vol. 55, No. 1, pp. 5–16, Menasha. 1953.

BLACK, GLENN A., and PAUL WEER
"A Proposed Terminology for Shape Classification of Artifacts." *American Antiquity,* Vol. 1, No. 4, pp. 280–294, Menasha. 1936.

BRINTON, DANIEL G.
The American Race. Philadelphia. 1901.

BYERS, DOUGLAS S.
"The Eastern Archaic: Some Problems and Hypotheses." *American Antiquity,* Vol. 24, pp. 233–256, Salt Lake City. 1958.

CALDWELL, JOSEPH R.
Trend and Tradition in the Prehistory of the Eastern United States. Memoir No. 88, American Anthropological Association, Springfield. 1958.

COLTON, HAROLD S.
Potsherds. An Introduction to the Study of Prehistoric Southwestern Ceramics and their Use in Historic Reconstruction. Flagstaff. 1952.
Pottery Types of the Southwest. Flagstaff. 1955.
Check List of Southwestern Pottery Types. Flagstaff. 1955.

DIXON, ROLAND B.
The Racial History of Man. New York. 1923.
The Building of Cultures. New York. 1928.

DOCKSTADER, FREDERICK J.
The American Indian in Graduate Studies. A Bibliography of Theses and Dissertations. Contributions from the Museum of the American Indian, Heye Foundation, Vol. 15, New York. 1957.

DRIVER, HAROLD E. and W. C. MASSEY
Comparative Study of North American Indians. Transac-

tions of the American Philosophical Society, Vol. 47, Philadelphia. 1957.

FENEGA, FRANKLIN (ed.)
The Plains Anthropologist, Number 2. Lincoln. 1954.

FENNEMAN, NEVIN M.
Physiography of the Eastern United States. New York. 1938.

FENTON, WM. N. and J. GULICK (ed.)
Symposium on Cherokee and Iroquois Culture, Bureau of American Ethnology, Bulletin 180, Washington. 1961.

FORD, JAMES and GORDON R. WILLEY
"An Interpretation of the Prehistory of the Eastern United States." *American Anthropologist,* Vol. 43, No. 3, pp. 325–363, Menasha. 1941.

GRIFFIN, JAMES B. (ed.)
Prehistoric Pottery of the Eastern United States. Ann Arbor. 1950–1954.

"The Pursuit of Archeology in the United States," *American Anthropologist,* Vol. 61, No. 3, pp. 379–389, Menasha. 1959.

HADDON, A. C.
The Races of Man and Their Distribution. New York. 1925.

HARRINGTON, J. C.
"Archeology as an Auxiliary Science to American History." *American Anthropologist,* Vol. 57, No. 6, pp. 1121–1130, Menasha. 1955.

HICKERSON, HAROLD
The Southwestern Chippewa. Memoir No. 92, American Anthropological Association, Menasha. 1962.

HODGE, FREDERICK W., editor
Handbook of American Indians North of Mexico. Bureau of American Ethnology, Bulletin 30, Pts. 1 and 2, Washington. 1907–10.

HOLMES, WILLIAM H.
"Areas of American Culture Characterization Tentatively Outlined as an Aid in the Study of Antiquities." *American Anthropologist,* Vol. 16, No. 3, pp. 413–446, Lancaster. 1914.

Handbook of Aboriginal American Antiquities. Part I: *Introductory: The Lithic Industries.* Bureau of American Ethnology, Bulletin 60, Washington. 1919.

HRDLIČKA, ALES

"Catalogue of Human Crania in the United States National Museum Collections: The Algonkin and Related Iroquois; Siouan, Caddoan, Salish and Sahaptin, Shoshonean and California Indians." *Proceedings of the U.S. National Museum,* Vol. 69, Art. 5, Washington. 1927.

"Anthropological Survey in Alaska." *Forty-sixth Annual Report, Bureau of American Ethnology, 1928–1929,* pp. 19–374, Washington. 1930.

"Anthropology of the Sioux." *American Journal of Physical Anthropology,* Vol. 16, No. 2, pp. 123–166, Philadelphia. 1931.

"Catalogue of Human Crania in the United States National Museum Collections: Pueblos, Southern Utah Basket-Makers, Navaho." *Proceedings of the U.S. National Museum,* Vol. 78, Washington. 1931.

"Early Man in America: What Have the Bones To Say?" In *Early Man* (George G. MacCurdy, ed.), pp. 93–104, Philadelphia. 1937.

"Catalogue of Human Crania in the United States National Museum: Indians of the Gulf States." *Proceedings of the U.S. National Museum,* Vol. 87, pp. 315–464, Washington. 1940.

HURT, WESLEY R., JR.

"The Comparative Study of the Preceramic Occupation of North America." *American Antiquity,* Vol. 18, pp. 204–222, Salt Lake City. 1952.

The Inter-Agency Archaeological Salvage Program After Twelve Years, The Committee for the Recovery of Archaeological Remains, University of Missouri, Columbia. 1958.

JENNINGS, JESSE and E. NORBECK

"Great Basin Prehistory: A Review." *American Antiquity,* Vol. 21, pp. 1–11, Salt Lake City. 1955.

JOHNSON, FREDERICK, editor

Man in Northeastern North America. Papers of the Robert

S. Peabody Foundation for Archaeology, Vol. 3, Andover. 1946.

JUDD, NEIL M.

"The Present Status of Archaeology in the United States." *American Anthropologist,* Vol. 31, No. 3, pp. 401–418, Menasha. 1929.

KIDDER, ALFRED V.

An Introduction to the Study of Southwestern Archaeology. New Haven. 1924.

The Artifacts of Pecos. New Haven. 1932.

KNOBLOCK, BYRON W.

Bannerstones of the North American Indian. La Grange. 1939.

KRIEGER, ALEX D.

"A Comment on 'Fluted Point Relationships' by John Witthoft." *American Antiquity,* Vol. 19, pp. 273–275, Salt Lake City. 1953.

MACWHITE, EÓIN

"On the Interpretation of Archeological Evidence in Historical and Sociological Terms." *American Anthropologist,* Vol. 58, No. 1, Menasha. 1956.

MASON, RONALD J.

"Fluted Point Measurements." *American Antiquity,* Vol. 23, pp. 311–312, Salt Lake City. 1958.

MCGREGOR, JOHN C.

The Pool and Irving Villages, A Study of Hopewellian Occupation in the Illinois River Valley. Urbana. 1958.

MINER, HORACE M.

"The Importance of Textiles in the Archaeology of the Eastern United States," *American Antiquity,* Vol. 1, No. 3, Menasha. 1936.

"Guide Leaflet for Amateur Archaeologists." *Reprint and Circular Series,* Number 93, Washington. 1930.

"The Role of the Amateur in Archaeology." *Museum News,* W. H. Over Museum, State University of South Dakota, Vol. 22, Nos. 11 and 12, Vermillion. 1961.

ROBERTS, FRANK H. H., JR.

"The Folsom Problem in American Archeology." *Annual*

Report of the Board of Regents of the Smithsonian Institution for 1938, pp. 531–546, Washington. 1939.

"Developments in the Problem of the North American Paleo-Indian." In *Essays in Historical Anthropology of North America,* Smithsonian Miscellaneous Collections, Vol. 100, pp. 51–116, Washington. 1940.

SHEPARD, ANNA O.

Ceramics for the Archaeologist. Washington, D.C. 1956.

STAUFFER, ALVIN P., and CHARLES W. PORTER

"The National Park Service Program of Conservation for Areas and Structures of National Historical Significance." *Mississippi Valley Historical Review,* Vol. 30, No. 1, pp. 25–48. 1941.

PHILLIPS, PHILIP and G. R. WILLEY

"Method and Theory in American Archeology: An Operational Basis for Culture-Historical Integration." *American Anthropologist,* Vol. 55, No. 5, pp. 615–633, Menasha. 1953.

STRONG, WILLIAM DUNCAN

"The Value of Archeology in the Training of Professional Anthropologists." *American Anthropologist,* Vol. 54, No. 3, pp. 318–322, Menasha. 1952.

SWANTON, JOHN R.

Indian Tribes of the Lower Mississippi Valley and Adjacent Coast of the Gulf of Mexico. Bureau of American Ethnology, Bulletin 43, Washington. 1911.

Early History of the Creek Indians and Their Neighbors. Bureau of American Ethnology, Bulletin 73, Washington. 1922.

"Social Organization and Social Usages of the Indians of the Creek Confederacy." *Forty-second Annual Report, Bureau of American Ethnology, 1924–1925,* pp. 23–472, Washington. 1928.

"Religious Beliefs and Medical Practices of the Creek Indians." *Forty-second Annual Report, Bureau of American Ethnology, 1924–1925,* pp. 473–672, Washington. 1928.

"Aboriginal Culture of the Southeast." *Forty-second Annual Report, Bureau of American Ethnology, 1924–1925,* pp. 673–726, Washington. 1928.

"Social and Religious Beliefs and Usages of the Chickasaw Indians." *Forty-fourth Annual Report, Bureau of American Ethnology, 1926–1927,* pp. 169–273, Washington. 1928.

"Some Neglected Data Bearing on Cheyenne, Chippewa, and Dakota History." *American Anthropologist,* Vol. 32, No. 1, pp. 156–160, Menasha. 1930.

"Notes on the Cultural Provinces of the Southeast." *American Anthropologist,* Vol. 37, No. 3, pp. 373–385, Menasha. 1935.

Source Material on the History and Ethnology of the Caddo Indians. Bureau of American Ethnology, Bulletin 132, Washington. 1942.

The Indians of the Southeastern United States. Bureau of American Ethnology, Bulletin 137, Washington. 1946.

Tax, Sol (ed.)

Indian Tribes of Aboriginal America: Selected Papers of the XXIXth International Congress of Americanists. Chicago. 1952.

Townsend, Earl C., Jr.

Birdstones of The North American Indian. Indianapolis. 1959.

Voegelin, Carl F., and Erminie W. Voegelin

"Linguistic Considerations of Northeastern North America." In *Man in Northeastern North America* (Frederick Johnson, ed.), Papers of the Robert S. Peabody Foundation for Archaeology, Vol. 3, pp. 179–194, Andover. 1946.

Von Bonin, Gerhardt, and G. M. Morant

"Indian Races in the United States. A Survey of Previously Published Cranial Measurements." *Biometrika,* Vol. 30, Pts. 1 and 2, pp. 94–129, London. 1938.

Webb, William S. and R. S. Baby

The Adena People—No. 2. Columbus. 1957.

Wedel, Waldo R.

An Introduction to Pawnee Archeology. Bureau of American Ethnology, Bulletin 112, Washington. 1936.

The Direct-Historical Approach in Pawnee Archeology. Smithsonian Miscellaneous Collections, Vol. 97, No. 7, Washington. 1938.

"Culture Sequence in the Central Great Plains." In

Essays in Historical Anthropology of North America, Smithsonian Miscellaneous Collections, Vol. 100, pp. 291–352, Washington. 1940.

"Culture Chronology in the Central Great Plains." *American Antiquity,* Vol. 12, No. 3, pp. 148–156, Menasha. 1947.

WHEAT, JOE BEN

Mogollon Culture Prior to A.D. 1000. Memoir No. 82, American Anthropological Association, Menasha. 1955.

WHEAT, JOE BEN, *et al.*

"Ceramic Variety, Type Cluster, and Ceramic System in Southwestern Pottery Analysis." *American Antiquity,* Vol. 24, pp. 34–47, Salt Lake City. 1954.

WILLEY, GORDON R. and P. PHILLIPS

"Method and Theory in American Archeology II: Historical-Developmental Interpretation." *American Anthropologist,* Vol. 57, No. 4, Menasha. 1955.

WITTHOFT, JOHN

"Smooth-base Projectile Points from Eastern Pennsylvania." *The Pennsylvania Archaeologist,* Vol. 16, No. 4, pp. 123–130, Milton. 1947.

"A Note on Fluted Point Relationships." *American Antiquity,* Vol. 19, pp. 271–273, Salt Lake City. 1953.

WORMINGTON, HELEN M.

Ancient Man in North America. Denver Museum of Natural History, Popular Series, No. 4, third edition. Denver. 1949.

Analysis

ANDERSON, ROGER Y.

"Pollen Analysis, A Research Tool for the Study of Cave Deposits." *American Antiquity,* Vol. 21, pp. 84–85, Salt Lake City. 1955.

BOYD, W. D. and L. G.

Science, #78 (Paleoserology). 1933.

Journal of Immunology, #33 (Paleoserology). 1937.

American Journal of Physical Anthropology #25 (Paleoserology). 1939.

CALEY, EARLE R.

"Technique for Obtaining Uncontaminated Small Samples

of Ceramic Glazes and Other Hard Siliceous Materials."
Analytical Chemistry, 19, p. 360. 1947.

CANDELA, P. B.
American Journal of Physical Anthropology, Vol. 27
(Paleoserology). 1940.
American Journal of Physical Anthropology, Vol. 24
(Paleoserology). 1939.

COOPER, F. G.
Munsell Manual of Color, Baltimore. 1929.

DAVIDSON, J., and W. D. TAYLOR
"Staining of Mammalian Hair." *Journal of the Quekett
Microscopical Club.* Serv. iv, no. 1. 1943.

DODD, BRITISH
Journal of Experimental Pathology, # 33 (Paleoserology).
1952.

DOLLAR, A. T. J.
"Cellulose Acetate Mounts For Rock and Mineral Fragments," *Nature,* p. 226, London. 1944.

EASTMAN KODAK COMPANY
Infrared and Ultraviolet Photography, 4th ed., Rochester,
New York. 1951.

HARDY, A. C.
Handbook of Colorimetry. Cambridge, Mass. 1936.

HEDDEN, MARK
" 'Surface Printing' As A Means of Recording Petro-
glyphs." *American Antiquity,* Vol. 23, pp. 435–439, Salt
Lake City. 1958.

HIRSFELD, L. and H.
Lancet (Paleoserology). 1919.

INSTITUTE OF ART RESEARCH.
"Studies on Art Objects Through Optical Methods."
Bijutsu Kenkyu, No. 159, pp. 174–190, Tokyo. 1950.

MATSON, G. A.
Journal of Immunology, # 30 (Paleoserology). 1936.

McKERN, T. W. and E. H. MUNRO
"A Statistical Technique for Classifying Human Skeletal
Remains." *American Antiquity,* Vol. 24, pp. 375–382, Salt
Lake City. 1959.

MORGAN, W. T. J. and W. M. WATKINS
British Journal of Experimental Pathology # 29 (Paleoserology). 1939.

MOURANT, A. E.
The Distribution of the Human Blood Groups. Oxford. 1954.

Munsell Book of Color. Abridged Edition, Baltimore. 1929.

PHILLIPS, E. W. J.
Identification of Softwoods by Their Microscopic Structure. London, H.M.S. Off. (Gr. Brit. F.P.R.L. Bulletin No. 22). 1948.

RIGBY, G. R.
The Thin-Section Mineralogy of Ceramic Materials. British Refractories Research Association, London. 1948.

SCHATZER, L.
"Microscopic Methods for Ceramics." *Die Glashutte,* 76, pp. 141–143. 1950.

SMITH, MADELINE.
"Blood Groups of the Ancient Dead." *Science,* Vol. 131, # 3402, March. 1960.
Nature, # 184, p. 867. 1959.

STOVES, J. L.
"The Histology of Mammalian Hair." *The Analyst,* 67, pp. 385–387. 1942.
Chemical Abstracts, 37, p. 1347. 1943.

THIEME, *et al.*
American Journal of Physical Anthropology # 14. 1956.

TOOMBS, H. A. and A. E. RIXON.
"Use of Plastic in The Transfer Method of Preparing Fossils." *Museums Journal,* 50, pp. 105–107. 1950.
Chemical Abstracts, 45, 4975h. 1950.

WEATHERHEAD, A. V.
Petrographic Micro-Technique. . . , London. 1947.

WILDMAN, A. B.
"The Microscopy of Textile Fibers—Aids to Their Identification." *Journal of the Textile Institute,* 38, No. 10, pp. 468–473. 1947.
Chemical Abstracts, 42, 1058. 1948.

WINCHELL, HORACE and MATT S. WALTON
    An Inexpensive Petrographic Microscope. *American Mineralogist,* 34, pp. 688–691. 1949.
WRIGHT, W. D.
    The Measurement of Colour. London. 1944.
WYMAN and BOYD
    American Anthropologist, # 39 (Paleoserology). 1937.

Archaeological Methods

ATKINSON, R. J. C.
    Field Archaeology. London. 1946.
ALBRIGHT, WILLIAM F.
    Archaeology and the Religion of Israel. Baltimore. 1942.
    From the Stone Age to Christianity. Baltimore. 1946.
    The Archaeology of Palestine. Harmondsworth. 1960.
American Anthropologist. American Anthropological Association, Andover, Mass.
American Antiquity. Society for American Archaeology, Ann Arbor.
American Journal of Archaeology. Archaeological Institute of America, New York.
Annals of Archaeology and Anthropology. Liverpool.
Archaeology. Archaeological Institute of America, New York.
BARROIS, GEORGE
    Manuel D'Archéologie Biblique, I–II. Paris. 1939, 1953.
BARTON, G. A.
    Archaeology and The Bible. Philadelphia, 1937.
BERNAL, IGNACIO
    Introduccion a la arqueologia. Panuco, Mexico. 1952.
Biblical Archaeologist. American Schools of Oriental Research, New Haven.
Bulletin of the American Schools of Oriental Research. American Schools of Oriental Research, New Haven.
BURROWS, MILLAR
    What Mean These Stones? American Schools of Oriental Research. New Haven. 1941.

CERAM, C. W.
  The March of Archaeology. New York. 1958.
COLTON, HAROLD S.
  Field Methods in Archaeology. Flagstaff. 1952.
DETWEILER, A. H.
  Manual of Archaeological Surveying. American Schools of
  Oriental Research, New Haven. 1948.
n.a. "Exploring by Electronics: Resistivity Equipment." *Science News Letter* #78, October 1960.
FINEGAN, J.
  Light From the Ancient Past. Princeton. 1959.
GETTENS, RUTHERFORD J. and BERTHA M. USILTON, compilers
  Abstracts of Technical Studies In Art and Archaeology.
  Freer Gallery of Art, Occasional Papers, Vol. Two, Number Two, Washington, D.C. 1955.
GLUECK, NELSON
  The Other Side of the Jordan. American Schools of Oriental Research, New Haven. 1940.
  Rivers In The Desert. New York. 1959.
GRIFFIN, JAMES B., ed.
  Archaeology of Eastern United States, Chicago. 1952.
HEIZER, ROBERT FLEMING, ed.
  A Manual of Archaeological Field Methods, 3rd rev. ed.
  Palo Alto. 1958.
HEIZER, ROBERT F. (ed.)
  The Archaeologist at Work. Berkeley. 1959.
HOURS, MAGDELEINE
  Les Méthodes scientifiques au Service de L'archéologie.
  Comptes rendus de l'academie des inscriptions, et belles lettres. 1952.
Israel Exploration Journal, Jerusalem, Israel.
KENYON, KATHLEEN
  Beginning Archaeology. London. 1952.
  Archaeology in the Holy Land, Benn. 1960.
MILLER, WILLIAM C.
  "Uses of Aerial Photographs in Archaeological Field
  Work." *American Antiquity,* Vol. 23, pp. 46–62, Salt Lake City. 1957.

MOHD, KHAN BAHADUR and SANA ULLAH
"Notes On The Preservation of Antiquities in The Field."
Ancient India, No. 1 (January), pp. 77–82. 1946.
Palestine Exploration Quarterly. London.
n.a., "Preserving the Monuments of Nubia, The U.A.R. Government's Contribution." *The Arab Review,* Vol. 1, # 9, December 1960.
PRITCHARD, JAMES B.
Archaeology and The Old Testament. Princeton. 1958.
Gibeon, Where The Sun Stood Still. Princeton. 1962.
Quarterly of The Department of Antiquities. Jerusalem, Hashemite Kingdom of Jordan.
Revue Biblique. Ecole Biblique, Jerusalem, Hashemite Kingdom of Jordan.
SMITH, WATSON and LOUIE EWING
Kive Mural Decoration. Harvard University Peabody Museum of Archaeology and Ethnology, Papers, Vol. 37, Cambridge. 1952.
STIRLING, MATTHEW W.
"Exploring Ancient Panama by Helicopter." *National Geographic,* Vol. 97.
TOOMBS, H. A., and A. E. RIXON
"Removal of Bones From Other Matrix." *Antiquity,* 24, p. 141. 1950.
n.a., "Underground Camera Aids Scientist . . .". *Popular Photography,* # 42, February. 1958.
n.a., "Weatherproof Digging." *Archaeology,* # 13.
WHEELER, SIR MORTIMER
Archaeology From the Earth. Harmondsworth, England. 1956.
WRIGHT, G. ERNEST
Biblical Archaeology. Philadelphia. 1957.
The Pottery of Palestine. American Schools of Oriental Research, New Haven. 1957.

Care and Handling: General

BIEK, LEO
"Protective Coatings For Silver." *Museums Journal,* 52, pp. 60–61; *Chemical Abstracts,* 46, 9866a. 1952.

ORMSBEE, THOMAS HAMILTON
  Care and Repair of Antiques, New York. 1949.
PLENDERLEITH, HAROLD JAMES
  "Preservation of Museum Specimens." *Thorpe's Diction-
  ary of Applied Chemistry,* 4th ed., Vol. 8, pp. 247–252.
  1947.
  The Conservation of Antiquities And Works of Art. Lon-
  don and New York. 1956.
STOUT, GEORGE L., CHARLES M. RICHARDS and ROBERT S.
SUGDEN
  "Packing and Handling of Art Objects." *Museum News,*
  26, September, pp. 7–8. 1948.
SUGDEN, ROBERT P.
  Care and Handling of Art Objects. The Metropolitan Mu-
  seum of Art, New York. 1946.

Dating

ANDERSON, E. C., J. R. ARNOLD, and W. F. LIBBY
  "Measurement of Low-level Radiocarbon." *Review of Sci-
  entific Instruments With Physics News and Views* 22, pp.
  225–232, Lancaster, Pa. 1951.
ANTEVS, ERNST
  "Geologic-Climatic Dating in the West." *American An-
  tiquity,* Vol. 20, pp. 317–335, Salt Lake City. 1955.
ARNOLD, J. A. and W. F. LIBBY
  "Radiocarbon Dates." *Science,* 133, pp. 111–120. 1951.
BARTLETT, H. H.
  "Radiocarbon Datability of Peat, Marl, Caliche, and Ar-
  chaeological Materials." *Science,* 114, pp. 55–56. 1951.
BELL, ROBERT E.
  "Tree Ring Chronology." *Chicago Naturalist,* Vol. 6, No.
  1, pp. 2–8, Chicago. 1943.
BRIGGS, LYMAN J. and K. F. WEAVER
  "Carbon 14 Dating . . . ." *National Geographic,* Vol. 94,
  August. 1958.
BRINDLEY, G. W.
  *X-ray Identification and Crystal Structures of Clay Min-
  erals.* The Mineralogical Society, London. 1951.

BUSHNELL, G. H. S.

"Prehistoric America: Comments on Some C14 Dates." *Antiquity,* 25, pp. 102–103. 1951.

COLLIER, DONALD

"New Radiocarbon Method For Dating The Past." *Chicago Natural History Museum. Bulletin* 22, pp. 6–7; *Biblical Archaeologist.* 14, pp. 25–28, 1951; *Museums Journal.* 51, pp. 41–43. 1951.

CRANE, H. R.

"Dating of Relics by Radiocarbon Analysis." *Nucleonics,* 9, pp. 16–23. 1951.

CURTIS, GARNESS H.

"A Clock For the Ages: Potassium-Argon." *National Geographic,* Vol. 120, October. 1961.

n.a. "Dating by Thermo-luminescence." *Archaeological News, Archaeology,* Vol. 13. 1960.

DOUGLASS, A. E.

"Notes on the Technique of Tree-Ring Analysis. IV: Practical Instruments." *Tree-Ring Bulletin,* Vol. 10, No. 1, pp. 2–8, Tucson. 1943.

GIDDINGS, J. L., JR.

Dendrochronology in Northern Alaska. University of Arizona Bulletin, Vol. 12, No. 4, Tucson. 1941.

GINDEL, J.

"Aleppo Pine as a Medium for Tree-Ring Analysis." *Tree-Ring Bulletin,* Vol. 11. No. 1, pp. 6–8, Tucson. 1944.

GLADWIN, HAROLD S.

Tree-Ring Analysis. Methods of Correlation. Medallion Papers, No. 28, Globe. 1940.

GLOCK, WALDO S.

Principles and Methods of Tree-Ring Analysis. Carnegie Institution of Washington, Publication No. 486, Washington. 1937.

GODWIN, H.

"Relationship of Bog Stratigraphy to Climatic Change and Archaeology." *Proceedings of the Prehistory Society,* 12, pp. 1–11, London. 1946.

HAWLEY, FLORENCE

Tree-Ring Analysis and Dating in the Mississippi Drain-

age. University of Chicago Publications in Anthropology, Occasional Paper, No. 2, Chicago. 1941.

HERZOG, L. F.

"Age Determination by X-Ray Fluourescence Rubidium-Strontium Ratio Measurement in Lepidolite." *Science,* Vol. 132, June. 1960.

HOROVIC, A.

"Procédé appliqué pour établir l'ancienneté des objets et des localités archéologiques au moyen du carbone radio-actif." *Recueil des Travaux sur la Protection des Monuments Historiques.* 3, pp. 13–24, Belgrad. 1952.

JOHNSON, FREDERICK, assembler

Radiocarbon Dating: A Report on the Program to Aid in the Development of the Method of Dating. Society for American Archeology, Memoir No. 8, Salt Lake City. 1951.

"Radiocarbon Dating." *American Antiquity,* 17, Menasha. 1951.

LIBBY, W. F.

Radiocarbon Dating. Chicago. 1952.

LIBBY, WILLARD F., *et al.*

"Age Determination by Radiocarbon Content: World-wide Assay of Natural Radiocarbon." *Science,* 109, pp. 227–28. 1949.

LOWTHER, A. W. G.

"Dendrochronology." *The Archaeological News Letter,* March, London. 1949.

ROBERTS, FRANK HAROLD HANNA

"The Carbon 14 Method of Age Determination." *Smithsonian Institution. Annual report of the Board of Regents,* pp. 335–50. 1951; *Transactions of the American Geophysical Union,* 33, pp. 170–174. 1952.

SELLERS, O. R.

"Date of Cloth From The 'Ain Fashka Cave." *Biblical Archaeologist,* 14, February, p. 29. 1951.

SCHULMAN, EDMUND

"Dendrochronology in Pines of Arkansas." *Ecology,* Vol. 23, No. 3, pp. 309–318, Lancaster, Pa. 1942.

"Dendrochronology in Mexico, I." *Tree-Ring Bulletin,*

Vol. 10, No. 3, pp. 18–24, Tucson. 1944.

"Tree-Ring Work in Scandinavia." *Tree-Ring Bulletin,* Vol. 11, No. 1, pp. 2–6, Tucson. 1944.

n.a. "Soil Phosphorus Measures Organic Waste." *Science News Letter,* # 72, August, 1957.

STEWART, T. D.
"Antiquity of Man in America Demonstrated by The Fluorine Test." *Science,* 113, pp. 391–392. 1951.

STROSS, FRED H.
"Authentication of Antique Stone Objects by Physical and Chemical Methods." *Analytical Chemistry,* 32, No. 3, March. 1960.

ZEUNER, FREDERIC EBERHARD
Dating The Past: An Introduction to Geochronology, 2d ed. rev. and enl., London. 1950.

Dyes and Inks

BARROW, WILLIAM J.
"Black Writing Ink of The (American) Colonial Period." *American Archivist,* 11, pp. 291–307. 1948.

BENDER, MAX
"Colors for Textiles: Ancient and Modern." *Interchemical Review,* 4, pp. 75–87. 1945.

LEECHMAN, JOHN DOUGLAS
Vegetable Dyes From North American Plants. St. Paul and Toronto. 1945.

LEGGETT, W. F.
Ancient and Medieval Dyes. Brooklyn. 1944.

Metals

BLACK, GEORGE and JACK SINNER
"Identification of Plated Coatings." *Metal Finishing,* 41, pp. 529–530. 1947.

BRAIDWOOD, ROBERT J., JOSEPH E. BURKE and NORMAN H. NACHTRIEB
"Ancient Syrian Copper and Bronzes." *Journal of Chemical Education,* 28, pp. 87–96. 1951.

BRIGHT, WILLARD M.
"The Treatment of Iron Antiquities." *Museums Journal,* 46, April, pp. 1–5. 1946.

CALEY, EARLE R.
"Estimation of Composition of Ancient Metal Objects." *Analytical Chemistry,* 24, pp. 676–681. 1952.

COUGHLAN, H. H.
Notes on The Prehistoric Metallurgy of Copper and Bronze in The Old World. London. 1951.

DELBART, G.
"Iron and Steel Metallurgy Through The Ages." *Journal of The Iron and Steel Institute,* 159, p. 350, London. 1948.

ENSKO, STEPHEN G. D.
American Silversmiths and Their Marks. priv. print., Robert Ensko Inc., New York. 1948.

HILL, DOROTHY KENT
"Ancient Metal Reliefs." *Hesperia,* 12, pp. 97–114. 1943.
"More About Ancient Metal Reliefs." *Hesperia,* 13, pp. 87–89. 1944.
"The Technique of Greek Metal Vases and Its Bearing on Base Forms in Metal and Pottery." *American Journal of Archaeology,* 51, pp. 248–256. 1947.

JACK, J. F. S.
"The Cleaning and Preservation of Bronze Statues." *Museums Journal,* 50, pp. 231–236. 1951.

MANTELL, CHARLES L.
Tin: Its Mining, Production, Technology. . . . 2d ed., American Chemical Society, Monograph Series, No. 51, New York. 1949.

MARYON, HERBERT
"Metal Working in The Ancient World." *American Journal of Archaeology,* 53, pp. 93–125. 1949.
"The Sutton Hoo Helmet." *Antiquity,* 21, pp. 137–144. 1947.
"The Sutton Hoo Shield." *Antiquity,* 20, pp. 21–30. 1946.

OLSON, GILLIS, and BENGT THORDEMAN
"Cleaning of Silver Objects." *Museums Journal,* 50, pp. 250–252. 1951.

O'NEILL, H.
"Metal Founding Through The Ages." *Foundry Trade Journal*, 86, pp. 575–581; *Journal of the Iron and Steel Institute*, 163, p. 366, London. 1949.

QUIRING, HEINRICH
Geschichte des Goldes. Stuttgart. 1948.

RICKARD, T. A.
"Homeric Metallurgy." *Transactions of the Canadian Institute of Mining and Metallurgy*, 52, pp. 58–63, 1949; *Journal of the Iron and Steel Institute*, 163, p. 366, London. 1949.

TERNBACH, JOSEPH
"The Archaic Greek Helmet in St. Louis." *Archaeology*, 5, March, pp. 40–46. 1952.
"Restoration of Ancient Bronzes." *Museum News*, March 1, pp. 7–8. 1949.

VOGEL, HERMINE
"The Cleaning of Metal Objects of Antiquity, Museum Pieces, and Bronze Monuments." *Metalloberflache, 1*, pp. 107–111. 1947.

WAINWRIGHT, G. A.
"Egyptian Bronze Making." *Antiquity*, 17, pp. 96–98. 1943.
"Egyptian Bronze Making Again." *Antiquity*, 18, pp. 100–102. 1944.
"Early Tin in The Aegean." *Antiquity*, 18, pp. 57–64. 1944.

WILSHAW, C. T.
"Identification of Metals and Alloys by Chemical Spot Testing." *Metallurgia*, 45, pp. 102–106. 1952.

WITTER, WILHELM
"Metal Investigation (Copper and Bronze) in The Service of Archaeology." *Nova Acta Leopoldina*, 12, pp. 197–214, London. 1943.

Numismatics

BALOG, PAUL
"Aperçus sur la technique du monnayage Musulman au Moyen-âge." *Bull. Inst. Egypt*, 31, pp. 95–105. 1948–49.

Caley, Earle R.
"Methods of Distinguishing Cast From Struck Coins."
Numismatic Review, Vol. 2, No. 4, pp. 21–24. 1945.
"Restauración electrolítica de monedas antiguas de cobre
y bronce," *Cienciae e invest.,* 6, pp. 100–105, Buenos Aires.
1950.

Hudson, Douglas Rennie
"Coinage Metals in Antiquity. Parts I–V: I. Punjab and
Egypt." *Metallurgia,* 30 (October), pp. 313–320. 1944.

Miles, George C.
The Coinage of the Umayyads of Spain. American Nu-
mismatic Series, Monograph No. 1, pp. 96–101, New
York. 1950.

Numismatic Review. New York. The *Numismatist.* American Numismatic Association. Wichita.

Paints and Paintings

Augusti, Selim
La Tecnica dell' Antica Pittura Parietale Pompeiana.
Naples. 1950.

Barker, J.
"Identification of Pigments." *Journal of the Oil and
Colour Chemists' Association,* 25, pp. 240–246, London.
1942.
*Review of Current Literature Relating to the Paint Colour,
Varnish and Allied Industries,* 15, p. 205, London. 1942.

Bliss, Wesley L.
"Preservation of the Kuaua Mural Paintings." *American
Antiquity,* 13, pp. 218–222. 1947–48.

Bontinck, Ed.
"Comment Étudier les Anciennes Techniques de la Pein-
ture Artistique." *Chimie des Peintures,* 8, pp. 75–84. 1945.
Physique et Peintures, Les Editions Lumière, Paris-
Bruxelles. 1944.

Borrelli, Licia
"Primi provvedimenti nella Casa dei Grifi sul Palatino."
Bollettino dell'istituto centrale del restauro, 9–10, p. 49.
1952.

BRADLEY, MORTON C.
The Treatment of Pictures, Cambridge, Mass. 1950.

BRYSON, H. COURTNEY
"The Earliest Known Paints," *Paint, Incorporating Paint Manufacture,* 22, pp. 243–246, 257. 1950. *Abstract Review,* no. 1832, p. 165. 1952.

BUCK, RICHARD D.
"Conservation and Mounting of Drawings." *News Bulletin, The International Council of Museums,* pp. 11–12. 1949.

CARSON, MARIAN SADTLER
"Early American Water Color Paintings," *Antiques,* 59, pp. 54–56. 1951.

COCHE DE LA FERTE, E.
Les Portraits Romano-Egyptiens du Louvre. Musées Nationaux, Paris. 1952.

CONSTABLE, W. G.
"A Discovery and A Warning." *Bulletin of the Museum of Fine Arts,* 41. No. 245, pp. 51–54, Boston. 1943.

COREMANS, PAUL B.
"Depose des Peintures Murales Découvertes en 1940 à Tournai et à Nivelles, *Bulletin des Musées Royaux d'Art et d'Histoire,* No. 6, pp. 125–132. 1941.
"Peintures Murales Anciennes; Procédés Altération, Nettoyage et Transfert." *Bulletin des Musées Royaux d'Art et d'Histoire,* 3e ser., 12th annee, pp. 133–136. 1940.

DURUP, G.
"Standardization of Color Science Terminology." *Peintures, Pigments, Vernis,* 25, pp. 171–177, Paris. 1949.
Review of Current Literature Relating to The Paint, Colour, Varnish and Allied Industries, 22, p. 491. 1949.
Abstract Review, No. 156, p. 90. 1950.

GETTENS, RUTHERFORD, J. and EVAN H. TURNER
"The Materials and Methods of Some Religious Paintings of Early 19th Century New Mexico." *El Palacio,* 58, pp. 3–16. 1951.

KECK, SHELDON
"On The Conservation of Early American Paintings." *Antiques,* 53, pp. 52–54. 1948.

"The Technical Examination of Paintings." *Brooklyn Museum Journal*, pp. 71–82. 1942.

KRONSTEIN, MAX

"Ancient Surface Technology." *American Paint Journal*, 32, No. 8, pp. 39, 42–43, 46, 48, 51–52; No. 10, pp. 16, 18, 22, 24, 26–27. 1947. *Abstract Review*, No. 132, p. 36. 1948.

MARGIVAL, F.

"Colors and Coatings in Antiquity." *Peintures, Pigments, Vernis*, 26, pp. 467–474. 1950. *Abstract Review*, No. 170, p. 140. 1951.

PEASE, MURRAY

"A Treatment For Panel Paintings." *Bulletin of The Metropolitan Museum of Art*, 7, pp. 119–124. 1948.

RAWLINS, FRANCIS IAN GREGORY

"Physics in Paintings." *Reports on Progress in Physics*, 9, pp. 334–348. 1942–43.

Kodak Bulletin. Current Photographic Information, No. 76/81, p. 62. 1943.

Review of Current Literature Relating to The Paint, Colour, Varnish and Allied Industries, 18, p. 245. 1945.

"Scientific Examination of Paintings." *Journal of The Oil and Colour Chemists' Association*, 34, pp. 337–345. 1951.

ROSEN, DAVID

"Notes on The Preservation of Panel Pictures." *Journal of the Walters Art Gallery*, 4, pp. 123–127, Baltimore. 1941.

ROTH, JAMES

"The Separation of Two Layers of Ancient Chinese Wall-painting." *Artibus Asiae*, 15, pp. 145–150. 1952.

SCHENDEL, A. VAN

"The ICOM Commission for the Care of Paintings and the Problems of Cleaning." *Museum*, 4, pp. 63–66, Paris. 1951.

SMITH, WATSON and LOUIE EWING

"The Painted Walls in the Jeddito; Materials and Methods Employed in Their Construction." *Kiva Mural Decoration At Awatovi and Kawaika-a* . . . , pp. 13–32, Papers of the Robert S. Peabody Foundation of Archaeology, Vol. 37, Cambridge, Massachusetts. 1952.

STOPPELAERE, ALEXANDRE

"Introduction à la Peinture Thébaine." *Valeurs,* Nos. 7/8, pp. 3–13. 1947.

"Dégradations et Restaurations des Peintures Murales Egyptiennes," *Annales du Service des Antiquités de l'Egypte,* 40, pp. 941–950. 1942.

WERNER, A. E.

"Scientific Examination of Paintings," *Royal Institute of Chemistry, Lectures, Monographs and Reports,* No. 4, London. 1952.

WULKEN, H. E.

"What Do We Know About The Paints of The Old Egyptians?" *Verfkroniek,* 23, pp. 41–46. 1950.

Photography

BEUTTNER-JANNSCH, JOHN

"Use of Infrared Photography in Archaeological Field Work." *American Antiquity,* Vol. 20, 84–87, Salt Lake City. 1954.

COOKSON, M. B.

Photography for Archaeologists, London. 1954.

Kodak Data Book, Infrared and Ultra-violet Photography. Eastman Kodak Co., Rochester.

LERICI, C. M.

"Periscope on the Etruscan Past." *National Geographic,* Vol. 116. 1959.

Pottery, Glass and Cement

BOUSQUET, J., and P. DEVAMBEZ

"New Method in Restoring Ancient Vases in The Louvre." *Museum,* 3, pp. 177–179, Paris. 1950.

HEDVALL, JOHAN ARVID, ROBERT JAGITSCH and GILLIS OLSON

"The Problem of Restoring Antique Glass, Part II." *Official Technical Service Reports, Rept. PB 105977.* 1951.

HONEY, WILLIAM BOWYER

Glass: A Handbook For The Study of Glass Vessels of All Periods and Countries and A Guide To The Museum Collection (Victoria and Albert). London. 1946.

KELSO, JAMES LEON, and J. PALIN THORLEY
"The Potter's Technique at Tell Beit Mirsim, Particularly in Stratum A." *Annual of the American Schools of Oriental Research,* 21–22, pp. 86–142, New Haven. 1943.

MATSON, FREDERICK R.
"Composition and Working Properties of Ancient Glasses." *Journal of Chemical Education,* 28, pp. 82–87. 1951.

PARKINSON, A. ERIC
"The Preservation of Cuneiform Tablets By Heating To A High Temperature." *Museum News,* 27, pp. 6–8. 1951.

n.a., "Pottery Reconstruction." *Museums Journal,* 45, p. 22, London. 1945.

RIEFSTAHL, ELIZABETH
Glass and Glazes From Ancient Egypt. Institute of Arts and Sciences, The Brooklyn Museum, Brooklyn. 1948.

SHEPARD, ANNA O.
"Technological Observations on Mesa Verde Pottery in O'Bryan, Deric." *Excavations in Mesa Verde National Park,* private printing, pp. 89–91, 93–98, Globe, Arizona. 1947–48.

UNWIN, MAX
"Treatment For The Preservation of Glass." *Museums Journal,* 51, p. 10, London. 1951.

VASTAGH, GÁBOR and ÉVA IVÁN
"The Chemistry of The Ancient Roman Mortars of Lime and Powdered Brick." Magyar Kémiai Folyóirat, 54, pp. 42–45. 1948.

WARD, LAURISTON
"Suggested Outline For Description of Pottery." *Far Eastern Ceramic Bulletin,* No. 3., pp. 17–19. 1948.

Wood, Textiles and Leather

ASTBURY, WILLIAM THOMAS
Textile Fibers Under The X-rays. Imperial Chemical Industries, Ltd., London. 1943.

BELLINGER, LOUISA
"Textile Analysis; Early Techniques in Egypt and The

Near East. Parts I–III." *Workshop Notes, Papers, Textile Museum,* No. 2–3, 6 (June 1950, April 1951, November 1952), Washington, D.C.

GREENE, FRANCINA S.
"Cleaning and Mounting Procedures for Wool Textiles." *Workshop Notes, Papers, Textile Museum,* No. 1 (n.d.), Washington, D.C.

LEASK, HAROLD GRAHAM
"Ancient Objects in Irish Bogs and Farm Lands." *Ulster Journal of Antiquaries,* 6, p. 147. 1943.

LEECHMAN, JOHN DOUGLAS
"Preservation of Fibre Cordage in Ethnological Objects." *Museums Journal,* 44, p. 112, London. 1944.

MARX, ERIC
"Ancient Egyptian Woodworking." *Antiquity,* 20, pp. 127–133. 1946.

MORI NOBORU
"Experiments on the preservation of ancient fabrics." *Scientific Papers on Japanese Antiques and Art Crafts,* No. 3., January, pp. 21–26. 1952.

MOSS, A. A.
"Preservation of a Saxon Bronze-bound Wooden Bucket With Iron Handle." *Museums Journal,* 52, pp. 175–177, London. 1952.

O'NEALE, LILA MORRIS
Textiles of Pre-Columbian Chihuahua. Pub. 574, Carnegie Institution of Washington. Washington. 1948.

n.a. *Standard Methods of Identification of Fibers in Textiles* (A.S.T.M. Designation: D 276–49), pp. 67–85, plates, tables, Philadelphia, 1949.

TEXTILE INSTITUTE
The Identification of Textile Materials, The Institute, (Handbook of Textile Technology, No. 3), Manchester, England. 1949.

TRUDEL, VERENA
"Textilkonservierung." *Zeitschrift für schweizerische Archaeologie und Kunstgeschichte,* 12, pp. 227–230. 1951.

VOGT, EMIL
"The Birch As Source of Raw Material During The Stone

Age." *Proceedings of the Prehistoric Society,* 15, pp. 50–51, London. 1949.

VON BERGEN, WERNER and WALTER KRAUS
Textile Fiber Atlas; A Collection of Photomicrographs of Old and New Textile Fibers. rev. ed., Textile Book Publishers, Inc. New York. 1949.

WRIGHT, E. V. and C. W.
"Prehistoric Boats from North Ferriby, East Yorkshire." *Proceedings of the Prehistoric Society,* 13, pp. 114–138, London. 1947.

Writing Materials and Documents

ARIAS, A. CHARRO
"New Method For Restoring Falsified or Faded Documents." *Farmacia Nueva,* 7, pp. 480–485, Madrid. 1942.

BARROW, WILLIAM J.
Procedures and Equipment Used in The Barrow Method of Restoring Manuscripts and Documents, W. J. Barrow, Richmond. 1952.
"Restoration Methods." *American Archivist,* 6, pp. 151–154. 1943.

BECKWITH, THEODORE D., W. H. SWANSON and THOMAS MARION ILIAMS
"Deterioration of Paper; The Cause and Effect of Foxing." *University of California at Los Angeles, Publications in Biological Science* 1, No. 13, pp. 299–356, pls. 13–20. 1940.

HUNTER, DARD
Papermaking; The History and Technique of An Ancient Craft. London. 1947.

JAFFAR, S. M.
"Protection of Paper." *Museums Journal (Pakistan)* 4 *News Bulletin published by the International Council of Museums,* 5, p. 33. 1952.

PLENDERLEITH, HAROLD JAMES
"Some Aspects of The Preservation of Museum Materials of Organic Origin: Paper, Textiles, Wood." *Nieuwsbulletin van de Koninklijke Nederlandse Oudheidkundige Bond,* pp. 39–42. 1952.

RADLEY, J. A.
"Deciphering of Charred Documents." *The Analyst,* 75, pp. 628–629; *Chemical Abstracts,* 45, 914i (1951). 1950.

Miscellaneous

BURGESS, S. G., and R. J. SCHAFFER
"Cleopatra's Needle." *Chemistry and Industry,* pp. 1026–1029. 1952.

CALEY, EARLE R.
"Archaeological Chemistry." *Chemical and Engineering News,* 27, pp. 2140–2142. 1949.

DYER, AGNES S.
"Oriental Lacquer Work." *Interchemical Review,* 4, pp. 35–46. 1945.

JAKLITSCH, J. J., JR.
"Archaeology—'Briefing the Record'." *Mechanical Engineering,* 71, pp. 678–679. 1949.

LUCAS, ALFRED
Ancient Egyptian Materials and Industries, 3rd ed., Edward Arnold & Co., London. 1948.

n.a. "Masterpieces in Cast Resin." *Pacific Plastics,* 6, p. 41. 1948.

PRICHETT, WILLIAM KENDRICK
"Liquid Rubber For Greek Epigraphy." *American Journal of Archaeology,* 56, pp. 118–120. 1952.
"Further Notes On Liquid Rubber." *American Journal of Archaeology,* 57, pp. 197–198. 1953.

Canadian Archaeology General

BARBEAU, MARIUS
"Totem Poles." National Museum of Canada, *Bulletin # 119,* I-II, *Anthropological Series # 30,* Ottawa. n.d.

BARBEAU, MARIUS
"Indian Days on the Western Prairies." National Museum of Canada, *Bulletin # 163, Anthropological Series # 46,* Ottawa. 1960.

BARBEAU, MARIUS
  "Huron-Wyandot Traditional Narratives in Translations and Native Texts." National Museum of Canada, *Bulletin* # 165, *Anthropological Series* # 47, Ottawa. 1960.

CLARK, ELLA E.
  Indian Legends of Canada. Toronto. 1960.

HOUGHTON, FREDERICK
  "Indian Villages, Camp and Burial Sites on the Niagara Frontier." *Bulletin of the Buffalo Society of Natural History,* No. 3, IX, Buffalo. 1919.

HUNTER, A. F.
  "Sites of Huron Villages." *Appendix to The Report of The Minister of Education,* Ontario. 1899.

JENNESS, D.
  "The Indians of Canada (5th ed.)." National Museum of Canada, *Bulletin* # 65, *Anthropological Series* # 15, Ottawa. 1960.

JOHNSON, FREDERICK (ed.),
  "Man in Northeastern North America." *Papers, Robert S. Peabody Foundation for Archaeology,* 3, Andover. 1946.

LEECHMAN, JOHN DOUGLAS
  "Native Tribes of Canada." Ontario Provincial Museum, *Annual Archaeological Report,* Toronto. 1957.

MacNEISH, RICHARD S.
  "A Speculative Framework of Northern North American Prehistory As of April 1959." *Anthropologica,* N.S., Vol. 1, Ottawa. 1960.

MacNEISH, RICHARD S.
  "Iroquois Pottery Types." National Museum of Canada, *Bulletin* # 124, *Anthropological Series* # 31, Ottawa. 1952.

MacNEISH, RICHARD S.
  "Archaeological Projects in Canada 1959." *Archaeology,* Vol. 13, pp. 194–201. 1960.

MᴄIʟᴡʀᴀɪᴛʜ, T. F.
"Archaeological Work in Huronia 1946: Excavations Near Warminster." *Canadian Historical Review,* Vol. 27, pp. 394–401, Toronto. 1946.

Mᴏᴏʀᴇʜᴇᴀᴅ, Wᴀʀʀᴇɴ Kɪɴɢ
Stone Ornaments Used by Indians in The United States and Canada . . . Andover. 1917.

Mᴏʀɢᴀɴ, Lᴇᴡɪs H.
The Indian Journals 1859–62 (L. A. White, ed.). Ann Arbor. 1959.

Nɪᴄᴏʟᴀs, Fʀᴀɴᴋ (compiler),
Index to Paleontology. Canadian Geological Survey, Ottawa. 1925.

Mᴜʀᴅᴏᴄᴋ, Gᴇᴏʀɢᴇ Pᴇᴛᴇʀ
Ethnographic Bibliography of North America, 3rd ed. Human Relations Area Files, New Haven. 1960.

Osʙᴏʀɴᴇ, Dᴏᴜɢʟᴀs, *et al.*
"The Problem of Northwest Coastal-Interior Relationships As Seen From Seattle." *American Antiquity,* 22, Salt Lake City. 1956.

Sᴍɪᴛʜ, Hᴀʀʟᴀɴ I.
"An Album of Prehistoric Canadian Art." Victoria Memorial Museum, *Bulletin* # 37, *Anthropological Series* # 8, Ottawa. 1923.

Wᴀʟʟɪs, Wɪʟsᴏɴ D. and R. S. Wᴀʟʟɪs
The Micmac Indians of Eastern Canada. Minneapolis. 1955.

Wᴀᴜɢʜ, F. W.
"Notes on Canadian Pottery." *Annual Archaeological Report,* Minister of Education, Ontario, Toronto. 1902.

Wɪɴᴛᴇᴍʙᴇʀɢ, W. J.
"The Geographical Distribution of Aboriginal Pottery in Canada." *American Antiquity,* 8, pp. 129–141, Menasha. 1942.

WINTEMBERG, W. J.
"The Middleport Prehistoric Village Cite." National Museum of Canada, *Bulletin* # 109, *Anthropological Series* # 27, Ottawa. 1948.

Periodicals

Annales de l'association canadienne-franc pour l'avancement des sciences. Montreal.

An Anthropological Bibliography of the Eastern Seaboard. Eastern States Archeological Federation. Trenton, New Jersey, U.S.A.

Bulletin de la Société de Géographie de Quebec. Quebec.

Bulletin. The Eastern States Archeological Federation, Trenton, New Jersey, U.S.A.

Canadian Antiquarian and Numismatic Journal.

Canadian Historical Review. Toronto.

Le Bulletin des Recherches Historiques. Quebec.

Le Courrier du Livre. Canadiana. Quebec.

INDEX